THE TRAUMA OF GENDER

THE TRAUMA OF GENDER

A Feminist Theory
of the English Novel

HELENE MOGLEN

University of California Press

Berkeley · *Los Angeles* · *London*

University of California Press
Berkeley and Los Angeles, California

University of California Press, Ltd.
London, England

© 2001 by the Regents of the University of California

Library of Congress Cataloging-in-Publication Data

Moglen, Helene, 1936–
    The trauma of gender : a feminist theory of the
English novel / Helene Moglen.
        p.   cm.
    Includes bibliographical references and index.
    ISBN 978-0-520-22589-3 (pbk. : alk. paper)
    1. English fiction—18th century—History and crit-
icism.   2. Feminism and literature—Great Britain—
History—18th   century.   3. English   fiction—Male
authors—History and criticism.   4. Sex role in literature.   5. Sex in literature.   6. Gender identity in
literature.   7. Feminist literary criticism.   8. Women
in literature.   I. Title.

PR858.F45 M64 2001
823'.509353—dc21

                                              00-055965

Manufactured in the United States of America
16   15   14   13   12   11   10   09   08

10 9   8   7   6   5   4   3   2
The paper used in this publication meets the minimum
requirements of ANSI/NISO Z39 0.48—1992 (R 1997)
(Permanence of Paper).

To Seth,
my empathic witness

Contents

Acknowledgments   ix

Introduction: The Gender Politics of Narrative Modes   1

1. Daniel Defoe and the Gendered Subject of Individualism   17

2. *Clarissa* and the Pornographic Imagination   57

3. (W)holes and Noses: The Indeterminacies of *Tristram Shandy*   87

4. Horace Walpole and the Nightmare of History   109

   Conclusion: The Relation of Fiction and Theory   139

   Notes   149
   Works Cited   185
   Index   195

Acknowledgments

Many acts of generosity and friendship sustained me in the writing of this book. A year's fellowship from the American Association of University Women gave me the precious gift of time, while several faculty grants from the University of California, Santa Cruz, helped to fund my research. Christine Berthin, Susan Derwin, Jody Greene, Donna Haraway, and Myra Jehlen read and commented on one or another of the chapters. Greg Forter put aside his own work at a crucial moment to give me the benefit of his wonderfully analytic mind. Wendy Brown was my intellectual and emotional support: a wise, thoughtful and informed reader, a tactful critic, and a loving friend. Carol Mavor placed her creativity at my service and brought my search for a felicitous cover image to a happy end.

I have also been fortunate in the help I have received in the book's preparation and production. Ann Speno, Jessica Breheny, and Jessica Goodman, my research assistants, were both inventive and assiduous in their efforts. Betsy Wotten and Barbara Lee provided superb staff support for this project, as they have for many others over the years, and Cheryl Van de Veer and Zoe Sodya prepared the manuscript with the exquisite competence I have come, because of them, to expect. At the University of California Press, Linda Norton has been the editor about whom every writer fantasizes: she had confidence in the project from the earliest moment and shepherded the manuscript through the complex review and publication process with calm good humor, intelligence, and warmth. Dore Brown proved her genius for book production once again—and left me even deeper in her debt than I had been before.

Finally, there is my family: a family composed—with a single exception—of men. Each in his own way has influenced the worldview upon which this project rests. With Sig—my closest friend for more than fifty years and, for just a few years less, my husband—I have lived out and endeavored to understand the meanings of gender differences: how those differences are constructed and how those

Acknowledgments

constructions can be mined, adapted and transcended. In my three sons, I have watched the evolution of subjectivities that are intricately gendered. Eben—astute historian, lover of literature, intellectual omnivore—who has brought a populist vision of the cyber future to the theory and practice of law. Damon, an activist whose courageous struggle for social change has been animated by great personal integrity, cultural insight, and the abhorrence of power's misuse. And Seth, a gifted critic and dedicated teacher who recognizes others as they would want to be known and is committed to making the good things of society available to all.

Seth was, in all respects, the first reader of this book. He understood its aspirations from the earliest moments and helped me to embody them at every stage. To work with him as my editor, colleague, and friend was to discover how luminous a flowering the primal root of the mother-child relation can achieve. It is to him that *The Trauma of Gender* is dedicated.

Introduction

The Gender Politics of Narrative Modes

I want to challenge two linked assumptions that most historians and critics of the English novel share. The first is that the burgeoning of capitalism and the ascension of the middle classes were mainly responsible for the development of the novel. The second is that realism represents the novel's dominant tradition.[1] I want to propose instead that, as surely as it marked a response to developing class relations, the novel came into being as a response to the sex-gender system that emerged in England in the seventeenth and eighteenth centuries.[2] My thesis is that from its inception, the novel has been structured not by one but by two mutually defining traditions: the fantastic and the realistic.[3] The constitutive coexistence of these two impulses within a single, evolving form is in no sense accidental: their dynamic interaction was precisely the means by which the novel, from the eighteenth century on, sought to manage the strains and contradictions that the sex-gender system imposed on individual subjectivities. For this reason, to recover the centrality of sex and gender as the novel's defining concern is also to recover the dynamism of its bimodal complexity. Conversely, to explore the interplay of realist and fantastic narratives within the novelistic tradition is to explore the indeterminacy of subjectivities engaged in the task of imposing and rebelling against the constraining order of gender difference.

The historical foundation of the project is the recognition that the alteration of class structure in this period was inseparable from the reconceptualization of gender differences and the reconfiguration of gender relations. Synthesizing a simple story from complex accounts, one can say that by the middle of the seventeenth century, there was a shift away from a feudal and Puritan patriarchalist order that saw cosmos, state, and family as analogically related and social position as established through inherited status. As the authority of the father and husband were distinguished from the authority of the

1

sovereign, the family became a distinct unit of organization, with the evolving role of women more restricted than the emerging role of men.[4] While sexual difference had been less significant than rank in earlier forms of social organization, the modern form of patriarchy that replaced it was organized according to essentialized, biological distinctions.[5] So, at the same time that permeable boundaries of class were replacing inflexible differentiations of inherited position, the boundary that separated male from female was increasingly experienced as too formidable to be crossed. Qualities of masculinity and femininity, seen as natural and treated as immutable, anchored personal identity as they grounded the sociocultural order.

Socioeconomic changes that accompanied the rise of capitalism contributed significantly to the transformation of the sex-gender system. Although the recent work of feminist historians emphasizes the dependence of these changes on class status and geographical location, there is broad agreement that the situation of women in England altered radically from 1600 to 1750. In the sixteenth century, when women had been involved in production for the subsistence of their households and for market, they had participated in a range of economically significant functions. The next hundred and fifty years saw the breakdown of domestic economy, as lands were enclosed, estates consolidated, and work that had traditionally been performed at home was removed from domestic space and professionalized within a public sphere to which women were barred entry. The family ceased then to be the primary unit of production, and the interdependency of its members was replaced by a division of labor structured along gender lines.[6]

As middle-class men moved into an expanding public world—as political citizens, legal subjects, and aspiring economic individuals—their female counterparts were restricted to a diminished private sphere in which they performed their duties as mothers and as wives. Infantalized by her legal, social, and economic dependence on her husband, a woman was likely to be an object of ambivalence for her children, whose psychic lives she dominated. Her sons defined themselves in opposition to her maternal qualities, while her daughters read their futures in the functional limitations of her life. Both were prepared by the patterning of the nuclear family to assume the attitudes, roles, and forms of subjectivity that were required by emerging gender arrangements. In this bisected world, male interiority was identified with reason, female interiority with feeling. With masculine rationality enabling the creation and command of culture, female sensibility, while valued, required cultural embodiment and control.[7]

In the same way that the sex-gender system was reinforced by the division of labor, with its comprehensive discriminations between public and private spheres, it was strengthened by a shift in scientific ideology, which identified the female body as the center of the binarized new order. No longer understood to be a variant of the male's, as it had been since the work of Galen in the second century, a woman's body was perceived as fundamentally different from a man's.[8] Nowhere was that essentialized difference more remarked than in the redefined areas of her sexual and reproductive functioning. Although female sexuality had been thought throughout the Renaissance not only to have mirrored man's, but to have been more intense than his—more voracious and demanding—the eighteenth century thought her desire to be more subject to the self-discipline of a female character that was naturally mature and morally developed.[9] By the century's end, when scientists had ceased to regard female orgasm as relevant to conception, there was assumed to be much less libido for a woman to control. Her sexuality was detached conceptually from her maternity, and the ideological commitment to her sexual passivity was reinforced.[10] Once her normalcy was associated with her maternity rather than her sexuality, it remained for her sexuality to be displaced onto the prostitute, her abnormal counterpart, who was often represented as ambiguously gendered, even mannish, with an enlarged and ejaculating clitoris.[11] Further, as sexual activity in women became more suspect, so did sexual passivity in men, along with other forms of sexual anomaly. It was in this context that the passive, feminized male sodomite joined the sexually initiating whore as one whose aberrant status was crucial to the maintenance of the emergent sex-gender system.[12] Heterosexuality was prescribed not just as normal but as compulsory, and marriage—ideologically based in mutual feeling rather than in property—became the romanticized site of its expression.

It would be difficult to overestimate what it meant for masculinity and femininity to be defined not just as different from one another but as mutually exclusive. Conceptions of the self were shaped by that opposition, as was the self's experience of others. Differences of class, race, and nationality were filtered through the lens of sexual alterity, and they were tinged by fears and desires that such alterity produced. With manners, linguistic expression, and morality dictated by gender as well as class affiliation, society became a more ambiguously charted territory, which men and women had to negotiate at risk. And because the sex-gender system helped to determine which aspects of the self would flourish and which would be suppressed, the psychological reverberations of differentiated social practices were profound.

It was in the novel, more than in any other expressive form, that the social and psychological meanings of gender difference were most extensively negotiated and exposed. At one level, these innovative fictions demonstrated how the ideals of masculinity and femininity were translated into social roles, and they established norms for that translation. At another level, they expressed resistance to the wrenching system of differentiation and revealed the psychic costs that it incurred. By combining social and what we would now call psychological perspectives, novels facilitated acculturation while also formulating damning cultural critiques. Through their detailing of character and situation, they enacted the feelings and desires of their authors and exposed the ambivalence that underlay the fabrication of gendered subjectivities. Through the full range of their expressivity, and their availability to fantasy and dream, they disclosed psychic excesses that were unassimilable to the coercive sexual order.

The novel imposed and resisted the sex-gender system through a bimodal narrative form that was molded by another major cultural transformation. At the same time that radical changes were occurring in socioeconomic and sex-gender systems, a significant form of self-awareness was created by the development of individualism. Like the class and gender systems, this new structure of consciousness saturated every aspect of social, psychological, and epistemological interaction. Self-aware individuals experienced themselves as preeminent in their relationships and were intensely focused on themselves. At the social level, they believed themselves to be autonomous and independent: active agents in a world available to rational comprehension and control. Stamped by the spirit and practices of capitalism, they were acquisitive, pragmatic, and competitive. When they encountered others, they treated them instrumentally, as objects. At the psychological level, the individual's obsession with its own interior life produced a division between the self that scrutinized and the self that was watched. Subject and object simultaneously, the socially self-possessed individual was psychologically riven.

The historian Norbert Elias has traced the progress of the "civilizing process" through which individuals became increasingly self-centered and aware.[13] Detailing changes in everyday behavior over a period of two hundred years, he shows how modern individuals differentiated themselves, socially and psychologically, from the collectivities with which they had previously identified. As self-interest was asserted against the traditional practices of the group, the management of behavior became an increasingly private matter, handled by the family on one side and by personal conscience on the other. When social prohibitions were internalized and experienced as self-control, the psychic self was deepened and divided.[14] Manners increasingly achieved the intensity of morality, and morality constructed desire as perversion. Pervasive feelings of guilt and shame marked the partitioning of the self into the judging and the judged, and inexpressible resistance to social interdiction signaled the existence of the unconscious mind.[15] In this same period, affective impulses, which should have bound individuals to one another, were incorporated into a claustral psychic economy that defined them as private and interior. Men and women shared this solipsistic structure of self-awareness, but the conscious and unconscious contents of their minds were not the same. Different social relations produced different aspirations and forms of self-control, as they also produced different fantasies, resistances, and desires.

The novel's two narrative modes reflected the outward- and inward-looking aspects of the consciousness of individualism. Realism, the more familiar of the two, was fundamentally a social form. Its narratives were shaped by the consciousness of the self in its moral, ethical, and psychological relationships with others. Representing the hegemonic order of individualism, as Ian Watt and other critics have suggested, realist narratives described a world that was appropriate to the aspirations of middle-class subjects, in terms that reflected their cultural assumptions and beliefs. They erased signs of class inequity by naturalizing social differences—which were crucial to the construction of the bourgeois subject—in order to present them as timeless and inevitable. Mediating between the power of self-interest and the need for social integration, they showed how modern self-awareness could produce an egotism threatening to society, and they delineated strategies for its containment. The formal methodologies of these narratives supported their ideological suppositions. Creating coherence from a single overarching perspective, they affirmed the possibility of psychic wholeness and structured desire in conformity with communal need. Projecting the reader into the omniscient narrator's place, they confirmed social consensus formally and rejected subversive eccentricity. Presenting truth as a function of reliable representation, they employed language as if it could be adequate to its object, projected characters that were possessed of intelligible interiorities, and shaped linear narratives that synchronized personal and collective histories.

In the same way that realistic narratives functioned to disguise signs of class inequity in the interests of the bourgeois subject, they also functioned to disguise, by naturalizing, inequities of gender. The stories that they told concerned the sons and daughters who struggled to accommodate themselves to rapidly changing social and personal relations. In the modified picaresque, the bildungsroman, and the novel of psychological realism (all genres written predominantly in the realistic mode), the son who either bears or must discover his father's name also assumes his father's place: his property, social position, capacity for economic survival in the public world, and authority as founder of a family. His is ultimately a fiction about autonomy achieved and competitions won—in material, epistemological, psychological, and vocational terms. His emotional detachment from social and spiritual communities may be noted, but the costs of his affective disengagement are not explored.

The daughter's story is recorded in the domestic novel, which assumes the female's embeddedness in family. Tracing the father's replacement by the aspiring suitor, it maps the complexities of courtship and carries the protagonist to the threshold of marriage: what follows, unspoken in the eighteenth century, is her maternity. Often it is the girl's first name that supplies the novel's title—Pamela, Cecilia, Evelina, Emma—emphasizing the extent to which her social identity is suspended as she moves from the shadow of one patronymic into the shadow of another. It is in this liminal moment, when she selects a husband, that her potentially subversive sensibility is subordinated to her socially responsive moral consciousness. The "correctness" of her choice is signaled by the improvement of her class status and, with it, the class status of her family. Once that is accomplished, her particularized narrative is appropriated for a universalized female plot. Her future happiness, which is presented as secured, rests on the foreclosure of agency prefigured by her mother's insignificance in, or absence from, the text. So while the son assumes the father's active position at the fiction's end, the daughter slips into the invisibility of the maternal role. For both, the marital union, which is romanticized as healing isolation, reinscribes the differences that contribute to isolation's cause. This is made explicit in nineteenth-century realistic novels, where the wedding is prelude rather than conclusion, and marriage focuses the strains created by the oppositional structure of gender arrangements.

In contrast to the social emphasis of the realistic mode, fantastic narratives had an intrapsychic focus. They mapped interior states produced by possessive and affective forms of individualism, and they exposed the anxious melancholy that the modern order of social differences induced. Unmasking the belief in autonomy as false, they bared its roots in the fear of psychic vulnerability. Revealing the link between materialism and desire, they exposed the libidinal investments of patriarchal capitalism. They demonstrated that obsessive self-awareness could yield to madness and that paranoia was the product of a guilty conscience. Most significantly, they uncovered the psychological dynamic that helped to structure the new sex-gender system. Focusing on the fundamentally divided nature of the self, fantastic narratives depicted a subject who knew itself predominantly as object: a subject who struggled for integration, but learned that fragmentation was its doom.[16] Proliferating characters who were both themselves and versions of one another, they enacted the processes through which the subject found itself reflected in others and others reflected in itself. And, finally, in the specular self's fearful but pleasurable transgression of boundaries that guarded its social identity, they suggested the awesome attraction of an indeterminacy that would undermine oppositional categories of difference.

There were elements of the fantastic in most eighteenth-century realistic texts, but it was only in the late part of the century that fictions written predominantly in the fantastic mode started to appear. The gothic, which was the first of the fantastic genres, established the subjectivist form that was elaborated later in Romantic, modernist, and postmodern genres. Its narratives rejected the values of realism, interrogating moral judgment with psychic need, reason with affectivity, and the fiction of objective truth with relative perspectives. Desiring subjects were the focus of both male- and female-centered versions of the gothic, but because the desires of men and women were conceptualized differently, their narratives assumed quite different shapes.[17] In coded forms, which represented indirectly what women were not allowed to speak, the female gothic unveiled the psychic costs of affective individualism and revealed the price that women paid to achieve their places in a sexually segregated social order.[18] Excluded from the protective family by her parents' death, the female protagonist was subject to a predatory patriarchy concerned with the material value of her sexuality. Dependent for knowledge on the sensibility by which she was defined, she moved among sexual and economic horrors that, although imagined, reflected a world that was genuinely fearsome for dependent women. Because intensity of feeling was associated with passion unacceptable in a lady, she strove for self-control, which meant the suppression of her expressivity and the denial of threatening realities. In learning to reject the evidence of her feelings, she refused her own capacity for self-awareness and gave to others the authority to mold her life. Identified with their appropriative power, she complicitously adopted a masochistic model of desire, which signaled her socialization while revealing its fundamentally disabling nature.[19] In the text, her fate is shadowed by the lives of women who are represented as possible versions of herself: bad women whose passion leads them to madness or to death, and good women who cannot survive the hardships of their marriages to sadistic men.[20] The female protagonist can escape her tragic fate only if the fantastic narrative yields to the impulse of romance. Then she marries not the sadistic gothic hero to whom she is magnetically drawn, but the feminized hero whose passivity precludes his participation in the gothic plot.[21]

The character of the anti-hero, who dominates the gothic narrative, is fully elaborated in the male-centered text.[22] His tragic story exposes the dark side of possessive individualism as unrestrained egotism, greed, and lust, and it shows how the materialistic urge, which is fostered by capitalism, permeates sexuality. In him, the solipsistic tendencies of modern self-awareness are intensified as a toxic masculinity that femininity cannot alloy. Possessed by paranoia, he tries to resist objectification by objectifying and exploiting others. Motivated at once by misogynistic heterosexuality and homophobic homosexuality, he defines love as erotic domination, in which the domination that is practiced is always his.[23] Although he needs a male or female counterpart to complete himself, he is doomed to eradicate or be eradicated by the subjectivity of the other whom he desires. And because he destroys himself when he destroys that other, his story culminates in madness or in death.

Situated in a psychic past that haunts a social present, predominantly fantastic narratives suggest that desire is structured and deformed within the family. Saturated with incestuous longings, these stories expose intrafamilial relations as psychologically determining and the sexuality of parents and children as multiple, ambiguous, and complex. In these narratives, the absence of the mother is as crucial to her sons and daughters as her presence: it is a spectral reminder of the lost other, which is also a lost aspect of themselves. The female protagonist recalls the mother's nurturance and love as a powerful but now foreclosed alternative to sexual difference and erotic domination by the male. As anti-hero, the son experiences her in the perilous, interior void, which his denial of affectivity has created, and in the sexually voracious woman, who threatens him with boundary loss and psychic appropriation. As the feminized hero, he finds her reflected in the desexualized woman whom he loves and ultimately marries. For female and male protagonists alike, the father is an object of intense desire and fear. His sadistic sexuality terrifies and attracts the daughter, whom he craves, and arouses in the son virulent competitive feelings and an ambivalent homoerotic fascination. For both of them, he holds the magnetic power of the eroticized patriarchal family in which children remain mired throughout their lives.

While realism takes the individual's accommodation to society as its subject, then, the fantastic reveals the psychic costs of social deformation. While realism traces the generational displacement of parental authority, the fantastic exposes ways in which intrafamilial identifications, which are etched into the psyche, reproduce themselves in subsequent relations. While the trajectory of realism is toward an improving future, the movement of the fantastic is backward toward a regressive past. While realism poses the possibility of the self's union with another, the fantastic insists on the self's alienation from others and itself. Finally, while realistic narratives struggle for textual intelligibility, completeness, and coherence, fantastic narratives gesture toward an affectivity that lies outside of language and, therefore, outside the text. Eighteenth-century philosophers defined that intense experience of affectivity as the sublime, while Freud later calls it the uncanny, Lacan associates it with the Real, and Kristeva explores it, in its positive and negative moments, as the semiotic and abject. For all of these speculative thinkers writing in the fantastic mode, it represents a realm of indeterminacy that is rooted in the unconscious mind. Utopically a place of subversion, it is also a place potentially of madness. It is that place which fantastic narratives struggle, repeatedly, to reach.

I want to argue, therefore, that the modern form of self-awareness born of individualism was articulated through two narrative modes that represented distinct, but related, ways of knowing and of telling. These modes constituted each other through diverse genres that were shaped by changing cultural assumptions and shifting relations of desire.[24] Together they suggest the interpenetrability of fantasy and reality, and the mutual dependence of the unconscious and the social. Early fantastic fictions, which were rooted in a long romance tradition, revealed the price paid in the Enlightenment for the increasing rigidity of epistemological, racial, national, and, above all, sexual boundaries, which realism functioned to perpetuate. First, in the gothic novels of the late eighteenth and early nineteenth centuries, the anxieties and wishes that had been excluded from realistic fictions appeared in a supernatural—but incipiently psychological—form to belie realism's myths of distinct differences, progressive histories, and integrated texts.[25] Then, as realist fictions used sexual, social, and racial "others" thematically in order to reinforce hierarchical orders of difference, fantastic fictions (which had acquired an explicitly psychological focus) dissolved the distinction between self and "other" and revealed how the "other" serves instrumentally in the self's construction. With the advent of modernism, reality was filtered through a subjectivist lens and fantastic narratives tended to move, in most novels, from the periphery to the center.[26]

Literary historians have generally aligned themselves with the values and assumptions of one of these two narrative modes, ignoring or devaluing the other. Those who have constructed realism as the novel's dominant tradition have dismissed subjectivist fictions as popular and ahistorical, while those who have privileged fantastic texts see realism as bound to the hegemonic values of an ascending middle class. By separating social from psychological discourses, both groups have repeated the gesture that divides the internal from the external world and one aspect of modern self-awareness from another. As a result, they have tended to overlook the full interactive spectrum of ideology, subjectivity, and narrative structure.[27] Pursuing an alternative route, I will argue that few fictions are actually elaborated through one narrative form alone. Most are composite structures that reveal personal ambivalences and ideological contestations through interactive modes and genres. Because the male-authored, canonical novels that serve as my case studies overflow the definitional categories to which they have been assigned, they implicitly call those categories into question. For example, *Robinson Crusoe*, which is ordinarily read as formal realism's founding fiction, reveals in its fantastic subtext an obsessive, claustral, appropriative, and haunted subjectivity that is defined through the projections and introjections of gendered—as well as racial and class—"others." A classic study of modern psychosexuality, *Clarissa* has generally been read as a novel of psychological realism. In fact, its realistic narrative—which examines the encounter of sexual with socioeconomic interests—is interrogated by a fantastic fiction, which exposes psychic fragmentation and social alienation, sexual anxiety and gender confusion, and interpretive relativity and authorial uncertainty. *Tristram Shandy*, which has been dismissed as formally anomalous by theorists of realism and ignored altogether by theorists of the fantastic, explores the limits and possibilities of both narrative modes in their mutually constitutive dynamic. In that text, it is the repeated conflict between the need for sexual definition and the desire for indeterminacy that creates the contestation of epistemological perspectives and modal forms. And, finally, *The Castle of Otranto*, which is the first English novel in which the fantastic mode is dominant, shares many of the thematic concerns and formal realistic strategies that Walpole, its author, explicitly wrote against. More importantly, it unmasks the sexual obsessions that derive from intrafamilial relations and lays open the melancholic nature of the loss incurred by the cultural imposition of gender difference.

Together and separately, these canonical texts explore, from male perspectives, the relation of gender identity to social authority and unconscious impulse. Charting the cultural dynamic through which the gendered subject is constructed, they also examine the psychological processes through which it attempts to deconstruct itself. Revealing how modern subjectivity is configured by the sex-gender system, they demonstrate how it resists, and at times subverts, that patterning. They show us that from its inception, the novel placed a self that is socially armored and coerced against one that suffers from, and even at times evades, the difficulties caused by that coercion. They enable us to see that the problem of gender lies at the heart of the process of subjectification and that while the novel has functioned to produce the gendered subject, it has also revealed that subject's radically ungendered and complexly sexual nature.

To the extent that eighteenth-century novels examined the production and destabilization of gendered identities, they anticipated the psychoanalytic project that Freud initiated at the nineteenth century's end. The problems that were thematized by fantastic narratives were also problems that he and his successors tried to solve. Like the protagonists of fantastic fictions, the subjects of Freud's case studies were governed by desires they could not understand. Torn by conscious and unconscious impulses, they revealed the self to be not unitary but divided. Compelled to action by their affective inclinations, they testified to the limits of the Enlightenment's rationalist ideal. Freud set out to explore the underworld of feeling and desire that the civilizing process had produced. Considering psychic resistance to culture as inevitable, he subordinated moral to psychological imperatives. He devised interpretive and therapeutic strategies that gave him access to the unconscious and invented a language that captured the symbolic meanings of fantasy and dream. Like the novelists whom he resembles, Freud was centrally concerned with the ways in which the self is sexualized and gendered; and like those novelists, he was implicated in the elaborate system of differences that he explored. In his blind spots, as much as in his explanations, he revealed that the sexual division of labor, which contorts individuals in the process of gendering them, limits their comprehension of the effects that the gendering process has had upon them. Like the male novelists whom I examine, Freud and, after him, Lacan have been the products and producers of male-centered histories of subjectivity and sexuality. They use sexual difference to anchor psychic and linguistic meaning, and male sexuality to anchor the meanings of sexual difference. In their narratives, which—although not fictions—are still fictive, they structure the contingencies of subjectivity and sexuality as necessarily male and female.[28] At the same time, they reveal the inevitable failure of the socializing process by exposing the depth of psychic resistance to any absolute identity, as well as to gender roles that are culturally prescribed.

I make use of Freud's interpretive method to bring fantastic narratives to the surface of realistic texts and to locate the deep layers of meaning that fantastic narratives contain. Just as the juxtaposition of text and subtext forces revisionary readings, so too does the conjunction of revisionary readings with appropriate psychoanalytic theories.[29] For example, Heinz Kohut's theory of narcissism illuminates Defoe's conception of character, at the same time that Defoe's early modern fictions provocatively interrogate the ideological assumptions of Kohut's bourgeois self-psychology. Read together, the narratives of Kohut and the narratives of Defoe expose the palimpsestic formation of modern self-awareness and the collaborative psychological and social shaping of subjectivity. In a similar way, *Tristram Shandy* is uncanny in its Lacanian presumptions. It reveals how the male body is castrated by the cultural mind and suggests the nature of the compensations that men seek for their deprivation. Lacan's formulations elucidate Sterne's view that the restrictions of language reflect and reproduce all other lacks. At the same time, Sterne's comic vision provides a critique of Lacan's misogynistic assumptions: assumptions which—to some extent—Sterne also shares. The work of the feminist object-relations theorist Jessica Benjamin strengthens and is reinforced by a reading of *Clarissa* as a developmental story that shows how the individual's struggle for autonomy and recognition yields relations of erotic domination, which are gender coded and culturally specific. And, finally, Walpole's two gothic texts, *The Castle of Otranto* and *The Mysterious Mother*, exemplify and extend Nicolas Abraham and Maria Torok's speculations about the relation of desire to personal and cultural loss.

Whether fictive or psychoanalytic, all of the texts that I consider in these chapters are shaped by conscious and unconscious loss: psychic losses inflicted by social accommodation, intrapsychic losses that have taken social form, cultural losses that testify to the haunting presence of the past. Hostage to memory and dependent upon fantasy for substance, these ghostly exclusions stamp the novel, as they fashion personality and culture. Experienced symptomatically, they are never completely recognized and are therefore never mourned. Their product is melancholia, which is represented as personal in the fantastic text and as a cultural effect in the realistic narrative. Like psychoanalytic theory, the novel charts the development of gendered subjectivities in the face of traumatic deprivation. Because deprivations imposed on men are different from those that women must endure, male- and female-authored fictions are structured by divergent fantasies of desire and employ distinct strategies of expression, resistance, and containment.

In the chapters that follow, I initiate a theory of the gender politics of narrative modes, examining developmental stories about men and women that have been conceptualized by men.[30] All are authoritative texts, popular in their own time and canonical in ours. It is their familiarity that recommends them for my purposes. Because they have been accepted as characteristic of either realistic or fantastic traditions, and middle-class and masculinist ideologies, they can usefully be read against the grain. In my interpretations, their fantastic and realistic narratives interact to form composite texts that function to manage gender relations even as they reveal the precariousness of selfhood and identity. Although these novels are male-centered, and can even be called misogynistic, they powerfully represent the ambivalent yearning that lies at the heart of misogyny: a yearning that originates not in hatred, but in love and loss. It is the unacknowledged nature of that loss that is inscribed, as melancholia, in the texts.

This book's implicit claim is that fantastic narratives unman these master texts with their persistent urge for indeterminacy. That urge expresses itself in the text's struggle for the experience of sublimity: an experience that, associated with the earliest stages of subjectification, survives in memory as a reminder that gender differences are disguises that the self assumes but that it wishes also to discard. The fantastic narrative answers to that urge when, in its shaping of characters and its development of themes, it demonstrates that to establish a radical distance from the biological other is to deny that kind of otherness in the self: to reject it altogether is to undergo a form of psychic mutilation. The entombment of fantastic narratives within realistic texts and the burial of the subtexts of fantastic narratives are both symptom and cause of the social intransigence that blocks the personal and cultural work of mourning. To make those invisible narratives visible is to facilitate mourning's productive, recuperative work. That is the primary project of this book.

1

Daniel Defoe and the Gendered
Subject of Individualism

A pivotal and provocative figure, Daniel Defoe embodied in his own life the ideology of individualism: the powerful fantasy of social, economic, and psychological autonomy that was central to the development of capitalism. Emphasizing his frequently illicit exploits and adventures, his biographers have represented him as the social outsider who improvised himself, seeking survival or, better still, success in a world that eluded his mastery, despite his resourcefulness and wit. Born in 1659, a year before the Restoration of Charles II and the initiation of a new political order, Defoe was marginal from birth: a child of Dissenters, whose civil and religious rights were legally restricted. Not simply a matter of inheritance or the result of hostile social forces, marginality was also a position that he continually chose: professionally, politically, and personally. Abandoning an early plan to join the Presbyterian ministry—with its assigned responsibilities and its community of values—Defoe selected the secular, morally ambiguous, and materially uncertain life of business: the brave new world of capitalist investment and expansion by which Puritanism had itself been overtaken.

Initially successful in a variety of merchant and trading ventures, Defoe plunged—within ten years—from affluence to insolvency. Perilously overextended in the boom that followed the Glorious Revolution, he tried desperately to recoup his losses, but by 1692 his failure as an entrepreneur was clear. Hounded by creditors, he was sued for the nonpayment of contracted debts, for mismanaging his factoring responsibilities, for trying fraudulently to corner the perfume market based on civet cats, for appropriating a patented invention for the recovery of buried treasure, and for cashing a bill of exchange that was drawn on a person who had died. Declaring bankruptcy, he endured the first of several imprisonments. His reputation went the way of his financial dealings as ethical judgment was over-taken by self-interest.

In adapting himself to a rapidly changing society, Daniel Defoe was an exemplary modern subject who continually reinvented him-self. As easily as he added a prefix to his name—changing it from the simpler "Foe" in 1695—Defoe assumed, discarded, and resumed disguises, declared affiliations, inhabited positions, and spoke in a chorus of dissonant voices. While some of his impersonations were ironically undertaken, their consequences were real. In 1702, he was arrested, imprisoned, pilloried for sedition, and fined for adopting the High Church point of view too persuasively in his tract "The Shortest Way with the Dissenters." Ten years later, he was impris-oned again, this time for writing anti-Jacobite pamphlets that em-ployed a pro-Jacobite perspective. Other impersonations were un-dertaken literally—with stakes that were equally as high. At the turn of the century, Defoe acted as a political spy for Robert Harley, one of Queen Anne's leading ministers, and for nine years (from 1704 to 1713), he single-handedly published *The Review* as an Independent, while being paid by Secret Service money. Beginning in 1715, he spied for the Whig ministry but wrote for Tory periodicals. Perhaps less self-consciously, but with equal inconsistency, he inhabited con-flicting, even contradictory positions on a range of important con-temporary issues. In his poem "The True-Born Englishman," he sat-irized a xenophobia with which he identified in other writings;[1] he participated in the slave trade while condemning slavery as evil; and he joined Monmouth's Rebellion against James in 1685—the last ep-isode of the democratic English Revolution—only to support Wil-liam and the Revolution of 1688. Throughout his adult life, he was a deeply secularized man of faith and a ruthlessly pragmatic ethicist.[2]

A great deal has been written about the prodigious versatility of Defoe. He was merchant, trader, entrepreneur, court adviser, editor, journalist, poet, novelist, essayist, travel writer, spy, double agent, and also (the fact usually emerges incidentally) a husband and a father. But it is difficult to learn how it felt to *be* Defoe: the nature of his affective ties to family and to friends; his emotional responses to financial failures, loss of reputation, and personal and political dou-ble-dealings; at what moment in his life optimism was overtaken by despair and how ambivalence was negotiated. To the extent that his biographers have submerged his psychological depth in the flat multiplicity of retold events, they have shaped his life (as he shaped the lives of his protagonists) in the mode of realism and in the genre of picaresque. But since most of his realistic narratives contain a strong fantastic strain, the nature of his interiority may be glimpsed in the divided subjectivities that he projected in his fictions. Indeed, while Defoe's protonovels have been read as founding texts because they chart the origins of the possessive individual and (in the case of Robinson Crusoe) a new political subject,[3] they are equally deserving of this status because of the insights they provide into the consciousness of individualism.

In his fictions, Defoe set out to represent men and women who successfully embraced the ideology of possessive individualism: men and women who could survive and even prosper under the volatile conditions of entrepreneurial capitalism. As he told their stories, Defoe inadvertently exposed the conflict of values and beliefs that the commitment to autonomy produced. Unconsciously charting the collision between the ideology of individualism and the sex-gender system, he revealed how that clash created insoluble dilemmas for men and, for women, contradictory demands of such intensity that the viability of female individualism itself was called into question. He told the double stories of his protagonists through the interplay of realistic and fantastic narratives—the former setting out the contradictions through which the illusion of autonomy was achieved, the latter tallying that illusion's psychic costs.

I will examine the constructions of the male and female subjects of individualism in three of Defoe's novels—*Robinson Crusoe, Moll Flanders,* and *Roxana*—and the relation of those constructions to narrative form. Long recognized as a founding text of literary realism, *Robinson Crusoe* articulated a powerful myth of the possessive, autonomous, and masculine individual through the interaction of three narrative modes, which were shaped by three forms of consciousness. An allegorical narrative, which reveals the fiction's origins in an earlier, religious system of belief, is contested and ultimately displaced by realistic and fantastic narratives, which trace the emergence of the social and psychological aspects of modern self-awareness. The realist narratives (in the midst of which the fantastic narrative is embedded) detail the dependencies upon which the illusion of autonomy relies and the forms of antisociality that follow from it. The fantastic narrative, which dominates the account of

Crusoe's island adventure, exposes psychic division as the dark underside of Crusoe's selfish egotism and shows how the solipsism of individualism turns into paranoia. In the contestation between its fantastic and realistic narratives—with the latter's ultimate appropriation of the former—the fiction represents the psychological and social processes that produce the self-dependent male as entrepreneurial capitalist, political agent, and imperialist. Fundamentally, it suggests that the erasure of the female and the displacement of the family are crucial to his definition.

In *Moll Flanders* and *Roxana,* Defoe attempted to represent a female individualist who would be equivalent to Crusoe, but his inability to think beyond the values of the emerging sex-gender system limited the possibilities of his representation. As Defoe applied to women a concept of social, economic, and psychological autonomy that was usually identified with men, he exposed the fundamental incompatibility of individualism with the normative categories through which women were defined. In *Moll Flanders,* Defoe assumes the ideology that aligns women with their reproductive bodies and their affective relations with children and with men. Because he subordinates maternity to his protagonist's entrepreneurial interests and comes close to erasing her emotional ties, he deprives the gender category he employs of its customary meaning. Writing his fiction exclusively in the mode of realism and the genre of picaresque, he is able to evade the psychological implications of the definitional disjunctions he creates, but the tonal fissures that develop in the text indelibly mark the places where the woman separates from the individualist.

In *Roxana,* Defoe makes visible the ideological contradictions that remain partially buried in *Moll Flanders.* In the realist narrative, which initially dominates the fiction, Defoe tells the story of an enterprising woman who, abandoned by her husband, abandons her children, signaling—as Moll had—the radical incompatibility of individualism with conventional maternity and the affective family. As she becomes mistress to increasingly affluent and statused men, Roxana invests her money and becomes a wealthy capitalist: truly a possessive individual. But the material success she is given in the realistic fiction is undermined when the reappearance of her children motivates an intense fantastic narrative. As the story of the abandoning mother engages the story of the prosperous whore, Roxana is forced to recognize the price she has paid for her rejection of a proper woman's role. The agonized consciousness of female individualism is explored by the fantastic narrative, which encounters, contests, and finally overwhelms the picaresque plot. The ultimate tragedy of Roxana suggests the intransigence of gender ideology: how it is internalized by women no less than men, and how it produces, in those who resist it, guilt and shame that are destructively turned back upon the self. Although Defoe's continuing ambivalence is recorded in the convoluted structure of the narrative, the balance of his feelings has shifted away from the celebratory impulses of *Moll Flanders,* and he aligns himself against his protagonist and with the party of misogyny.

Of these three studies of individualism, *Roxana* is the most formally sophisticated and insightful. Unlike *Robinson Crusoe,* where the fantastic narrative is cordoned off from the realistic, picaresque adventure, and unlike *Moll Flanders,* which is without an intrapsychic perspective, the realistic and fantastic narratives in *Roxana* are intricately conjoined. That coherence reflects the interpenetration of psychological and social forces in the construction of the subject, as it also reflects the entanglement of a personal past and present. The unassimilability of the fantastic narrative in *Crusoe* speaks to forms of psychic repression that follow from the belief in male autonomy, as the central metaphor of shipwrecked man suggests the fundamentally antisocial nature of individualism. The complete absence of a fantastic narrative in *Moll Flanders* signals the psychological inadequacy of Defoe's conception: his inability either to think past or to accept the gender assumptions of his time. And as the painful self-awareness of Crusoe on his island helps to identify the psychological deficiency in Moll, Moll's social embeddedness interrogates the limitations of Crusoe's definition. The representations of Moll and Crusoe inadvertently reinforce the oppositions of the sex-gender system, which Defoe resisted but in which he also was invested. It is in *Roxana* that Defoe achieves, for the first time in the English literary tradition, the full potential of the bimodal form. That form allows him to explore—through its integrated fantastic narrative—the psychological meanings of ideological contradictions that the realistic narrative imposes. Writing a story of a female individualist that demonstrates the impossibility of female individualism, Defoe lays bare a central paradox of the ideology that shaped his thinking, as it also shaped his life.

Defoe was situated at the boundary of two worlds, each with its own economic, political, and cultural imperatives, and each with its own system of belief. As Defoe's life reflected the influences of that particular transitional moment, so also did his novels. *Robinson Crusoe* is especially significant in its representation of old and new discourses. It is imprinted by the Puritan form of consciousness, which negotiated the shift from a decentered to a centered self, and it is stamped by individualism's double-sided self-awareness. In *Crusoe*, the Puritan sensibility expresses itself through the residual mode of allegory and the genre of spiritual autobiography, while the mindset of individualism is elaborated through the emergent forms of picaresque realism and the fantastic.[4] In their interactive dynamic, the three narrative modes chart a history of the emergence and development of modern consciousness.

In the adventures that precede the shipwreck, the text is dominated by a picaresque narrative, which maps the progress of Crusoe toward independence and autonomy. The family history that Defoe provides establishes the context for his protagonist's rejection of traditional values and inherited relationships. "Kreutznaer," the family's German surname, has already been changed to "Crusoe" by "the usual Corruption of Words in England."[5] The death in war of one brother and the mysterious disappearance of the other have left Robinson, the youngest son, in the position of unwilling heir. Crusoe's father has planted the seeds of individualism by moving from Hull to York and transforming his own worldly condition through successful entrepreneurial activities. Rejecting his inheritance of the "middle State," along with the subjection to authority that it requires, Crusoe chooses to oppose the "will" of his father and the "entreaties" of his mother. He is driven by an irrational "inclination" for prosperity and power, and by a "rash and immoderate desire of rising faster than the Nature of the Thing admitted" (38). Above all, he is motivated by a wish for autonomy: psychological, social, and economic.

For Crusoe, to be "free" of affective ties is to be self-possessed; to be materially independent is to be powerful in possession. Striving to create a self that is libidinally and economically autonomous, he wants to be the active subject of his life, never subject to others. But even as the realist narrative documents Crusoe's achievement of that desired condition, it also provides evidence that his success is more a function of his dependence and social embeddedness than it is of his autonomy. From the outset, Crusoe's rupture with his parents emerges as more apparent than real. He takes money from his mother and imitates the trajectory of his father's subversive adventure, reversing it by leaving York in order to return to Hull. Similarly, while he wishes to reject the complacency of his father's bourgeois position, he does so only to join him as a member of the rising middle class, acquiring capital on his African voyages and investing it in the purchase of his Brazilian plantation. After leaving home, he repeats the familial pattern in nonreciprocal relations with two captains and a widow, all of whom honor their commitments to him while he does nothing in return for them. The widow acts faithfully on his behalf as banker; the first captain befriends and instructs him in the value of investment; and the second rescues him, gives him free passage, and, by buying his goods, provides him with the capital he needs for the acquisition of property. At still another level, the falsity of his autonomy is suggested by the fact that voyages intended to demonstrate his independence mark him as implicated in a national imperialist project. That project is recapitulated in the order of his adventures: his journey down the African coast, his encounter with Islam, his crossing of the Atlantic, his plantation ownership, and, ultimately, his exportation to the Caribbean of Brazilian expertise.[6]

The egotism that makes Crusoe (and one assumes, Defoe) interpret the personal and social exploitation of others as autonomy and the selfishness that makes him oblivious to the social function of reciprocity are displayed and intensified in Crusoe's adventure in Sallee. Captured by the captain of a Moroccan ship, Crusoe learns what it means to be enslaved, a state which he describes as "the most miserable of all Conditions of Life" (34). But his knowledge of hardship makes him neither democratic nor empathic; instead, it strengthens his urge to self-preservation and hardens him to the instrumental use of others, particularly others who are different from himself. Behaving characteristically, he promises the young Muslim,

Xury, that if he will swear fidelity to him, he will "make [him] a great Man" (34). But while his fellow slave takes such an oath and risks his life to save him, Crusoe ignores the contract, claiming the heathen as his property so that he can sell him into slavery. Protestations aside, his selfish pragmatism easily wins the day. It is only later—when he needs free labor on his plantation and help in escaping from his island—that Crusoe decides that he "had done wrong in parting from my boy" (35). Xury's value changes with his potential uses, but there is never any question for Crusoe (or, apparently, for Defoe) that Xury's value belongs not to Xury himself, but to his self-created master. The objectification of others is, after all, a significant aspect of capitalist self-sufficiency.

The aspect of Crusoe's egotism that Defoe questions is not his treatment of others: it is his relation to God. Searching for the moral meaning of Crusoe's project, Defoe subjects his protagonist's entrepreneurial adventures to allegorical interpretation by a retrospective narrator—another, older Crusoe who imposes a religious reading on his early experiences and on the journal he kept when he was shipwrecked on the island.[7] The narrative strategy reflects Defoe's effort to understand the innovating individual through a typological symbology rooted in an earlier traditional order. Emphasizing not the uniqueness but the typicality of Crusoe as a sinner, the spiritual autobiography represents him as alienated from God by his refusal to obey his father. His sin carries him deeper into spiritual estrangement and despair until he is finally converted to religious faith: a healing of the soul that is also the integration of the self. Providence provides the integrative principle of the elder Crusoe's allegorical interpretation: it is the origin of prophetic warnings, which he discovers in the record of everyday occurrences, and it is the source of overarching patterns of meaning, which he associates with repeated events. Assuming time to be simultaneous instead of linear, Crusoe sees, with hindsight, that when he was living on his plantation in Brazil, he was "just like a Man cast away upon some desolate Island" (35).[8] In the storms that he endured in his first days at sea, he perceives a punishment for the "wicked leaving of my Father's house, and abandoning my duty" (9); and in desire itself, he finds "a secret over-ruling Decree that hurries us on to be the Instruments of our own Destruction" (14). Sign reading, he understands that he departed for his ill-fated voyage "in an evil hour—September 1—the same day eight year" that he "left his father and his mother" (40). Ending in shipwreck, this voyage initiates the spiritual crisis that will lead to Crusoe's reaffirmation of faith. It also initiates crises in the values of individualism and in the narrative structure itself.

In the journal that Crusoe keeps on the island, there is a contestation for dominance between the allegorical and the realistic narratives. From the beginning of the fiction, the thrust of the allegory is fundamentally at odds with the defining interests of the picaresque. While the former functions to embed the recalcitrant self in a network of symbolic relations, the latter seeks to free it from all affiliational ties. In the spiritual autobiography, Crusoe's confidence in his own powers must ultimately be supplanted by his recognition of the surpassing power of God, while in the realistic narrative, he must achieve a fully confident conviction of autonomy. As the narratives move toward Crusoe's conversion, allegory is itself transformed and is forced to serve the ends of realism.

Crusoe's crisis of belief is signaled by increasing despair, confusion, and irrational anxiety. Although the retrospective narrator attributes these feelings to Crusoe's faltering faith, the text also associates them with his horror of self-obliteration. To feel that one is abandoned by God is to lose one's conviction of autonomy and psychic wholeness—it is to be plunged into a cosmic darkness, which is also the disintegration of the self. After the shipwreck, an earthquake, and in the course of a severe illness, Crusoe experiences the psychic terror that marks the outer edge of Puritan introspection. Attempting to move Crusoe out of the spiritual and psychological paralysis that then besets him, Defoe is torn between the spiritual autobiography's urge to reconcile him with God and individualism's requirement that the illusion of autonomy be maintained. Identifying God's power with the power of his father, Crusoe has a "terrible dream" that gives a human shape to the divine. He sees "a Man descend from a great black Cloud, in a Bright Flame of Fire." His "dreadful" countenance is also "bright as Flame," and he holds a spear with which he threatens the life of the rebellious son who has not yet repented (87). Crusoe recognizes that "My dear Father's Words are come to pass: God's Justice has overtaken me, and I have none to help or hear me" (91). Reconciling himself only *symbolically* to his father by reconciling himself *explicitly* to God, Crusoe is able to maintain the *fact* of the familial rupture, which undergirds his illusion of independence. Further, by identifying himself with the omnipotence of God, Crusoe finds his own power and integrity affirmed. Conversion to God becomes, in this context, a conversion to the centrality of the self. After the transformative moment, in which the soul is replaced by the rational mind, there is no need for Defoe to extend the religious reading of Crusoe's experience.[9] Realism— the narrative of individualism—appropriates allegory, the narrative of spirituality. The problem of interiority remains, but it is associated now with the psychology of the autonomous self. Crusoe's psychic struggle is defined in relation to himself, not in relation to a higher being. That new struggle evokes and shapes the fantastic narrative, which interrogates the values that Crusoe self-consciously affirms.

In the realistic narrative, Crusoe describes his imposition of order on an alien environment, explains how he establishes ownership of the island through the efforts of his labor, and argues that he has achieved mental stability through the cultivation of practical reason and self-discipline. Adjusting private to public time, he chronicles the passing of days, weeks, months, and years, detailing his patterns of sleeping, eating, and working. In this mode, Crusoe presents himself as resourceful and resilient. He is capable initially of managing an economy based on use and is able then to accumulate surplus value with the grain and money that he saves. Experiencing himself as powerful and autonomous, he believes desire—which is inevitably "for Things which I had not" (129)—to be irrelevant to life in the "kingdom" of his island: "I had nothing to covet; for I had all that I was now capable of enjoying: I was Lord of the whole Mannor; or if I pleas'd, I might call my self King, or Emperor over the whole Country which I had Possession of. There were no Rivals. I had no Competitor, none to dispute Sovereignty or Command with me" (128). In this, as in other moments of unrestrained grandiosity, Crusoe experiences himself not only as integrated and whole, but actually as omnipotent.

At the same time, Crusoe's isolation intensifies anxieties that undermine his hard-won sense of internal mastery and coherence. In the fantastic narrative that emerges, the island becomes a mirror image of his mind. Crusoe's "reign" proves to be also his "captivity " (137), with himself the jailer, prisoner, and prison. His terror of annihilation by unseen forces is the projected terror of a self that is internally alienated and divided. From the moment of his arrival on the island, Crusoe is acutely fearful of others whom he does not see. On his first night, he sleeps in a tree with his truncheon; and, in the days and years that follow, he carries his gun everywhere, despite his belief that the island is uninhabited. His constant dread is that he will be "swallow'd up alive" by wild beasts or cannibals (82), as he was, very nearly, by the sea. Hiding himself in the "fortress" that he erects, he continues to extend his barricades at the same time that he enlarges and cultivates his domain. His anxiety is under rational control only when he believes his autonomy to be complete. At the same time, it is the illusory nature of that autonomy that continually threatens him with fear of existential alienation.[10]

In his eleventh year, as the fantastic narrative continues, Crusoe encounters a sign of indubitable otherness in the form of a single footprint on the beach. It is this uncanny presence—himself and not himself—that finally subverts the delicate emotional balance that, from time to time, he has been able to achieve. Standing "like one Thunderstruck," as if he "had seen an Apparition," he feels "perfectly confus'd and out of myself" (153)—effectively divided. Losing faith in his own integrity and power, he loses faith also in the omnipotence of the ideal other. "As wonderful Experience as I had had of his Goodness, now vanished," he observes, "as if he that had fed me by Miracle hitherto, could not preserve by his Power the Provision which he had made for me by his Goodness" (156). Distraught when he realizes that he cannot claim the footprint as his own, Crusoe experiences himself as an object in another's world. Paranoid, he frantically buries his possessions, builds fortifications, and plans strategies of defense. "In two Years Time," he explains, "I had a thick Grove and in five or six Years Time I had a Wood before my Dwelling, growing so monstrous thick and strong, that it was indeed perfectly impassable" (161). When he ultimately finds "the Shore spread with Skulls, Hands, Feet, and other Bones of humane Bodies," he recognizes the cannibals' "feasting spot" (165) and is thrust into the paranoid hell of his imaginings. As his anxiety puts an "End to all Invention" (176), his moods oscillate wildly; he is haunted by nightmares and, in the daytime, by fantasies of revenge. His intense desire for escape, which is a desire to elude himself, is satisfied only when the solipsism that entraps him yields to a form of sociality in which he can dominate others. This transformation is anticipated by Crusoe in a dream in which he rescues a savage from cannibals who would kill and then devour him. In the dream, the man he saves becomes his servant and helps him to flee the island. When that dream becomes reality, Crusoe's psychic economy begins to change. The narrative enters a transitional phase, which facilitates a movement away from the fantastic mode and toward a realistic resolution. A substantially extended version of his earlier relation to Xury, Crusoe's relationship with Friday is based on a series of contradictions, which help to explain how the illusion of male autonomy is created and sustained.

The consolidation of Crusoe's precariously balanced and divided self takes place through Defoe's imaginative manipulation of a complex, hierarchical system of racial, national, and gender differences, which structure Crusoe's relation to his servant. Together, these differences work to establish for Crusoe an apparently autonomous but actually exploitative male identity, which denies dependence on others. Snatching the savage from the mouths of his captors, Crusoe is no longer a son, but becomes at once a maternal, paternal, and godlike figure. Giving Friday a miraculous birth, he reinscribes the familial relation from a position of power, preparing the way for a new social persona. Treating the man as a clean slate upon which he alone can write, Crusoe names him for the day on which he is saved and designates himself as "Master." Defoe's fantasy is one of willing, even delighted subordination, with the kneeling Friday placing Crusoe's foot upon his head (203) as he offers appropriate signs of "Subjection, Servitude and Submission" (206).[11] Instructing Friday in English, Crusoe teaches him also what to eat and how to dress, deters him from cannibalism, and attempts to convert him to the Christian faith. Their relationship is written in the form of a domestic idyll. Friday, whose affections are tied to him "like those of a Child to a Father" (209), is feminized as well as infantilized by the paternalistic order. Crusoe begins to love the "Creature," who loves him more "than it was possible for him ever to love any Thing before" (213). They live together in Edenic bliss and Crusoe believes it to be "the pleasantest Year of all the Life I led in this Place" (213).

Defoe's representation of Crusoe's "natural" superiority rests on his assumption of an ideology of geographical diffusionism that is linked, on one side, to English nationalism and, on the other, to capitalist individualism.[12] The basic presumption of that ideology concerns the centrality of Europeans and Europe and the marginality of "others, " who are reduced to the level of childlike "primitives." As he had described Xury previously as "my boy," Crusoe now describes Friday as "my man." Both are as available for appropriative ownership as is the "empty" island that Crusoe has "discovered" and which he develops and exploits for his own use. Because Friday is at the periphery of Defoe's worldview, he is defined as uncivilized and savage. But if he were only that, he would threaten Crusoe's convictions of autonomy. Because he is also identified as the "good" native, he can be perceived as innocent and childlike—educable in his primitivity. In this way, Friday becomes the object of a love shaped by its partners' inequality. Caring for him as a child and, implicitly, as a wife, Crusoe is morally justified in requiring his obedience and fidelity. Friday's labor, like his affections, belongs "naturally" to his master. The colonial project is therefore rationalized through its domestication, and with Friday's conversion to Christianity, it is also sanctified.

Although the contradiction that structures the colonial relation can be disguised, it cannot be erased. In his interactions with Friday, Crusoe wavers between a fearful belief that the native is dangerous, even deadly in his difference, and the sense that *because* of his difference, he is attractive and deserving of sympathy. Mediating between these polar attitudes, Crusoe creates fantastic compromises which are intended to control an otherness that is threatening to his identity. So, by defining Friday's features as European and his skin as "tawny," Crusoe simultaneously accepts and denies the native's strangeness. Assigning him the role of an educable and loving child, Crusoe splits off menacing qualities of difference, constructing a benign hierarchical relation that allows the incorporation of the other into the masterful self. That mastery is shattered, however, when Friday dares to assert his own autonomy. Hearing Friday's expressions of joy when he sees his "country" and "nation" from a hill on the island (223), Crusoe experiences himself as subordinate to Friday's subject self. And as paranoia returns, his xenophobia also is aroused.

> I made no doubt, but that if Friday could get back to his own Nation again, he would not only forget all his Religion, but all his Obligation to me; and would be forward enough to give his Countrymen an Account of me, and come back perhaps with a hundred or two of them, and make a Feast upon me. (224)

Now, in Crusoe's mind, Friday is no longer separable from the other natives, and is therefore to be feared instead of desired. The realist psychic economy of self and other exposes its roots in the fantastic economy of the divided, intrapsychic self. The "jealousy" that Crusoe experiences for "some Weeks" marks the return of an anxiety of obliteration and abandonment that can only be calmed by the restoration of his dominance in socioeconomic and national as well as personal terms.[13]

Although Crusoe's jealous anxiety is assuaged by Friday's repeated affirmations of fidelity, it is his own rescue of Friday's father from the cannibals that proves decisive in ending his ambivalence— and the modal vacillations of the text. After effecting the symbolic substitution that installs Crusoe in the place of patriarch, the text authorizes the values of individualism and the mode of realism.[14] In psychological terms, Crusoe's relation to Friday enables the formation of the subjectivity of possessive individualism: a movement away from the self-obsession of fantastic consciousness toward the objectifications and hierarchies that belong to realist social discourse. The affectivity of their domesticity is unthreatening because it is grounded in inequity. It serves to naturalize the exploitation of Friday's labor while it masks the transition from a primitive island economy based on use value to a capitalist economy based on the alienation of land and the values of surplus and exchange. Although Crusoe had already established his possession of the land through his accumulation of grain and his right to political sovereignty through his holding of property, it is only when the island is populated—by Friday, Friday's father, and a Spaniard whom Crusoe has also rescued—that he is finally able to exercise the full social authority that he could, until then, only nominally claim.[15]

> My Island was now peopled, and I thought my self very rich in Subjects; and it was a merry Reflection which I frequently made, How like a King I look'd. First of all, the whole Country was my own meer property; so that I had an Undoubted Right of Dominion. 2dly, My People were perfectly subjected: I was absolute Lord and Lawgiver; they all owed their Lives to me, and were ready to lay down their Lives, *if there had been Occasion of it*, for me. (241)

Here, the passion for domination is revealed to be the other side of the liberatory spirit that initially motivated Crusoe's quest, and the individualistic self of capitalism is shown to depend for its consolidation on the instrumentalization and appropriation of nature and other human subjects.

As the population of the island begins to grows, Crusoe's fantasies of power proliferate. When he meets a ship full of mutineers with their deposed commander, he presents himself as a combination of conquering soldier and benign deliverer, with "a naked Sword by my Side, two Pistols in my Belt, and a Gun on each Shoulder" (253). The commander's response to his "Spectre-like" form is fully appropriate to the grandiosity of Crusoe's self-presentation. "Am I talking to God or Man," the commander asks, "Is it a real Man or an Angel?" Proclaiming that "I am a Man, an Englishman" (254), Crusoe locates himself at the intersection of individualism and nationalism, a location to which the religious identifications of an earlier moment are no longer relevant.[16] In an ecstasy of self-confidence induced by this strange new world of social, personal, and economic possibility, Crusoe tries out a variety of identities, playing "Generalissimo" (with Friday his lieutenant-general), the island's governor, and the governor's delegated representative. In this way, he redefines himself to accommodate the requirements of the society to which he is now ready to return.

In the final segment of the fiction, Crusoe is fully restored to the code of realism and to his newly integrated and socially adapted self. Having completely suppressed the fantastic form of self-awareness, he can tell the captain, with bravado, that "Men in our Circumstances [are] past the Operation of Fear" (260). Everywhere at once, he is a master of military strategy, an innovative planner, and a courageous leader of his motley band of men. His island is at first his empire—defended by arms—and then, as he prepares for his departure, his "Collony," a place that he organizes along class lines, delegating authority while sustaining economic and political control. After he returns to the mainland and finds himself rich from the rentier share of his Brazilian plantation, he comes to appreciate the power of capital for self-sustaining growth. Interpreting institutionalized privilege as personal success, Crusoe, like Defoe, celebrates a false autonomy that depends on the exploitation of racial, national, and socioeconomic others—and involves not so much the oppression but the erasure of women.

In order to be the free political subject and autonomous individual that the ideology of bourgeois capitalism affirms and specifically distinguishes as male, Crusoe needs to liberate himself from kinship ties, which have determined social position and limited personal identity in the past. As he struggles to achieve the class status to which he aspires, he must also learn to play the gender role that he has been assigned. This means that he will have to displace the father with whom, as a male, he identifies, while he tries to make himself invulnerable to the challenge that would be posed by the son he must produce if he is to play the patriarch at all. Further, in order to affirm his gender difference, he not only has to deny affiliation with his mother, he also must resist the sexual woman who, in replacing her, would bear him the son he needs but also fears. Arousing his desire, her sexuality would evoke his vulnerability; representing difference, her femininity would threaten his masculinity; promising love, she would explode his illusion of autonomy altogether. The realistic narrative seeks to resolve the profound contradictions that emerge from the historically defined dilemma, but the resolution it effects only serves to reproduce them.[17]

Initiated by filial disobedience, Crusoe's project is shaped by an anxiety of paternity that makes him want to supplant his father economically and psychologically, achieving property and status independently, without becoming a father who himself can be displaced. In order to accomplish this, Defoe makes a number of ingenious interventions. The father who is rejected and made invisible at one level reemerges at another in a disguised but recognizable form. In the allegorical mode, God serves as a father substitute, as we have seen, while the three ships' captains function, at the level of realism, in a similar capacity. Crusoe's transformation from son to patriarch is marked and facilitated by the text's erasure of the religious allegory, as it is by the inversion of Crusoe's relation to the Portuguese captain, who is indebted to Crusoe for his life and reinstatement to power. Crusoe avoids the threat of parricide by playing the paternal role with Friday, whose own father he supplants and who has no power for him to fear. Further, his claim to his island property is not legitimated and reproduced through Friday or through a biological child, but descends through the children who are born as—and to— subordinates: to the women captured for sexual purposes from the mainland (305), to those whom he exports for his colonists from Brazil (women "proper for Service, or for Wives"), and to those whom he transports with other "necessaries" from England, who are intended for higher-statused but still inferior Englishmen (306). The oedipal struggle, which the text covertly maps, is avoided by the introduction of an imperialist drama in which the threatening affective family is replaced.

In its representation of Crusoe's experience on the island, the text metaphorizes the implications of the sexual division of labor. At the heart of that representation is the need of the male to distinguish himself from the feminine, which he then controls, appropriates, and displaces. Exemplifying the male individual in the realistic narrative, Crusoe succeeds magnificently in his project of sublimation. Self-sufficient, he usurps the female role in the functions he performs: cooking, sewing, baking, and domesticating animals. He gives symbolic birth to Friday, first dreaming him into existence and then saving him from death, naming him, and treating him as a son. Later, installing him in the domestic space as surrogate wife, he develops an erotically tinged, homosocial relationship with the native that makes it unnecessary for him to establish affective ties to women, who are barely present in the text. The fact of his marriage ("and that not either to my Disadvantage or Dissatisfaction"), the existence of his three children, and the death of his wife are all disconcertingly announced in a single sentence at the novel's conclusion (305). These four family members are bracketed as irrelevant. They are secondary as a group to the families that proliferate on the island to which Crusoe's restless spirit repeatedly urges him to return. Because their relation to him affirms his masculine authority while hiding his potentially disruptive sexuality, the island families enable him to play the surrogate God who here, as elsewhere, safely assumes the father's place.

The disjunction that is created in the fiction between woman's literal absence and her metaphorical presence signals the tension that exists between the text's need to repress and its urge to disclose her. So, while male subjectivity is constructed through the appropriation, subordination, and erasure of the female, her existence is also continually, if covertly, reaffirmed. The text refuses the exclusion of women by representing the son's connection to the female and maternal in coded terms.[18] The feminine saturates representations of nature, which serve as the crux of gender displacements, enabling Crusoe's mastery while revealing its fragility. Presented early in the text as the primal maternal body, nature is simultaneously destructive and sustaining: the ocean, which has the power both to overwhelm and to deliver, and the fertile island into which Crusoe initially burrows for protection and from which he derives security and nourishment. The primal fear of engulfment—which is a fear of the omnipotence of nature and the mother—reverberates in Crusoe's obsessive terror of the cannibals, a terror that is made more frightening when it is projected onto alien others, who become more alien as a consequence of the projection. In this sense, the island offers Crusoe a transitional space—an opportunity to differentiate himself from a feminized world that he is also able to control. Establishing distance from the body of the island, he appropriates it first for his own use, then alienates it as his possession, and finally cultivates and commodifies it through the exploited labor of others. In domesticating nature, Crusoe affirms his masculine autonomy. By taking possession of the island body, which he has cultivated, he establishes himself as a political individual. By populating it and governing its people, he asserts his authority within the social community. Representing Crusoe's transformation of nature from untamed wilderness to orderly polis, Defoe participates in the dominant political and scientific discourses of his time. Constructed by—and also helping to construct—the sexual division of labor that was then in the process of revision, those discourses placed rational masculinity against a feminine nature, subordinating the latter to the former, as feminine feeling was subordinated to the masculine mind.

When Crusoe leaves the island—ostensibly rejecting the gender indeterminacy that is typical of the male fantastic narrative—he has become a political agent, an entrepreneurial capitalist, an imperialist, and a self-dependent male: the last is the identity that undergirds them all. Friday has become his faithful mate, effectively forswearing father and country for Crusoe. After returning to civilization, Friday kills a bear and Crusoe kills a pack of wolves. Both incidents are described in the realistic mode of the fiction's final segment and suggest that the acculturated male individual, with his representative, has masculinized female nature and then conquered it. As the obsession of fantastic self-awareness has been absorbed by the hierarchical relations of realism, so also has the problematic relation of male and female been absorbed in the male's relation to himself, to a masculinized nature, and to other men. The realistic narrative of the possessive male individual, as Defoe constructs it, is a narrative that has no place for women.

Constructing Crusoe as a possessive individualist, Defoe reveals contradictions that he tries to contain in the tensions of the realist narrative, and that he exposes as psychic pain in the fantastic. Mainly, the novel demonstrates that the illusion of autonomy rests upon the transformation of relations of dependence into relations of exploitation. Because men's dependence upon women is the deepest and most threatening dependency of all, any evidence of it must be thoroughly expunged. In *Moll Flanders* and *Roxana,* Defoe sets out to construct female individualists who will be equivalent to Crusoe. But as he applies to women a concept that the sex-gender system associates exclusively with men, he inadvertently exposes the social paradoxes that it is the function of the ideology of individualism to disguise. Given their definition as women, Moll and Roxana cannot disavow the sexual and affective needs that Crusoe either denies or satisfies through substitution, nor can they dismiss their affiliation with the family, which for them is the locus of emotional connection. In the accounts of his female protagonists, Defoe exposes the discrepancy that exists between the instrumentalization of others, which is central to capitalist individualism, and the normative significance for women of sexual desire and maternity.[19]

Clearly, the metaphor of man creating himself in isolation on his desert island has little in common with the pragmatic circumstances of Crusoe's female counterparts, who are always embedded in social relations. Conventionally seen as wives and mothers, and forbidden legitimate routes to capitalist enterprise, women in this period were defined biologically and relationally, not in terms of their autonomy. Although Defoe accepts the normative categories of femininity, he subordinates them to the requirements of an essentially masculine individualism and deprives them of their ideological content. So, while his mistress/whore shares with the idealized mother/wife a sexual body that connects her to children and to men, Defoe denies her affectivity and represents her motivation as purely instrumental. Because he both exaggerates and perverts the female stereotype, he creates tonal disjunctions in the text that many readers have interpreted as authorial irony—particularly in the case of Moll. These textual fractures are not in fact ironic, but testify to the contradictory nature of Defoe's imaginative construction—as they do to the rigidity of his culture's gender categories.

Defoe's assumption about his whores can be seen as oddly similar to the assumptions that eighteenth-century novels make about respectable women's lives. Although status may differ, the essentials of women's experience remain, in many ways, the same. Defoe ironizes courtship, family life, and marriage, but he recognizes the value—even the necessity—of such institutionalized forms for women, even when those forms are utterly deprived of substance. Drawn to conventional roles, Moll and Roxana do not choose entrepreneurial adventure, as Crusoe does. It is forced upon Moll by the faithlessness of her first lover and upon Roxana by the abandonment of her husband. It is only after they have been deprived of licit relationships with men upon whom they can economically rely that they are willing to consider their alternatives. Resisting membership in an exploited, laboring underclass, they can be supported as mistresses or they can work as prostitutes. What the text reveals is that the differences among their possibilities are more imagined than real, and that none of their options will produce autonomy. If they choose to be protected by a man, they are subject to his whims, as well as to the misogyny of patriarchal institutions. If they decide to live at the margins of the fathers' law, they can seek economic self-sufficiency by removing their bodies from the cycle of reproduction in order to alienate them as marketable commodities. Whichever path they choose, they remain subject to the contingencies of their female roles and bodies. But when their sexuality is detached from desire and maternity, it becomes merely entrepreneurial, and the children who mark what becomes a parodic family must either be commodified or ignored.

Although Defoe's male and female narratives are necessarily enabled by the rejection of familial relationships, which ultimately return to haunt them, the ghosts that are laid to rest in *Robinson Crusoe* indelibly stamp the female-centered fictions. All three texts resonate with anxieties that are aroused by the transition from an extended kinship structure, which is crucial to an agricultural economy, to the nuclear family, which is responsible for socializing its members to bourgeois capitalism and its gender roles.[20] All three expose the tension that exists between the ideology of individualism, which privileges autonomy and instrumentalizes relationships, and the individual's need for affective, reciprocal, and sexual connection. Testifying to the power of male sublimation, *Robinson Crusoe* shows how needs and desires that ordinarily seek satisfaction in the family can be redirected to the production of culture and the exploitation of others. (In that novel, as we have seen, women who are too threatening to be exploited must be eliminated altogether.) But in *Moll Flanders* and *Roxana*, the tensions that exist between the demands of individualism and those of the sex-gender system prove to be intolerable. Perverting normative conceptions of femininity, they also provide a distorted image of the nature of the family.

For women, there is no world elsewhere: no desert island, no place beyond society. But the domesticity that binds women to society also deprives them of choice, of agency, and therefore of a story. As Moll herself points out, a woman without a man is "left alone to shift for [her]self"—and it is precisely such a shifting that provides Moll her adventures and Defoe his plot.[21] The empty spaces and silences within Moll's adult narrative are those in which she lived "as if married" and "like a woman": bearing children with a single man. To the extent that she functions outside of the legitimate domestic sphere—as a mistress, whore, and finally thief—Moll does appear to be a social and an economic agent. But her reference is always back to the private female world that continues, however perversely, to mold her experience. Marriage provides the model from which she diverges, and which she also cynically duplicates: legitimate marriages which she contracts, bigamous marriages in which she participates, and illusory marriages which she feigns. The children whom she bears (and who identify her with the female sphere) are ubiquitous despite the fact that she relinquishes them with as little ceremony as her mother had relinquished her. And although they slip as easily into death as they do from her memory, each one is immediately replaced.

Just as Moll reproduces the family through distorted versions of the wife and mother, so she also acts as a daughter in perverse relationships with several older women. There is the "nurse" who is Moll's foster mother in her childhood and the "governess" who, after helping to rid her of an unwanted child, educates her in the strategies of thievery. There is also her biological mother, whom she accidentally encounters as a respectable plantation manager in America after she herself has been deported as a thief. All of these women live autonomously, without dependence on men, and all have pragmatic skills to teach her. In this regard, they are similar to "real," respectable mothers who socialize their daughters to the values and expectations of the world in which they will have to make their way. But because the survival techniques that Moll must learn involve the instrumentalization of others, they are incompatible with the female stereotype. These are the techniques that the false mothers know through their own experience and that they must help her to acquire.

Still, perverse as familial relations in *Moll Flanders* may seem to be, that perversity is merely an exaggerated rendering of the influence that patriarchal capitalism exerts on affiliational ties. The twinned fear and desire that the new, affective nuclear family produces in the culture are reflected in the incest anxiety that haunts this and other fictions of the period.[22] Moll's discovery that she inadvertently married her brother in England, and is living with him, their children, and her mother in Virginia, suggests at once the fragility and indissolubility of familial bonds in a society that fosters independence and anonymity.[23] Moll's response to "the odd and surprizing" situation ("tho' I was not much touched with the crime of it, yet the action had something in it shocking to nature, and made my husband even nauseous to me" [78]) reflects a deep uncertainty about the relation of "natural" to social prohibition. This is also true of Moll's mother's simultaneous expression of horror at her daughter's "lying with" her son and her advice to Moll that she should not abandon the marriage but should simply "bury the whole thing" (85). Throughout the novel, Moll's continuing references to her "husband/brother" mark an anxious return to problems of consanguinity. That anxiety is evident also in the obliquely incestuous attraction that Moll feels for Humphrey, the son whom she meets years later when she is transported to America as a thief. "About two hours after [Humphrey] was gone," she explains, "he sent me a maidservant and a Negro boy to wait on me, and provisions ready dressed for my supper; and thus I was as I had been in a new world, and began almost to wish that I had not brought my Lancashire husband from England at all" (291). Although it is difficult to understand to which of Moll's several appetites Humphrey is intended to appeal, her urge to displace her husband with her son is relatively clear.

Again through exaggeration, the primal scene of the novel suggests how desire is constructed and distorted within the vaguely incestuous family of capitalist individualism. This is the scene in which Moll is seduced by the son of the surrogate family in which she functions as almost-daughter and as maid. When her would-be lover kisses her passionately and then thrusts five guineas into her hand, she observes: "I was more confounded with the money than I was before with the love; and began to be so elevated that I scarce knew the ground I stood on" (23). It is to this experience that the commodification of Moll's desire can be traced: the redirection of her sexuality into a material form that appears to weaken her erotic energy.[24] Greed and sexual "inclination" become so hopelessly entangled that when her suitor asks her to become his mistress, her "colour came and went at the sight of the purse, and with the fire of his proposal together" (27). Although it is not evident which of the two leads more directly to her compliance, greed ultimately triumphs when she comprehends that she could have sold herself more prudently if she had not given immediately into inclination. "I had been trick'd once by that cheat call'd love," she observes, "but the game was over; I was resolv'd now to be married or nothing, and to be well married or not at all" (53). Although Moll's discourse of desire draws increasingly on the languages of biological instinct and bourgeois respectability, it is shaped throughout by the capitalist form of economic relations, which is doubly exploitative of women. Feeling is experienced as a snare and a delusion. Coins alone are real and their value is the sole measure of success. Much like the capitalist worker who, devoid of property, has only his labor to sell, Moll's body is her only marketable commodity. She can trade it contractually in marriage, which brings her some degree of security and legitimacy, or she can make other less formal, less permanent—and less reputable—arrangements. Either way, as wife or whore, she is likely to find that alienation is the price she pays for the self-commodification required of women by the social system that organizes their existence.[25] Moll's warped form of femininity heightens a truth that normative female roles function to disguise.

The commodification of desire that produces alienation in Moll (as it did also in Crusoe) is part of a larger process of reification that transforms the relation of the self to itself and to others into relations between things.[26] It is in just such a reified environment that Moll perversely comes to thrive. This apparent contradiction is at the heart of the tonal dissonance of the novel, which both confuses and disturbs the reader. Because her world is deprived of affective and symbolic meaning, it is oddly insubstantial: devoid of depth, as Moll herself is without interiority. With nothing stable to which social and psychic significations might be anchored, all appearances are equally valid and all are equally misleading. Seeming to anticipate the late modern subject, Defoe's realistic, early modern self creates an always shifting identity through the roles it copies, adapts to its own purposes, uses, and discards. Each semblance is designed for a specific end: an illusion invented to mediate between the individual's experienced needs and the resistances of others. Moll plays at mistress as she plays at wife, and she plays at both as she will later play at thief. Indeed, it is from her thieving that she derives the greatest pleasure. Released from the more restrictive roles that are associated with her sexuality, the older Moll can "appear in new shapes every time [she goes] abroad" (229), pretending to be everything from a shoplifting male to a gentlewoman as fine as those whose pocket watches she steals to a beggar woman dressed "in the coarsest and most despicable rags I could get" (221). But despite the range and multiplicity of her performances, Moll persists in her belief (it is the belief also of Defoe) that she is possessed of a "real" self. She knows it because it is the very thing that she is always driven to hide, protecting it from others like "the grand secret" that is her name. This illusion of coherence disguises the dissociation implied by her many roles and shifting practices, and it is identified—significantly—with the mystery of her "worth," which no relationship (not that of son, husband, lover, or friend) can persuade her to unveil.

Because she is deprived of the traditional moral values that would be linked to normative femininity, Moll recognizes pragmatic self-interest as the only appropriate guide she has to individual behavior. Driven to criminality by whatever she defines at the moment as an authorizing "necessity," she has plenty of judgments to make, but all are of her victims, none of her own conduct. She blames the mother, whose child she almost murders, for vanity in adorning her daughter with the necklace that she steals (169). She condemns the gentlewoman, whose watch she tries to take, as a "naive fool" because she is ignorant of Moll's thieving stratagems. And she comforts herself that by stealing money from a man whom she seduces, she might dissuade him from running a daily risk of being "undone"

(198). Not content with *being* a hypocrite, Moll chooses at times to "play the hypocrite," an identity that is as valid—and without self-consciousness—as any other (121). From the beginning of the fiction, Moll denounces everything but herself for her plight: everything from the "unenlightened" state that, by not providing care for children who have been orphaned by the deportation of their mothers, is responsible for the "scandalous" life which she has lived (9), to the devil who bestowed upon her the enjoyment of thievery, which prevented her from repudiating criminality even when "my necessities were not so terrifying" (176).

Self-enclosure, which is both cause and effect of individualism, justifies belief in one's own supremacy and in the relative unimportance of others. (For this reason, it is ordinarily linked to masculine, not feminine, "nature.") Locating creativity in the pragmatic making of identities, it identifies power with various forms of falsity. Symptomatically, when Moll describes how she discouraged the proposals of her first lover's brother, she explains that she "said everything to disswade him that I could imagine except telling him the truth" (28). In this novel, it is truth that is literally and figuratively unimaginable. Because it cannot be manipulated to serve defensive purposes, it is also dangerous to what is paradoxically experienced as the integrity of the isolated self. Moll is conscious of the loneliness of individualism only when, caught between identities, she is forced to face reality: in moments of stasis when, without a role to play, she actually feels the psychic disjunction that it would be the function of a fantastic narrative to explore. One of these moments is in midlife, when she sees the appearance fading upon which her sexual identities have relied. It is then that she perceives herself to be an object that others might, to their advantage, use: "When a woman is thus left desolate and void of council," she observes, "she is just like a bag of money, or a jewl dropt on the highway, which is a prey to the next comer" (112). By becoming a thief when she is no longer attractive enough to be a whore, however, she is restored to a masculine form of subjectivity that allows her to be exploitative rather than exploited. It is only later, when she is imprisoned for her crimes, that she falls again into a psychic limbo. In prison, she finds it difficult to inhabit the role of penitent until she believes herself about to die. Understanding then that she has "forfeited all hope of happiness in the eternity that I was just going to enter into" (250), Moll ensures the availability of identities in the next world by lamenting those that she has embodied in this one. The moral pieties she subsequently mouths recall an earlier religious discourse and substitute for the self-reflection that a fantastic narrative would articulate. They become increasingly vacuous and finally disappear after deportation, when she and her Lancashire husband are able to live "as new people in a new world" (264).

Of course, the one obvious role that we never see Moll play is that of conventional mother. It is the role that would openly challenge her status as an individualist by aligning her with a stereotypical femininity. With the intriguing exception of her grown-up son, Moll's children are notable only in their absence. As we have seen, it is this absence that frees Defoe from binding her to a legitimate domestic plot. Still, the frequent pregnancies and births, which are the side effects of her work, subvert Defoe's representation by exposing the reproductive relations that underlie (however tenuously) relations of production in a woman's life. They make Moll's embeddedness in nature visible, and they shatter the illusion of her social freedom and control. Marked by its own temporality and rhythm, the reproductive cycle invokes forms of connectedness that implicitly challenge the alienated relations of capitalism. That the alternatives it raises cannot find a place within this text is indicated by the absence of a fantastic narrative. Defoe can maintain his realistic rendering of possessive individualism's female configuration only by appropriating the female body's reproductive energies for capitalist enterprise, while foreclosing the self-awareness that would suggest that appropriation's psychic costs.

The subordination of maternity to an appropriate individualism is achieved through the interventions of Moll's "governess," Mother Midnight. A thief who has "left off the trade," Mother Midnight becomes a midwife "of the right sort" (140), operating at the threshold between male and female worlds of value: reifying, professionalizing, and commodifying. As a business woman, she transforms the reproductive into the productive body, acting as procuress and abortionist, and profiting from other women's labor by buying and selling the infants that her clients bear. As Moll understands, the children who cannot be accommodated by the market are simply done away with: "muther'd or starv'd by neglect and ill-usage, which was much the same" (148). Mother Midnight takes cares of Moll through one of her unwanted pregnancies, delivering and disposing of her child so that she can continue to function in an individualistic world in which sexuality is commodified and separated from maternity. When Moll becomes a thief, Mother Midnight serves as mentor once again, acting as "fence" and pawnbroker for Moll's stolen goods and assigning her a "schoolmistress" who instructs her in the tricks of her new trade. With a harsh pragmatism that reduces all value to the values of exchange, Mother Midnight makes explicit the antifeminine motivations and practices that drive entrepreneurial capitalism. Her ability to apply her managerial skills with equal competence to the criminal and sexual underworlds suggests the commonality of these diverse activities within the dominant economic system.

While Defoe cannot allow Moll's maternity to interfere with an aspiring individualism in which he clearly has substantial stakes, he is not finally able to separate her success as a bourgeoise from the ideology that is associated with female identity. Although Moll achieves prosperity as a capitalist in the New World, advancing to plantation owner from self-sufficient farmer, her respectability—and even her redemption—as a woman must be established in the private sphere. Ironically, the appearance of gentility (which is all the gentility that Moll or Defoe desires) rests ultimately on her enactment of the roles of wife and mother. Accordingly, her melodramatic reconciliation with Humphrey toward the end of the novel is offered as compensation for the lack of feeling that has characterized all of her previous relations to her children. Unaccountably described as her "own and only child" (288), the adult (and desirable) Humphrey is apparently intended as a substitute for his sisters and brothers who, once abandoned, are now forgotten. Anticipating her meeting with her long-lost son with "a confus'd mixture of joy and fright," Moll describes how "lying on my face [I] wept, and kiss'd the ground that he had set his foot on" (280). Having succinctly displayed Moll's credentials for a devoted maternity, Defoe swiftly vindicates her as a proper wife. He accomplishes this with the death of her husband/ brother and the legitimation of her bigamous, if long-standing, marriage to Jemy. The concluding scene of the novel is one of connubial happiness, with the wealthy old couple spending their last years "in sincere penitence for the wicked lives we have lived" (297). Having followed an extremely circuitous route, Defoe concludes his picaresque fiction with a peaceful domesticity that is as undisturbed by analysis or self-reflection as Moll's previous career has been. While Defoe's concluding effort to suture individualism to the normative sex-gender system is as unbelievable in *Moll Flanders* as it was at the end of *Robinson Crusoe*, it cannot be undertaken at all in *Roxana*. There, an integrated fantastic narrative suggests that the need to choose between autonomy and maternity produces a tragic dilemma, which is endemic to the situation of the female individualist. In the realistic narrative, Roxana's history is a variant of Moll's. Initially embedded in the domestic sphere, Roxana is sold on the marriage market by her father to an "Eminent Brewer" whom she describes as "not ungentle," "handsome," and "a sportsman," but "[o]therwise a weak, empty-headed, untaught Creature," who was essentially "a Fool."[27] Abandoned by him and left penniless, with five children to support, Roxana pawns her possessions so that she will not see "my Children starve before my face" (46). Since her primary concern is with her own survival, however, she fears that in her hunger she might behave "like one of the pitiful Women of Jerusalem . . . eating up my very Children" (50–51). In fact, she turns out to be only slightly less ruinous in her selfishness. Because, as she explains, "the Misery of my own Circumstances hardened my Heart against my own Flesh and Blood" (52), she forsakes her offspring to the uncertain care of relatives and the certain cruelty of the parish. Once forsaken, they are, for fifteen years, forgotten.

Relieved of the children who would have bound her to the domestic plot, Roxana—like Moll—initiates her adventures by commodifying her body, trading it to her landlord for security and comfort, a transaction in which eroticism is diverted to meet the material aim that then appropriates it. Although Roxana acknowledges that she has some "inclination" for sex, she also insists that "my Spirits were far from being high; my Blood had no Fire in it, to kindle the Flame of Desire" (75). Like Moll, her desire is subordinated to acquisitive instrumentality and is reduced and deformed by that subordination. Also like Moll, her alienation facilitates her career, as she fornicates upward, a mistress to merchants and noblemen who represent rungs on the ladder that she climbs to prosperity. Not content with the uncertainties of a courtesan's life, she carefully constructs an economic safety net, investing and saving in order to advance "from a Lady of Pleasure, [to] a Woman of Business, and of great

Business too, I assure you" (169). Her shrewdness keeps her from confusing—as Moll does—the relatively unconstrained circumstances of a mistress with the subjugation of a wife. She insists that after her "bad luck" with marriage, she has no desire to become a wife again:

> I found, that a Wife is treated with Indifference, a Mistress with a strong Passion; a Wife is look'd upon, as but an Upper-Servant, a Mistress is a Sovereign; a Wife must give up all she has; have every Reserve she makes for herself, be thought hard of, and be upraided with her very *Pin-Money*, whereas a Mistress makes the Saying true, *that what the Man has,* is hers and *what she has,* is her own; the Wife bears a thousand insults and is forc'd to sit still and bear it, or part and be undone; a Mistress insulted, helps herself immediately and takes another. (170)

She remains resistant to wedlock even when she is pregnant with the merchant's child, despite his insistence that if they should marry, he would not claim any part of her estate. Acknowledging that "it is not you . . . that I suspect, but the Laws of Matrimony [that] puts the Power in your Hands" (190), Roxana provides a sweeping condemnation of the patriarchal order, contending that a woman who marries becomes a willing slave, surrendering her "Liberty, Estate, Authority and Everything, to the Man" (187). Her protofeminist position distinguishes her from Moll, but its inconsistencies suggest the extent of Defoe's own ambivalence. At a later point, she claims that her rejection of the merchant "was the most preposterous thing that ever Woman did," a mark of her possession by the devil (197), and she names vanity instead of principle as her motivation, explaining that she was driven by "nothing less than being Mistress to the King" (201).[28] Her vanity proves to be well-justified and she defers marriage repeatedly until she perceives the decline of her beauty and her reputation when middle age puts "an End to . . . the intriguing Part of my Life" (287). Her marriage to the merchant returns her to domesticity and marks the end of the predominantly picaresque fiction.

Although in the realist narrative Roxana, like Moll, instrumentalizes normative female roles, unlike Moll, she is conscious of the similarities between normativity and perversity. And because she is intensely self-conscious, her feelings are always mixed. Her vacillations about the value and desirability of marriage are matched by fluctuating assessments of her own motivations in living the life of a whore. She argues material need, for example, claiming that love is "a Point so ridiculous to me, without the main thing [which is] the Money" at the same time that she describes herself as so "immensely rich" that "even Avarice itself seem'd to be glutted" (225). She explains that after twenty-six years in the profession, she has become "so long habituated . . . to a life of Vice, that really it appear'd to be no Vice to me" (229), just before she proclaims herself thoroughly disgusted with her wickedness, although "without the least Hint . . . from what may be call'd Religion or Conscience, and far from anything of Repentance" (243). And while she attributes her early behavior to the "Devil's doing," she acknowledges that it was really "that greater Devil of Poverty [that] prevail'd" (243). At one point, in a spirit of resolution, she acknowledges that while she "lov'd it for the sake of the Vice, and . . . delighted in being a Whore as such," poverty and necessity also stimulated in her excesses of avarice and vanity (244). The mixture of moral judgment, pragmatism, and desire characteristic of Roxana's self-reflections is significantly different from the rationalizations of Moll, who prefers any illusion to the truth. In his protagonist's struggle to understand the irrational desires by which she is driven, and in her inability to divorce herself effectively from her past, Defoe does manage to create the impression of psychic depth for the first time in his novels. It is this more complex interiority that prevents a simple attribution of Roxana's discrepant views to a disjunction of personality (like Moll's) or to Defoe's own ambivalent misogyny. Rather, the odd combination of Roxana's superficial materialism and her increasingly tortured self-awareness suggests a complicated if contradictory conception of subjectivity, which is reflected in an equally radical (and quite prophetic) textual form.

In *Robinson Crusoe*, as we have seen, the fantastic narrative dominates the island experience but is bracketed by the protagonist's picaresque adventures. In *Roxana*, the fantastic narrative continually interrupts the picaresque and, after the protagonist's marriage, subverts it completely by focusing on Roxana's feelings of guilt and shame. As Defoe moves toward the secular self-reflexivity and inwardness of the fantastic mode, which will not develop fully until the late eighteenth and nineteenth centuries, he defines a powerful new form of female subjectivity. The dilemma he sets out is one that will ultimately yield the hysterical women of Freud, and his representation of the divided consciousness of his protagonist anticipates sophisticated formal strategies that will not emerge until much later.

It is Roxana's female body that seals her within the fantastic form of consciousness, initiating a deep interior division that Defoe ultimately shapes in tragic terms. Although Roxana instrumentalizes her family in the interests of self-preservation and autonomy, she soon discovers that she cannot escape the contradictions of her perverse position. Like Moll, she is forced repeatedly to a maternity by which she is repelled—not least of all because "breeding" will ruin her value as a commodity, impairing the beauty which is "the Great Article that supported my Interest" (143). Wishing to preserve her appearance, she "is not sorry" when she sees some of her children die and, after experiencing "the first Touches of Affection" (142), she does not shrink from sending the others away—even to the "She-Butchers" who are certain to starve and murder them (116). But unlike Moll, whose consciousness functions in a continuous present that enables her to bury her infants without regret, Roxana cannot overcome a vexed relation to a past in which she has traded her body and abdicated her maternal responsibilities. Her pain is reflected in recurrent feelings of guilt about her "life of wickedness" and in her contradictory sense of herself both as a "sorrowful Penitent" (111), haunted by memory, and as one who, unable to repent, is possessed by "a silent, sullen kind of Grief, which cou'd not break out either in Words or Tears, and which was, therefore, much the worse to bear" (167). Because her moral urges are not animated by religious faith, they assume a psychological reference that embroils them in an obsessive, repetitive, and self-destructive dynamic. In this context, the crucial distinction to be drawn between the fixed subjectivity of Moll and the more fluid subjectivity of Roxana derives from the fact that Moll is socially alienated, while in Roxana, Defoe explores the internal division that self-alienation yields. While Moll's consciousness is flattened—composed of disjointed moments and contradictory positionalities—Roxana's consciousness is complex, shaped by irrational impulses of which she is herself aware. While Moll's world is solipsistic and self-enclosed, Roxana's comes to be characterized by collapsing boundaries between self and other, self as other, and other as the self. And although this fantastic aspect of Roxana's interiority is present in the "Dark Reflections" and "Heaviness of Heart" (83) that occur early in the fiction, it is mainly through her increasingly important relation to her servant, Amy, and later in her troubled association with her daughter Susan that Roxana's psychic fragmentation and ultimate breakdown are represented. It is also through her relation to them that the untenability of the contradiction between autonomy and normative femininity is fully articulated.

As several critics have noted, Amy serves as Roxana's "double" in the fiction, an other who is the self.[29] She functions as the site of Roxana's psychic fragmentation at the same time that Roxana finds in her a source of affectivity and a proof of personal continuity. Serving these several functions, the representation of Amy deepens the portrayal of Roxana's inner life, while it contributes a level of symbolic meaning that complicates the text. From the beginning of the novel, Amy works as an active agent on Roxana's behalf, often executing desires that are not explicitly articulated by her mistress. She is described by Roxana as "the Girl who lov'd me to an Excess" (64), "a cunning Wench, and faithful to me, as the Skin to my Back" (75), "an ambitious Jade, who knew my weakest Part" (275), and—perhaps most tellingly—as "Amy, who knew my Disease, but was able to do nothing as to the Remedy" (283). It is Amy who arranges and carries out the abandonment of Roxana's children and then persuades her mistress to succumb to the landlord's seduction. Frequent bedfellows themselves, their sexualities intertwine so that each acts as the instrument of the other's desire while enacting her own desire through the other. In the beginning of the fiction, after Amy has indicated to Roxana her willingness to "be a Whore, or anything, for your sake" (62), she participates in the landlord's game of seduction by playing pimp and acting as voyeur. Roxana then reverses their roles, undressing her maid, thrusting her into the landlord's bed, and remaining to watch their coupling. The ambiguous explanation she offers speaks to a compelling intermingling of their identities. "[A]s I thought myself a Whore," Roxana observes, "I cannot say but that it was something design'd in my Thoughts, that my Maid should be a Whore too, and should not reproach me with it" (81). Amy must not only be neutralized as Roxana's conscience; she must share her mistress's pleasure and desire.

Validating her mistress's behavior, Amy shadows Roxana through her picaresque adventures, preparing for the fiction's shift to the fantastic mode when the tension between autonomy and normative maternity explodes. While Roxana conducts her affair with a prince, for example, Amy sleeps "below," with the prince's gentleman. As Roxana amasses enormous wealth, Amy achieves more affluence, dressing "like a Gentlewoman," serving as Roxana's "companion" instead of as her maid (206), and ultimately becoming "a Woman of Business" capable of managing her mistress's economic affairs (290). She travels repeatedly as an emissary to the representatives of Roxana's past: to her lover and her first husband, to the Dutch merchant—and, finally, to the two daughters and the son who, of the five deserted children, are the only ones who have survived. This last mission completes the transition from a predominantly realistic narrative to one that is predominantly fantastic. It is undertaken by Amy to calm a tormented Roxana who looks back upon her life with "horror," "detestation," and "terror." But when Amy plays the role of mother in order to assuage Roxana's guilt, a crisis develops in their relationship. That crisis reflects Roxana's psychic disintegration and reveals its origins in the radical incompatibility of maternity, female sexuality, and individualism. Too ashamed "to think of ever letting the Children know what a kind of Creature they ow'd their being to, or giving them an Occasion to upraid their Mother with her scandalous Life" (248), Roxana delegates to Amy "the authority to manage everything in the Family" (239). But as Amy establishes herself as the benefactress of the children, she and the past elude Roxana's mastery, and the horror of her evil maternity overwhelms her life. It is at this point that Defoe loses the power to shape and bring his narrative to closure.

In its barely controlled, obsessive, and repetitive movement, this lengthy final segment of the fiction has much the feel of nightmare. Its focus is the confused and finally deadly relation of Roxana to Amy and Susan (who is Roxana's namesake as well as daughter), both of whom play out Roxana's most ambivalent desires and fears. Amy initiates the fantastic crisis, inadvertently compromising her mistress's anonymity by making "an unhappy Discovery of herself" to the girl, who is seeking passionately for her mother. Having worked as a servant in the establishment of the "Lady Roxana," Susan had seen her mother dance in the exotic guise of a Turkish princess (the performance that represents Roxana's unrestrained sexuality in the text). Although she knows the courtesan's "story," she is not certain of her "real" identity. It is that story of illicit sexual performance which a disguised Roxana hears Susan recount: "In a word," she says, "I was in a kind of silent Rage; for the Force I was under of restraining my Passion, was such, as I never felt the like of: I had no Vent; nobody to open myself to" (331). Objectified by Susan, Roxana experiences the full horror of self-knowledge as the rejecting sexualized mother. It is this that makes her hate her daughter and wish for her destruction. Unable to resolve Roxana's dilemma, the narrative is trapped between the intensity of Susan's desire to complete herself by discovering her mother's identity and Roxana's desire to avoid self-shattering shame by evading her daughter's discovery. The compulsive pursuit by the daughter of the compulsively fleeing mother prefigures the fantastic journey of Frankenstein and his monster. Like that deadly interdependence of father and son, which marks the impossible but inevitable division of the self, Roxana can rid herself of the psychic continuities of the past only with a murder that seals her own psychic destruction. Acknowledging that she "would shed but very few tears" for Susan if the girl were to die "naturally" (350), Roxana shrinks overtly from the murder that she then calls implicitly upon Amy to commit. It is as though the mother's sexuality poisons the maternity to which it is opposed.

The ambivalence of Roxana's desire is expressed through her contradictory behavior toward her faithful double: implicitly encouraging while condemning the crime, and turning her self-hatred as rage on the only one who has shared "the Secret History of my Life" (365). Although she recognizes that "to have fall'n upon Amy, had been to have muther'd myself," Roxana initiates a fight so serious that Amy leaves "and was gone for almost good-and-all" (350). The revelation of the murder's circumstances is continually promised by the text and continually deferred as Roxana distances herself from the action to which she felt herself compelled. That her connection to Amy is ineradicable is suggested by the final passage of the novel, which works simultaneously to affirm it and obscure it:

> Here, after some few Years of flourishing, and outwardly happy Circumstances, I fell into a dreadful Course of Calamities, and Amy

also: the very Reverse of our former Good Days; the Blast of Heaven seem'd to follow the Injury done the poor Girl, by us both; and I was brought so low again, that my Repentance seem'd to be only the Consequence of my Misery, as my Misery was of my Crime. (379)

As Roxana acknowledges Amy's crime to have been her own, the distance between them disappears and their fates are merged. The story that began by placing instrumentalized sexuality in opposition to maternity ends by demonizing the sexual mother, who cannot be saved from moral failure and psychic dissolution. This demonization will motivate fictions written by men and women over the next two hundred years, often in novels that duplicate *Roxana*'s central formal strategy.[30] It can also be found in accounts of the hysterical women whose divided minds psychoanalytic theory will explore.

A contradictory, inconsistent, and ambivalent fiction, *Roxana* is also Defoe's most fully realized study of individualism. In *Robinson Crusoe* and *Moll Flanders,* Defoe identifies with the entrepreneurial aspiration of his protagonists and vindicates it in the social discourse of realism. This identificatory relation causes him to appropriate the paranoia of Crusoe's island adventure for the grandiosity of his colonizing effort and leads him to preserve the autonomy of Moll by disavowing, while affirming, her female nature. As the fantastic narrative overwhelms *Roxana*'s realistic plot, Defoe fully exposes the price that women pay for the cultural role that they have been assigned. In the process, he achieves a formal breakthrough that brings individualism's divided form of consciousness to the surface of the text.

That Defoe should anatomize possessive individualism most effectively through the representation of a female subject, to whom possessive individualism is foreclosed, suggests what the writings of future generations of male authors will confirm. The gendered division of labor, which celebrates women's capacity for feeling, encourages men to articulate culturally devalued aspects of their own psychic lives through cross-gender representations. And although these representations are not free of misogyny, they are more than simply misogynistic. Misogyny is clearly woven into Defoe's representation of Roxana, but the female struggle for self-awareness that he describes offers an implicitly radical, even protofeminist critique of the individualism that he celebrated in *Robinson Crusoe* and tried, in his own life, to embody.

Finally, I want to speculate about an intriguing problem that is posed by Defoe's depictions of his male and female individualists and by our reception of them. Most contemporary readers have observed the heterogeneity of Defoe's characters, as well as their lack of intelligibly complex and integrated interior lives. The absence of coherence and interior depth (which Roxana ultimately achieves and which protagonists of nineteenth-century fictions will possess) has been attributed by some to authorial irony, by others to authorial naïveté. It is only recently, however, that some critics have found these characterizations to be uncannily familiar, convincing in a postmodern mode precisely because of their seeming discontinuity and flatness.[31] While one can readily comprehend how the discrepant values of Defoe's protagonists might reflect shifting structures of feeling in a moment of extraordinary social change,[32] it is more difficult to understand how that earlier form of subjectivity should have come to seem simultaneously primitive and eerily prophetic. Reading the temporal relation palimpsestically, so that the past prefigures a present through which the past is also seen,[33] we can surmise that the development of the modern subject, which began to crystallize in the early days of capitalism, contained the seeds of that subject's maturation and change, just as capitalist relations of production contained the promise of their own dialectical transformations.

In this context, Defoe's stories may be seen to have provided embryonic versions of selves that nineteenth- and twentieth-century fictions then explored and that psychoanalytic theory has dissected. His protagonists are familiar because we glimpse them at the deepest level of the palimpsest of modern subjectivity, in which we have also been inscribed. We recognize them as different but experience them as similar: a doubled perception that signals an affiliation of early and late modern structures of consciousness, ideology, and narrative form. I want to explore the nature of that affiliation through a brief comparison of Defoe's conceptions of the self with those of Heinz Kohut, the American object-relations theorist. Positioned on opposing sides of the Romantic, depth model of interiority, and representing anticipatory and nostalgic forms of individualism, Defoe and

Kohut can be seen as converse images of one another. Between the writing of *Crusoe* and the writing of *Roxana*, Defoe moved from a comic and realist representation of entrepreneurial capitalism to a tragic and fantastic focus on the self-alienation that is its cost. In his theorizing, Kohut specifically refused the fantastic perspective, which had achieved its apogee in Freud.[34] In its place, he installed an alienated subject whom he could restore, through therapy, to bourgeois sociality. When the realist fictions of Defoe are read in the context of Kohut's theory, their apparent prescience becomes explicable. And when Kohut's narratives are examined through the lens provided by Defoe's fictions, they suggest how the yearnings of entrepreneurial capitalism have persisted, not merely as economic motives but as fundamental psychic impulses.

Writing in the second half of the twentieth century, Kohut sought to replace the therapeutic technique he had inherited with a modified theory and practice appropriate to what he defined as a new form of subjectivity: the narcissistic personality.[35] Performing multiple roles and exhibiting extreme and contradictory behaviors, his estranged, narcissistic individual had only a void where an integrated self should have been. Not unlike Defoe's protagonists, who display an emptiness that would previously have been filled by the reflected presences of traditional authority, Kohut's wounded narcissists experience a hollowness that is the scar of their abandonment. In Kohut's judgment, the degeneration of previously supportive institutions (most notably, the family) has deprived these individuals of empathic authority figures who facilitate the development of inner coherence and strength. Without the introjected values of ideal "others," Kohut's hollow men and women are doomed to seek despairingly for "self-object" relationships that, mirroring them positively to themselves, will substitute for the authority figures they have lost. But because they are without a psychic core to which their introjected objects might cohere, the fleeting self-representations that they accumulate are merely added to a chaotic, unassimilable mass.

Anticipating the postmodern perspective, Kohut views the self "as a representation ... quite analogous to the representation of objects."[36] And because he conceptualizes his subjects as constructed surfaces (like Moll), he believes them to suffer not from the repression assumed by a depth model of the psyche—the barring of the past from present memory—but from a "narcissistic wounding": a rupture in the narrative of the self, which is expressed in inconsistency and incoherence.[37] Much like Defoe's protagonists, Kohut's narcissistic individuals fluctuate wildly between feelings of grandiosity and feelings of utter worthlessness. At times they are exhilarated and at times depleted by their interactions with "self-objects" that they encounter in the external world.[38] Both flattened and dispersed, they live in a depthless and foreshortened present. Described as drafts in progress, they write themselves while also waiting to be written.

According to Kohut's conception, the function of the analyst is to revise the deficient text that the analysand personifies.[39] Empathically enacting the role of the parental self-object, the therapist realigns the patients' self-representations, exerting an influence that moderates and channels grandiosity.[40] A process of "transmuting internalization" is enabled by this intervention: the draft of the self is ultimately "reformed," and the individual is successfully integrated (like Crusoe) and adapted to society. In his honoring of a self "restored," Kohut regressively rejects the fantastic form of subjectivity in order to reinstate the bourgeois (and realist) myth of autonomy. Attempting to enrich the patient's "impoverished personality," the Kohutian therapist transforms the narcissistic individual into a resourceful psychological entrepreneur, a "rational investor" who augments the value of its commodified self by cannily converting psychic "debits" into "assets."[41] In the happy ending of Kohut's realistic narrative, the individualistic self is made adequate, through the therapist's purchased intervention, to its aspiring project of mastery and self-creation. In this way, psychic and social organization are imagined in the materialist spirit of capitalist individualism that Defoe inaugurated in the novel.

In his nostalgic self-psychology, Kohut's intention is to return normativity to the increasingly dispersed and hollowed subject of late modernism, reconciling that subject's desires and needs to the requirements of a social world that eludes and overwhelms it. A liminal figure, Kohut has been shaped by a Romantic epistemological tradition that he rejects for a realism that cannot be disentangled from its fantastic roots. In the realistic narrative that he scripts, Kohut is the knowing subject who distances himself from a narcissistic other who is the fantastic actor of discontinuous roles. His goal is to integrate the multiple identities of the analysand in order to create a coherent personality from the fragments of that ruptured, psychic text. What is lost, imperceptibly, is that individual's psychic depth. As Kohut simplifies the Freudian narrative of interior conflict and unfulfillable desire, he transforms the complex, eccentric, and irrational subject of psychoanalysis into a two-dimensional character with psychic wounds that he, the analyst, can recognize and heal, and with an always available consciousness that can be manipulated at will.[42] But a fantastic effect ironically emerges from the strategy: the object of Kohut's rational exploration seems to become a projection of his own divided self, while his larger enterprise appears as a defense against the psychic alienation that he fears. By deploying the analysand as his alter ego, Kohut unwittingly reveals the Romantic aspect of his practice and his theory.[43]

Giving primacy to social accommodation, Kohut repeats a gesture that Defoe made in *Robinson Crusoe*. That repetition is provocative as well as disconcerting. Provocative because it establishes lines of continuity among ideological assumptions, structures of consciousness, and narrative forms across two hundred years; disconcerting because in abandoning the fantastic vision that lies at the heart of the psychoanalytic project, Kohut unwittingly reveals how profound and persistent the desire is to evade individualism's painful contradictions. Reading *Robinson Crusoe, Moll Flanders,* and *Roxana,* we see how those contradictions shaped the novel's bimodal form, and how the modal dynamic provides unique access to the ideological and psychological struggles of the modern subject. Considering Kohut's self-psychology, we can also see how psychoanalytic theory—which shares the bimodality of the novel—attempts to bring the conflicts of the modern subject into consciousness while laboring, at the same time, to evade them.[44] In succeeding chapters, I will examine the representations of these contradictions in the evolving English novel and in psychoanalytic theory—particularly as they relate to the imposition of and the resistance to gender identities.

2

Clarissa and the
Pornographic Imagination

Ian Watt placed *Pamela* and *Clarissa* at the center of the dominant
tradition of formal realism, but his defining category fractured and
dissolved beneath his own reading of the second of these texts. In
Pamela, Watt identified a social narrative shaped by middle-class consciousness and the ideology of individualism. He tried to fit *Clarissa*
into a similar realistic mold, but his theory could not accommodate
the fantastic elements that his analysis exposed.[1] Critics who suc-
ceeded Watt did not explore the anomalies that *The Rise of the Novel*
inadvertently laid bare. Instead of considering what the differences
between the novels might imply for narrative theory, they focused
on one or the other of these two seminal fictions. So Michael McKeon
and Nancy Armstrong, the most influential of Watt's revisionists,
made Richardson unproblematically pivotal in their accounts of realism by centering *Pamela* while omitting *Clarissa* altogether. Alter-
nately, the poststructuralist critics who produced the most extensive
studies of *Clarissa* disconnected the exhausting narrative from affil-
iated texts in order to explore it, exhaustively, alone.[2] They successfully suggested its contemporary relevance but did not consider its
influence on the development of novelistic form.

A critical consensus has emerged about *Pamela*, which supports
and extends the analysis that Watt provided. It recognizes Richardson's first novel as an ideological tour de force in which shifting
definitions of class are negotiated through the relations of an increasingly inflexible and binarized sex-gender system. When Mr. B., a
libertine member of the gentry, fails in his tireless efforts to seduce
the servant girl who resists his advances, he is forced to recognize
the power of her "virtue": the sign of a mystified and sublimated
sexuality. Their marriage proves her moral superiority, as it does the
responsiveness of the middle classes to social domestication and reform. Readers since Fielding have ironically observed that Pamela

(and her author) understood that she could acquire more money and status from her virtue than she ever could have from her body, and that for her—as for her suitor and her readers—desire resisted is desire intensified. In this view, it is by playing the good girl so effectively that Pamela gets the bad girl's pleasure, while avoiding the stigma of her reputation. Mr. B. can be seen to profit equally from the game. Although his marriage to Pamela signals the gentry's accession to a bourgeois respectability that has been feminized, his assiduous efforts at seduction suggest that the masculine libido is too powerful to be morally confined. Whether it is read as naively or ironically realistic, therefore, the narrative indicates that the sexual and moral division of labor might satisfy the needs of women as well as men, but it is ultimately masculine self-interest that shapes the institutional forms through which female desire is allowed expression.[3]

Acknowledged as the founding fiction of domestic realism, *Pamela* is generally understood to rationalize conformity to social regulation by naturalizing gender conventions. Once universalized, female virtue is deployed to disguise socioeconomic instability as class consolidation. The battle of the sexes, which is rooted in the categorical differences of the new sex-gender system, achieves its comic resolution in marriage, where gender antagonism is celebrated as complementarity. Since female desire is merged with virtue, and the body is disciplined by the socially instructed mind, the text does not distinguish between the moral and psychological aspects of Pamela's character. Alternate realities, which would interrogate the dominant fiction that *Pamela* propounds, are excluded from the novel's consciousness; and a clarity of perspective is achieved, which the writer, reader, and protagonist are all assumed to share. This is typical of predominantly realistic texts and it enables, in turn, the dominant critical construction.

Such a construction is not possible with *Clarissa*, an epistolary novel of a more fully bimodal sort. While the reality of *Pamela* is shaped solely by the letters of its protagonist, the contesting realities of *Clarissa* emerge from the epistles of four central and several subsidiary characters. The first reader to find the text exceeding the boundaries of his own interpretation was Richardson, who revised it several times as he tried to control the promiscuous responses of his audience.[4] For contemporary readers, the fiction has proven equally elusive. Watt fell into contradiction as he attempted to reduce its several narratives to a single form, while more recent critics have been attracted to it because of its multiplicity. Interested in problems of textuality and the politics of reading, they have exploited its ambiguities in order to make it an ally in our own critical and sexual wars.[5]

I want neither to establish an opposition between *Pamela* and *Clarissa*—assigning the latter to a second monologic tradition—nor to emphasize *Clarissa*'s idiosyncratic nature. Instead, I will examine Richardson's second novel in the context of its competing narrative modes, insisting that this kind of contestation was actually central to the development of the novel. Further, I will argue that *Clarissa* is a product of an emergent pornographic imagination, which Richardson, in both senses, represented. Although the pornographic imagination reflected a sensibility that was already visible in libertine literature of the seventeenth century, it was fundamentally structured by the ideology of capitalist individualism as it interacted with the modern sex-gender system. Produced at the intersection of public and private experience, collective practices and personal fantasies, shared beliefs and eccentric desires, it coalesced in the eighteenth century into a structure of feeling that had a specifically psychosexual reference. In its more extreme manifestations—which have evolved and persisted into our own time—it can be described as cultural psychosis.[6]

As *Clarissa* suggests, in realistic fictions (or in the realist strands of composite texts), the pornographic imagination eroticizes gender difference and the power relations by which that difference is organized and reproduced. These narratives are dominated by the perspective of a male character, for whom autonomy is a mainstay of identity and dependence a form of psychic death. The impulses of individualism block his recognition of others as self-conscious and self-determining agents, although he needs those others to recognize these same qualities in him. He struggles to maintain hierarchical structures of difference (which create the illusion of his own psychic wholeness) despite the fact that his illusion of psychic wholeness is threatened by those whose difference from him he accentuates. For this male protagonist, relationships involve manipulation and exploitation instead of mutuality. The wish to control slips easily into the desire to harm, and humiliation is the primary source of sexual pleasure. Through the protagonist's appropriation of the female body, the presumptively male reader is invited to bond with the explicitly male writer, reinforcing stereotypical gender identifications outside of, as within, the text.[7]

In fantastic narratives, the pornographic imagination exposes the psychic roots of toxic masculinity in the primal need for both individuation and connection. These narratives suggest how threats to male mastery and psychic wholeness evoke a condition before differentiation, which men identify retrospectively with the feminine and maternal. Because the conscious and socially supported urge for differentiation remains linked to the disavowed, but still powerful, wish for mergence, men's desire for heterosexual connection is fused to defensive forms of misogynistic hatred. Pornographic fantasies uncover the primal, psychic past that underlies the cultural present, and they expose the infantile experience that hovers at the outer edge of memory. For both the writer and the reader, these fantasies demolish conventional categories of gender to the extent that they reveal ungendered bodies, which are solipsistic and indeterminate in their desire. For those regressive bodies, the urge to power is, at times, submerged in the forbidden pleasures of impotence.[8]

A complex bimodal fiction that takes psychosexuality as its subject, *Clarissa* provides a field on which a range of psychic and social impulses can be played out. Its interactive narratives chart the processes through which desire is shaped by cultural requirements that it also actively resists. Eradicating gender differences while affirming them as ineradicable, Richardson's novel reveals at once the subversive and conservative implications of the pornographic imagination. In its realist components, it invites presumptive male readers to embrace a normative and sadistic heterosexual masculinity even as it represents the ways in which heterosexual relations fail tragically in a patriarchal and capitalist order that transforms sexual difference into an unbridgeable chasm. Where realism yields to the fantastic, that tragedy is tempered by an alternate form of knowledge that precedes the imposition of the sex-gender system in its primal psychic character. Because Richardson's fantastic pornographic narrative facilitates cross-gender identifications for the writer and his readers, it provides access to the ungendered, as well as the gendered, nature of the self.

Clarissa divides itself into three quite separate narrative moments. The mode of realism dominates the first, which focuses—through Clarissa's and Anna Howe's correspondence—on the conflict within the Harlowe family. It ends with the elopement of Clarissa and Lovelace. The fantastic mode is primary in the long middle section, which examines the conflictual psychological dynamic between Lovelace and Clarissa through the former's correspondence with Belford and the latter's with Anna. Finally, after the rape, the fiction reaches for the sublime—an aspiration enacted in both realistic and fantastic modes. In this last segment, Lovelace functions in increasing isolation while Clarissa's audience is expanded. Clarissa dominates the first and final portions of the novel, while Lovelace shapes and motivates the crucial middle section. The complexity of the text derives from the psychological elaboration of narrative modes and genres rather than from its plot, which is exceedingly straightforward and, for its time, familiar. Clarissa Harlowe, the daughter of a wealthy and aspiring middle-class family, is courted by Lovelace, an aristocratic libertine. Her parents oppose the match on her brother's behalf and try to marry her to Solmes, a man whom she detests. Driven by her family to despair, Clarissa is tricked by Lovelace into an elopement that places her completely in his power. His goal is seduction, and he is willing to marry her only if she succeeds in resisting his machinations. In order to accomplish his purpose, he brings her to a house of prostitution where he finally rapes her with the help of the brothel-keeper, Mrs. Sinclair. "Ruined" but uncompromised, Clarissa ultimately dies a spiritually satisfying death and Lovelace is murdered in a duel instigated by Clarissa's cousin.

In his initial depiction of Clarissa's family, Richardson established a realistic frame for the fantastic psychosocial portrait that he ultimately, in minute detail, creates.[9] Having already amassed substantial wealth through prudent marriages and investments, the Harlowes are described as seeking to "raise a family": not only to extend and to augment their holdings, but also to gain status and political power through the peerage to which James, their only son, aspires.

Clarissa stands as their most valuable asset and the most serious obstacle to their success. A good daughter and a paragon of female virtue, she accepts the dominant social fiction along with the role that she has been assigned, but it is her strict adherence to its values that brings to the surface the radical contradictions that the bourgeois ideology conceals. Having inherited her grandfather's estate, she demonstrates her own capacity for moral choice when she gives her father control of her inheritance, subordinating her own spiritual autonomy to his materialism. But while her character, like her beauty, is valued as a commodity, her ultimate refusal to be objectified unmasks the sexual and economic motives that have worked to perfect and sustain her "virtue."

As Richardson portrays them, the Harlowes represent the insatiable bourgeois family that would absorb all assimilable others into itself. They assert the crude materialism of the middle classes against the culture of the aristocracy, and they maintain male privilege against the rights of women. They all bathe in the glow of accomplishments that identify their daughter with an older, more beneficent order, which they want simultaneously to reject and to incorporate as their own. When Clarissa claims those accomplishments for herself, insisting upon her right to choose a husband, she leaves them exposed in their profound vulgarity. When she scornfully rejects the bourgeois Solmes and aligns herself with Lovelace, her actions radically threaten her family's class and sexual hegemony. Lovelace already distinguishes her from the other Harlowes, and if he were to marry her, he would claim her decisively for the upper classes. Since the family estate would then be settled on her (titled as she would probably be), her position in the class struggle is conceptualized as pivotal.

At the same time that Richardson details the socioeconomic motives of property marriage, he also reveals the sexual dimension of the bartering of women. Placed at the center of the transaction, Clarissa is both object of exchange and object of desire. "Winning" her signals entrepreneurial success in a business affair among men: it marks material power and provides symbolic proof of masculinity. Within the family, the question is who has the right of ownership and who is entitled, therefore, to the erotic pleasures of the sale. The fiction of the father's power is belied by the controlling interest of the son. The law, which makes the father a life-tenant on his heir's estate, inserts the son clandestinely in the paternal place. It is with impunity that James treats his father "as a superior would do,"[10] since his father is merely an agent of James's efforts to gain a peerage through the consolidation of the corporate estate. Daughters are mere "encumbrances" in this project: "chickens brought up for the tables of other men" (77). James tyrannizes his mother, as if he were her husband, and plots, "lover-like," with Arabella against their sister, placing himself at the apex of the erotic triangle of the sibling relation. Thinking it "proof of a *manly* spirit to be an utter stranger to the gentler passions" (139), James indulges his violent temper as an entitlement of patriarchal power, socioeconomic status, and sexual virility. But none of those entitlements are secure against the mocking presence of Lovelace, the "vile wretch" who tells James that Clarissa is his, "and *shall* be *his,* and he will be the death of any man who robs him of his *property*" (223). The privileges that James greedily struggles to obtain belong by birth to Lovelace, who assumes them gracefully. Refusing to recognize the crude upstart as his equal—barely recognizing James at all—Lovelace has "taught him to put his sword into his scabbard" (212), arousing sexual anxiety along with class resentment. If he "loses" Clarissa to Lovelace, James is vanquished in both the class and sexual wars. Once his social ambitions are defeated, the sexual power of his misogynistic sadism would also lose its force.

For these reasons, Solmes represents for the Harlowes an ideal solution to the problems posed by the upwardly mobile and resistant virgin. It is not only that he is willing to rob his own family in order to purchase Clarissa from hers; it is also that, bonded with the Harlowes, he enables them to participate in the sadistic sexualized cruelty of his pursuit. The Harlowes are untroubled by the fact that Clarissa is repelled by "the odious Solmes," who "squates" in his chair "with his ugly weight," pressing on her hoop, "with *so much assurance* in his looks" (87). Wishing her to be "humble and mortified," they berate her for resisting her disgusting suitor even as they spy with pleasure on the painful meetings of the two. The Harlowe males share Solmes's view that "[t]error and fear . . . looked pretty in a bride as well as in a wife," and "if *love* and *fear* must be separated in matrimony, the man who made himself *feared* fared best" (238). The insistence of Clarissa's oafish suitor makes her prey to the wrath of her family. They eavesdrop on her conversations, read her letters, peek at her through keyholes, and claim the right to ransack her belongings, her clothing, and, as much as it is possible, her self. Constructed as an object of the sadistic misogyny through which the pornographic imagination is articulated, Clarissa becomes a sacrificial victim. She is used to solidify the male, middle-class community, and to protect the complicitous female members of the group (her mother, her sister, her aunts, and her cousins) from being sacrificed themselves.

From the beginning of the novel, Clarissa seeks nostalgically for an alternative to the patriarchal family, by which she is manipulated and disrespected. Christianity provides her the perspective she needs to deny and even to transcend it. "[T]he world is but *one great family,*" she insists, "originally it was so; what then is this narrow selfishness that reigns in us, but relationship remembered against relationship forgot?" (62). It is a view that disadvantages her in a world that is organized by social exclusions, where "one half of mankind torment[s] the other, and [is] tormented themselves in tormenting" (224).

Because Anna Howe has a more peripheral relation to the patriarchal family than Clarissa, she can read its dominant fictions with more ironic distance. Living in a matriarchal household since her father's death, she is, as she observes to Clarissa, "fitter for *this* world than you, you for the *next* than me" (69). Her mother is not like Mrs. Harlowe, who "sacrificed" the "inward satisfaction . . . of a gentle and sensible mind" in order to maintain an "outward peace" with her husband and her son (54). Having quarreled her own husband into his grave, Mrs. Howe enjoys the independence of her widowhood, and the close if not always peaceful relationship it allows her with her daughter. Still, while Anna's situation permits her a woman-centered view of sexual relations, she is not immune to the social virus of patriarchal sexuality, which she examines with so cool a gaze. Much too sensible to have accepted James Harlowe as a suitor, Anna was not sensible enough to have rejected another lover, Sir George Colmer, who—according to Lovelace—was very like himself. Indeed, had it not been for Clarissa's interventions, Anna "would have followed him in all his broken fortunes, when he was obliged to quit the kingdom" because of his transgressions (635).

Portrayed as more experienced and as less a proper lady than Clarissa, Anna reveals a sexual ambivalence toward men that, while grounded in the inevitable conflict between desire and reason, is stamped specifically by the gender definitions and sexual proscriptions of her time. She is extremely scornful of Hickman, her current suitor. She finds him "bearable" because "he is humble and knows his distance" (68), but she also experiences him as profoundly unattractive. Refusing to be objectified herself, Anna wittily feminizes and objectifies *him* as a "fiddling" and "un-busy" man, "irresolute and changeable in everything," with too much "bustle in his manners" and without any "manliness in his aspect" (208). In a comic inversion of the clandestine, incestuous pattern that typifies relations within the Harlowe family, Anna repeatedly proclaims that Hickman would be a more appropriate suitor for her mother, "for what he wants in years, he makes up in gravity" (70). But ebullient as she is in her intelligent mockery of his "whining, creeping, submissive courtship" (466), her deep resistance to her suitor reveals the dark side of her conceptualization of the battle of the sexes. Her general view is Hobbesian. "If I do not make [Hickman] quake now and then, he will endeavor to make me fear," she writes. "All the animals in the creation are more or less in a state of hostility with each other" (487). And while, in her worldview, all may be at the throats of all, she knows that society validates the power of men, and gives to women only the days of courtship, "our best days," in which they can briefly play at domination (274). After that, they are the helpless victims of men's abusive power: "To be cajoled, wire-drawn and ensnared, like silly birds, into a state of bondage or vile subordination: to be courted as princesses for a few weeks, in order to be treated as slaves for the rest of our lives—Indeed, my dear, as you say of Solmes, I cannot endure them!" (133). Even her sober suitor is likely to change once he is certain of her, she half believes, and "the 'imperative husband' will come upon him while the obsequious lover will go off" (277). She likes to imagine that the equality of female friendship can provide an alternative to the power imbalances of heterosexual marriage, and she occasionally suggests that she and Clarissa would do well to run off together "and despise them all!" (133). But the fact is that she does not want "passion without passion" (466). She understands that "fear makes us more gentle obligers than love" (213), and that she is, despite herself, drawn powerfully to the Lovelacean man, as she is drawn, in fantasy, to erotic domination. Even after she learns that Lovelace has actually raped Clarissa, she continues to find Hickman "too meek" for her taste and, on the brink of marriage to him, acknowledges that she would have preferred him as a brother rather than have had him as a lover (1456).

The fluctuations that mark Anna's analyses of her own desire reflect the pervasive eroticization not only of gender difference but also of the power relations by which that difference is organized and reproduced. Seeking to affirm herself as an active sexual subject in a society that defines her as legally dependent and naive, Anna necessarily participates in the dominant social fictions that she also explicitly, even virulently, rejects. With a kind of outrage, she inquires of Clarissa: "[I]s it to be expected that I, who could hardly bear control from a mother, should take it from a husband?—from one too who has neither more wit, nor more understanding, than myself?" (1312). But "control" turns out to have deep psychological as well as significant social meanings. At times, Anna reproduces her mother's former marital situation, bullying a man whom she considers to be inadequately masculine and whom she then emasculates through her own attempts at domination. Doing this, she asserts her sexual agency by paradoxically denying her desire. The alternative is to accept control by a man whom she perceives as her superior, taking pleasure in being mastered and submitting. Lovelace understands her quandary since he represents its obverse side. Believing the "male-virgin," Hickman, to be disadvantaged because "women like not novices" (812), he confesses that he has imagined Anna to be in love with him because "your sprightly ladies love your smart fellows, and your rakes" (801). Although Richardson does not allow Anna to enact her ambivalent and masochistically tinged desire, in making her fantasies complementary to those of Lovelace he points to the pattern of heterosexual relations with which the pornographic imagination is most commonly identified. It is not the pattern that he finally chooses to center. In Clarissa, he does not provide a masochist for Lovelace's sadist, but creates a narcissist instead. Considered together, Clarissa and Anna suggest that female narcissism and masochism are both shaped by the modern sex-gender system, and are offered to women (in the way that Richardson offers them) as alternatives between which they have to choose.[11]

From the beginning of the novel, and until her turn toward death, Clarissa is not able—like Anna—to articulate the nature of her own desire. Constructed as a paragon of virtue, she serves as an exemplar for others of her class and sex. Guided by the motto "Rather useful than glaring" (40), she has defined herself through the services she performs for her doting grandfather, her proud, possessive parents, her admiring neighbors, and the recipients of her prudent charity—to whom she refers as "my deserving poor." Worthy to mediate between the crass materialism of her family and the more refined values of the upper classes, she is a "matchless young creature" (53), whose excellence marks her indelibly for sacrifice. Having assumed physical independence to be a function of spiritual autonomy, and having believed that virtue cannot help but be rewarded, Clarissa discovers the fictive nature of the reality she has lived when she claims the right to control the disposition of her body. At that point, she understands that others can, with impunity, enslave her: imprison her in increasingly restrictive spaces, allow her neither to speak nor to be heard, deprive her of her privacy, and cause her "never [to be] at liberty to follow [her] own judgment" (37). Male protection is revealed to be the pleasant face of unopposable privilege, and when the Harlowe household keys are taken from her, she finds that the role of surrogate mother is a symbolic one that she has only, through their sufferance, been allowed to play. Wishing to send her as his housekeeper to Scotland, her brother can readily transform her willing service to unwilling servitude, just as the inherited property that she has gifted to her father is lost to her forever if she does not gain the intercession of a sympathetic male trustee.

What is true of her familial situation proves to be true as well of her situation with Lovelace. Once she aligns herself with him, and until he extends to her the protection of a husband, she is socially and personally exposed—subject completely to his cruelest whim. No longer an exemplar, she is without social identity. Without a social identity, she is solely dependent on a belief in spiritual autonomy that sharply conflicts with her material condition. The ambiguity that surrounds her flight ("driven on one side and possibly tricked on the other" [405], according to Anna) reveals the absence of a strategy that would allow her any measure of independence. Denied viable alternatives, she is denied also the possibility of a moral decision. It is not simply propriety, therefore, that keeps her from knowing whether her "affections are engaged" and whether her cheeks "glow" and her heart "throbs" in Lovelace's presence. While she acknowledges that "there be not, if he be out of the question, another man in the world, I can think favorably of" (201), she is justifiably aware of the fact that given the pervasiveness of misogyny, she might not think favorably of any man. And while Anna can afford to theorize the erotic power of domination, Clarissa has had imposed upon her an understanding of its profound social and personal consequences. She asks, quite early in the novel, "[W]hat will not these men say to obtain belief and a power over one?" (171), and her experience provides the answer to her question: they will say—and do—anything she can imagine and a good deal more besides.

As Richardson constructs her situation, Clarissa is placed in a series of double binds. These reflect the contradictory nature of social fictions that require obedience to the father and fidelity to the self, and that call on propriety to constrain her while pronouncing her free to pursue the "dictates of her heart." The responses available to her all require a passively resistant stance. She has a minimal "power of the negative" that she can exercise against her family, against Lovelace, and, in a sense, against Richardson himself. This is finally how she uses the "great and invincible spirit" (593) on which she believes she must rely if she is to protect herself against the incursions of others and assure herself of her own effective subjectivity. Identifying seeming with being, Clarissa clings inevitably to a realist fiction of the self (of *her* self) as unitary, closed, and self-dependent. Believed to be reflected without mediation in its actions, that self is emptied of mystery, complexity, or desire—and it is the only self that she feels genuinely able to possess. The strength of her conviction about the verisimilitude of the narcissistic posture that she defensively assumes is suggested by the question she puts to Anna, when she is urged to be more forthcoming with her suitor: "And what mean you, my dear friend, when you say that I must throw off *a little more of the veil?—*Indeed I never knew that I wore one" (433). While she is adept at tracking down signs of inconsistency and self-deception in others, Clarissa cannot risk discarding, or even examining, the protective disguise in which the social masquerade has wrapped her. It is her obsession with what she calls "punctilio" that makes her decline the three proposals of marriage that Lovelace makes (only one of them deceptively), fatally reinforcing his construction of her as unassailable and strengthening his resolve to "penetrate" her hidden self.[12] It is this unassailability that makes her interpretable by the reader in a range of extreme, even parodic forms—as sacrificial victim (Castle), as metaphysical spirit (Watt), as mythic figure (Van Ghent), as ideological agent (Eagleton), or as narcissistic bitch (Warner)—but seldom, as Richardson discovered to his dismay, as a complex and fully realized subjectivity.

Lovelace is quite another matter. The obverse side of Clarissa, who supports the values by which she is tormented, Lovelace wants to unmask social hypocrisy while accepting the male privilege that the dominant ideology bestows upon him. To the extent that he is conceptualized through the discourse of realism, Lovelace is credible as the only son and single heir of a "considerable family." As Anna describes him: "From his cradle . . . as an *only child*, and a *boy*, humoursome, spoiled, mischievous: the governor of his governors. A Libertine in his riper years, hardly regardful of appearances; and despising the sex in general for the fault of particulars of it who made themselves too cheap to him" (498). The grandiose form of Lovelace's individualism is appropriate to his situation as a propertied and statused male. Financially independent, he need not, like James, aspire to the "building" of a family. On the contrary, his dominant fantasy (like Crusoe's) is to consolidate all past and future possessions in himself, neither marrying nor bearing children. Already orphaned, he has only to wait for his other, more distant relatives to die, which he does with remarkable complacency. Represented as resisting bourgeoisification at every level, he clings to a libertine ideology of subversive "freedom" that allows him to believe himself the subject who subjects others to his will. His relentless if ambivalent pursuit of Clarissa is stamped, as are all his interactions, by an appropriative spirit of competition to which he applies his not inconsiderable intellectual powers. Lovelace claims that his aspirations as seducer are grounded in the betrayal of "that quality-jilt, whose infidelity I have vowed to revenge upon as many of the sex as shall come into my power" (143). He adds to the sexual motive a wish for class revenge: "Then what a triumph it would be to the *Harlowe pride*, were I now to marry this lady?—A family beneath my own!—no one in it worthy of an alliance with but her! . . . Forbid it the blood of the Lovelaces, that your *last*, and let me say, not the *meanest* of your stock, should thus creep, thus fawn, thus lick the dust, for a *Wife*" (426). And, finally, his situation as "leader" of the dissolute young men he calls his friends depends upon the security of his reputation for a "manliness" evidenced by his limitless "success" with women.

Although Lovelace is presented effectively in realistic terms, unlike Clarissa, he is not conceptualized in that mode primarily.[13] So,
while Clarissa is trapped in social definitions and is unable,
therefore, to speak her own desire, the articulation of desire is Lovelace's obsession. While Clarissa has identified herself with the extended family, particularly with women, Lovelace has competitively
distinguished himself from all of his relations, particularly from
men. While Clarissa yearns nostalgically for the reestablishment of
community, Lovelace is motivated by his megalomania. While Clarissa strives to represent her self as unitary—a single point of interior
and exterior convergence—Lovelace projects himself as multiple,
fragmented, and inconsistent. And while Clarissa's efforts of self-
preservation appear as narcissism, Lovelace's performances of himself proclaim his radical dispersal.

Consistent and coherent, Clarissa's narrative contends with, struggles against, and is increasingly appropriated by the audacity of
Lovelace's desiring discourse. The narrative dynamic, which represents the personal incompatibility of the two characters, reveals the
radical disjunctions of the larger field of gender difference. Formally
and substantively, it suggests the impossibility of mutuality between
men and women who, having first been formed by the civilizing
process as self-dependent and enclosed, are then constructed by the
culture as so radically different that they are alien to one another.
Through the mutual interrogation of its modal forms, *Clarissa* tracks
the increasing separation of male from female and explores the conditions that maintain and deepen that divide. Finally, through the
fantastic mode, which is dominant from the moment of Clarissa's
elopement through her rape, efforts made to cross that profound
separation are shown to be emotionally deforming at best and, in
the worst case, psychically murderous as well as suicidal.

Quite early in the novel, Anna wisely asserts that "[t]he suiting
of the tempers of two persons who are to come together is a great
matter: and yet there should be boundaries fixed between them, by
consent as it were, beyond which neither should go: and each should
hold the other to it; or there would probably be encroachment in
both" (277). For her, the problem of establishing mutuality (the "suiting of tempers" without the inevitability of "encroachment") is potentially solved by a consensual creation of limits, which mark each
person's separateness and defend the integrity of each against the

invasive impulses of the other. Considered within the discourse of realism, hers appears to be a rational solution. When considered from the perspective of the fantastic, however, this drawing of boundaries reveals itself as one-half of a strategy that complicates mutuality by binding the need for separation to the needs for connection and recognition. At one level, Clarissa's wish to guarantee autonomy by delimiting self and other can be seen as the other side of Lovelace's desire to submerge the other in the infinite depths of the self. At another level, both impulses prove to be inseparable from the equally profound and apparently contradictory need of Lovelace and Clarissa to achieve recognition *from* the other: a need that, in this text, destroys the boundaries on which autonomy relies.[14]

Dependent upon Lovelace for her social status after she has fled her family's house, Clarissa's project is to mark off her psychic space while not foreclosing the possibility of connection. In response to each of Lovelace's "encroachments," she further retracts that boundary, as she engages in a continuous process of withdrawal. Lovelace, on the other hand, projects himself across the barrier she has constructed and seeks to claim her for a world of his own linguistic and imaginative creation. On both sides, the frustrating process is fraught with contradiction, for while each struggles for ascendancy—Lovelace by proliferating interpretations and Clarissa by withholding them—each also requires from the other acknowledgment of his or her own subjectivity. "We are both great watchers of each other's eyes; and indeed seem to be more than half afraid of each other" (460), Clarissa writes, suggesting the nature of their effort to know and to be known: to grasp one another's substance while fearing the knowledge that comes from such discovery. Afraid of his power, what Clarissa ultimately wants from Lovelace is confirmation of her social identity. She does not wish to lose herself in his (or in her own) desire or to become what he would clearly make of her: "a cipher, to give him significance and myself pain" (567). When she resists desire, however, she incites his rage. Once his rage is aroused, he cannot recognize, let alone respect, the boundaries that she has constructed for her own protection. As soon as his stratagems threaten her with erasure, subjugation, and even violent appropriation, Clarissa resists, withdraws, and, out of moral outrage, refuses to recognize him at all. Indifferent to his desire, she appears to be enigmatic and frighteningly inaccessible. Deprived of her resistance (which is itself a form of recognition), Lovelace's attempts at subjugation are also deprived of meaning. His sense of himself—both grandiose and fragile—is completely undermined.

While this psychic dynamic can appear as a universal existential phenomenon—as explored by Hegel and Sartre, for example, as well as by some psychoanalytic theorists—the novel suggests how indi-vidual struggles for autonomy and connection can yield relations of erotic domination that are gender-coded and culturally specific. In this relational configuration, as we have seen, male sadism demands female masochism as a response, but often produces narcissism as an effect.[15] The fantastic narrative problematizes the nature of those roles, particularly the role of sadist, which it centers. It maps the ways in which the positions are constructed and reveals the costs by which they are maintained. In the process, the fixity of the gendered terms is itself interrogated, and the sexual indeterminacy that un-derlies them is brought fleetingly into focus.

The realistic narrative of the novel establishes the complementary ways in which male and female identifications are constituted in response to cultural expectations and demands.[16] For Clarissa, no female model of autonomy exists. Her deepest tie is to her mother, whom she continues to "love and reverence" until her death, and whose idealized image she seeks in a range of mother surrogates from whom she futilely asks help throughout the fiction. Although she perceives the extent to which her mother has sacrificed first her-self and then her daughter in order to purchase peace with her dom-ineering husband and bullying son, Clarissa defines herself similarly through sacrifice in order to be worthy of the idealized feminine role she has internalized. Even with Lovelace, her initial hope is that she will be able to mediate his salvation by helping to effect his refor-mation; and when she recognizes that she cannot serve that function, she is unable to conceptualize another. Seeing her as "[s]omething more than a woman, an angel, in some things, but a baby in others: So father-sick! so family-proud" (521), Lovelace fears that she can love none but her parents, and his fear is not misplaced. Her mother's love and father's approval are the objects of her deepest longing until she turns at last to God, their final representative.

Lovelace acknowledges that he was brought up by a doting mother "to bear no control" (1431) and he seems to wish to repro-duce that idealized relationship—with himself the recipient of an

infinite, unconditional love—at the same time that he needs to distance himself from that love's potentially overwhelming source. He
looks to Clarissa to confirm the boundarylessness of a self that he
needs her also to delimit. Omnipotent, he is alone; vulnerable and
dependent, he can be destroyed. Believing that "if there was but the
shadow of a doubt in [Clarissa's] mind whether she preferred me to
any man living, I would show her no mercy" (387), Lovelace experiences his pride as "mortified" by the possibility that Clarissa would
be "governed in her behavior . . . by generosity merely, or by blind
duty" (669). On one hand, he wants to worship at the feet of his
"divinity," his "angel," his "exalted creature"; on the other, he is a
pure misogynist who questions whether there is "a soul in a sex,
created . . . only for temporary purposes" (1037). His ambivalence
yields rage, which he must inflict on others or turn back against
himself.[17] Lovelace's recollections of his boyhood suggest the extent
to which he claimed his maleness, from his early years, through a
sadistic form of self-expression that defined those external to him as
objects of his mastery. "When a boy, if a dog ran away from me
through fear, I generally looked about for a stone, a stick, or a brick-
bat," he writes to Belford, "and if neither offered to my hand, I
skimmed my hat after him to make him afraid for something. What
signifies power, if we do not exert it?" (610). Because he believes that
one can be certain of one's power only by seeing the effect it has in
causing pain, he finds it reasonable that "We begin with birds as
boys, and as men go on to ladies; and both perhaps, in turns, experience our sportive cruelty" (557). Perceiving no difference between
the careless torture of animals and the plotted victimization of
women—except for the challenge that is represented by each ("it is
more manly to attack a lion than a sheep" [610])—he acknowledges
that "Whatever our hearts are in, our heads will follow. Begin with
spiders, with flies, and what we will, the girl is the center of gravity,
and we all naturally tend to it" (419).

The girl does indeed prove to be the center of gravity for him—
and for reasons that concern "the heart" although, as the novel reveals, the heart has different secrets, which are probed by different
narrative forms. When those secrets are explored in the realistic
mode, they tell of heterosexual love and marriage in which differences are naturalized and social norms are reproduced—at times,
catastrophically. In the fantastic mode, the psychic meanings of

socialized "love" are interrogated, and its connection to heterosexuality is made problematic. Instead of examining the subject's connection to another, the fantastic exposes the mystery of desire and the self's complexly shadowed relation to itself. While Lovelace is obsessed, at one level, with Clarissa—with the question of what she wants and who, as a woman, she really is—at another level, his concern is with the secret of sexual difference, which Clarissa, in her impenetrability, seems to represent. Neither telling the story of her own desire nor responding to his, she acts for him as a mirror in which to rehearse his bafflement: a bafflement shaped at a specific historical moment and rooted in the personal histories of men.

At the level of realism, Lovelace assumes as natural the oppositional gender structure that marked women in Richardson's society as radically different from men and as anomalous in their own sexual nature. As female desire was split off from biological function, respectable women were defined by their maternity while sexual passion was interpreted as aberrant, a disjunction reflected in men's attitudes toward women as well as in women's experience of themselves.[18] Those women who were capable of eliciting feelings of "love" that were associated with early forms of affectivity were identified with the mother and placed out of sexual reach, while those perceived as sexual partners were deemed unworthy of emotional attachment or respect.[19] In order to distinguish wives from whores, men needed to read the signs of difference prospectively as well as retroactively: in women's knowledge, in their pleasure, in their bodies, and in their minds. And all the time, what they were reading were projections of their own desires and fears. It is in this way that Clarissa provides Lovelace (as she does Richardson) an image of his own ambivalence. On one hand, he wants her to be "an angel of a woman" (429), "pure" and virtuous, without desire—the desexualized mother who, as the essence of otherness, confirms his maleness while depriving it of a libidinal object. On the other hand, he wants her also to *be* that libidinal object, subject both to coercive control and to prurient investigation. Trapped in the incessant fluctuation of images that embody the double meaning of femininity, Lovelace exclaims, "Oh, why was this woman so divinely excellent!" only to ask, "Yet how know I that she is?" (694). Unable to believe that any woman "can be said to be virtuous till she has been tried" (430), he resolves to "try if I can awaken the *woman* in her . . . to try if she . . . be really inflexible as to the grand article" (431). "The grand article" is the mystery at the heart of the mystery of sexual difference, then: the sign of female pleasure that is visible even though its originary site is hidden. Excessive to her biological functioning, this "nothing to see" of woman eludes and therefore motivates a search for knowledge that is pornographic in its rejection of women's subjectivity.[20] Justifying his compulsive quest for the involuntary sign of her true nature, Lovelace insists that Clarissa "cannot bear to be thought a *woman* . . . and if, in the last attempt, I find her *not* one, what will she be the worse for the trial?" (868). Of course, if Clarissa were to prove herself proof against him, she would prove herself to be *the* woman who cannot be for him a woman: on the social level, the not-woman promoted by her culture; at a deeper level, the mother whom he both fears and wishes her to be; and, at the deepest level, the mother in himself which he has surrendered in order to become a man—the mother in himself to which he also clings.

Through Lovelace, Richardson suggests how the exclusion of sexuality from the definition of woman in the realistic mode produces in the fantastic an obsession with the mother's sexuality. More, he demonstrates how the pornographic fantastic with which Lovelace is identified does not focus on incest, as other fantastic genres tend to do, but regresses to a moment that predates the incest fantasy, revealing the solipsistic nature of infantile desire in which acculturated sexual relationships are rooted. In Lovelace, the pornographic imagination rehearses the struggle of differentiation, with all of its desire and rage, projecting it onto an adult world of erotic domination.[21] Genital confusions and oedipal conflicts collapse into archaic, preoedipal needs as bodily memory seeks to express itself in desublimated forms. The libertine desire for sexual conquest is shown to enact simultaneously the urge to social rebellion, the need of sadistic defense, the fear of impotence, the desire for sexual knowledge, the wish to merge with the body of the mother, and the need to resist, at any price, that merging.[22] Symptomatically, Lovelace's promiscuous sexuality is identified with exploits of his past. In the present of the novel, his is a sexuality related not to the body but to the mind. It is not behavioral excess that characterizes this descendent of Rochester and precursor of de Sade, but the insistence of compulsive curiosity. It is not pleasure that he seems to seek but knowledge, and it is in the interests of his epistemophilia that he finally undertakes Clarissa's rape.

The rape of Clarissa metaphorizes Lovelace's dilemma, suggesting the psychic complexity of his situation and the horror of its result. The reader's response mirrors the disjunctive levels of meaning: on one side, empathic recognition; on the other side, revulsion. The anticlimactic climax of the novel, the rape reveals the silence at the fiction's center by gesturing toward a scene that it refuses also to make visible. Although intended by Lovelace as solution, the rape fetishistically repeats the paradox it is called upon to solve. Neither able to seduce Clarissa nor willing to force himself to marry her— unable either to penetrate her virtue or to accept her virtue as impenetrable—Lovelace performs the function of pornographer, attempting to write her, against her will, as harlot in the house of prostitution over which Mrs. Sinclair presides. Failing to counter her resistance, he has her drugged in order to perform what he later calls "a notional violation" (916). In the aftermath he writes to Belford, "And now . . . I can go no farther. The affair is over. Clarissa lives" (883). Instead of discovering the "grand article" that would have proven her to be a woman, or the shudder of death that would have proven her transcendence of that fallen state, Lovelace has elicited— no sign at all. "I must own that there is something very singular in this lady's case[,]" he later says, "and at times I cannot help regretting that I ever attempted her; since not one power either of body or soul could be moved in my favour; and since, to use the expression of the philosopher, on a much graver occasion, There is no difference to be found between the skull of King Phillip and that of another man" (885). The contradiction remains: Clarissa is both "singular" and in all respects like every other person of her sex. Closed and impermeable, she is also only open: her vagina empty, like a skull—tokening not pleasure but a deathly void. Nothing marks her difference, except the thing that she proves finally not to have. Because difference is both everywhere and nowhere, the rape is itself both cataclysmic and unimaginable—unimaginable, at least, in the terms one would expect to find.[23]

When he describes the fire scene, Lovelace represents his first, failed effort to rape Clarissa in the excessive language of pornographic romance. He is strangely silent, however, about the rape that does succeed. Although he fantasizes endlessly about his appropriation of her, this ultimate appropriation has no narrative reality. It is the only event significant to them both of which only one account is given. Clarissa presents it as a nightmare that, while experienced in full horror, can only dimly be recalled: "I was so senseless that I dare not aver that the horrid creatures of the house were personally aiding and abetting: but some visionary rememberances I have of female figures flitting, as I may say, before my sight; the wretched woman's particularly" (1011). She says nothing more specific about the violation, but whenever she alludes to it, it is embedded in a scene that takes place among women dominated by "the wretched woman," rather than between Lovelace and herself.[24] Perceiving Mrs. Sinclair to be "a frightful woman—if she *be* a woman" (894), Clarissa remains more terrified of her "worse than masculine violence" (1011) than she is of Lovelace's attack. Lovelace also blames "the old beldame" for "ruining the fairest virtue in the world" (1217) and describes himself as impotent before her domineering powers. It is significant that Mrs. Sinclair intervenes in the rape scene at the approximate moment that Lovelace withdrew, without her intervention, in the fire scene: with Clarissa pleading, his own sympathies aroused. So, although Lovelace is not absolved of responsibility for the violation (as some have claimed), it can be argued that Richardson needs Mrs. Sinclair in order to complete the action that Lovelace has undertaken.

The nightmarish woman at the center of the text, Mrs. Sinclair functions as the subversive prostitute in the realist mode and, in the fantastic, as the uncontrollable, sexual mother. A brothel-keeper, she fosters a nonproductive sexuality that undermines the dominant fictions associated with the gendered division of labor. In her parody of the maternal role, she shows how mothers like Mrs. Harlowe serve the interests of the patriarchy, acting as the pimps and jailers of their daughters, performing their function as the heartless "breakers" of women through the socializing process which they oversee. As a grotesque figure of fantasy, she stands as Richardson's hallucinatory projection of unrestrained sexuality and boundless female power. Described as brutish, with a "masculine air and fierce look," "the old dragon" is shown with "her eyebrows erect, like the bristles upon a hog's back. . . . She pouted out her blubber-lips, as if to bellows up wind and sputter into her horse-nostrils; and her chin was curdled, and more than usually prominent with passion" (883). Not nurturant but destructive, the wicked witch instead of the virtuous godmother, a mentor not of pure but whorish daughters, she drugs Clarissa with her "bad London milk" and attempts to poison her body, soul, and mind. As an incarnation of the phallic mother, she is a man-woman who is autonomous and self-sufficient, a fetish object both denying and claiming difference. Not castrated according to cultural norms, she is, in her very presence, castrating: the primal object of hidden desires and secret fears. It is in this role that she serves as Lovelace's "other"—what Belford calls "the mother of your mind": the frightening embodiment of Lovelace's psychic and social ambivalence.

After the rape, Lovelace dreams that Clarissa manages to flee Mrs. Sinclair and her house of women with "a grave matronly lady"—a good mother who offers protection to "a most unhappy young creature who has been basely seduced and betrayed." Through "some quick transition, and strange metamorphosis," the benign old lady is transformed first into a version of Mrs. Sinclair and then, when she gets into bed with Clarissa, into Lovelace himself. The rape is replayed as "a strange promiscuous huddle of adventures" with "all the gentle and ungentle pressures of the lover's warfare" and is followed by "ensued recoveries, lyings in, christenings, the smiling boy amply, even *in her own opinion,* rewarding the suffering mother" (922). The dream concludes with one of Lovelace's recurrent fantasies: Clarissa "comparing notes" (922) about his sexual prowess with Anna Howe, who bears him a daughter who will ultimately marry Clarissa's son. The strategies of the dream—those of splitting and projection, condensation and displacement—repeat the strategies of the literary fantastic through which Lovelace is created and through which he continually and solipsistically creates himself.

Throughout the text, Lovelace's identification is split between Clarissa and Mrs. Sinclair: the good, pure mother and the bad, sexual mother, the ego ideal and a phantasm of the fallen self. The impregnation of Clarissa in his dream is grounded in his belief that with "that foundation laid," he can count on the "revived affection . . . which a woman seldom fails to have for the father of her first child, whether born in wedlock or out of it" (917). His wish for her maternity is grounded also in his desire to prove his own masculinity by proving Clarissa's difference as a woman. And, finally, it is grounded in his longing to *be* Clarissa's child. "Let me perish, Belford," he writes, "If I would not forego the brightest diadem in the world for the pleasure of seeing a twin Lovelace at each charming breast, drawing from it his first sustenance" (706). In varying contexts, Lovelace affirms his connection to the nurturant mother, attempting to claim the totality of her love while seeking permission to be a womanish man. It is this which motivates his pathological possessiveness and expresses itself, theatrically, as an urge to the performance of androgyny. Perceiving himself to have been a "bashful whelp," Lovelace concludes that "a bashful man has a good deal of the soul of a woman: and so, like Tiresias, can tell what they think and what they drive at, as well as themselves" (441). Significantly, Lovelace chooses to interpret Tiresias not as masculine *and* feminine, but as a man who can use his understanding of women to serve his masculine ends. In this way, he is himself the Tiresias figure he imagines—a bisexual subject who needs to be perceived as gendered. The comparison suggests how psychic longing is transformed by social necessity, how the fantasy of identification slips into the need for possession, how the fear of impotence gives way to a wish for omnipotence, and how the desire for erotic connection disguises itself in sadism. To be a womanish man, after all, is to be Hickman, despised by men and women alike. An alternative is to convert the feminized self into the mannish woman, as Lovelace does within his dream, and as he (and Richardson) do, finally, in the rape.

Of course, the conversion can never, for Lovelace, be decisive—oscillation is inevitable. Through the lengthy middle section of the novel, Lovelace struggles with a sense of his own vulnerability, moving between the rage of love and the rage of revenge. The first takes Clarissa as its object, the second strives for articulation through Mrs. Sinclair. In both love and revenge, aggression dominates. Lovelace's small triumphs in outwitting his "vigilant charmer" fill him with a sense of his own omnipotence: "I am taller by half a yard, in my imagination, than I was!—I look DOWN upon everybody now" (402). And when he tricks Clarissa into taking up residence at Mrs. Sinclair's, the sexual resonance of that sense of omnipotence is clear: "What a matchless plotter thy friend! Stand by and let me swell!—I am already as big as an elephant; and ten times wiser! mightier too by far! Have I not reason to snuff the moon with my probiscus?" (473). His sadistic fantasies proliferate from a desire for sexual power that masks his dread of impotence and fear of castration.[25] Because he cannot bear the threat of a friendship between Clarissa and Anna from which he is excluded, he fantasizes repeatedly that he will "teach [Anna] submission without reserve" (637). The form of that lesson is always rape, once with the help of "a dozen of her own pitiless sex" (635), once in the company of her mother (671), once in the presence of Clarissa (864), but always as a way of punishing her independence. He can imagine Clarissa living with her friend only if, as in his dream, both are pregnant with his children, both marked and dominated by his phallic power. What incites him to the greatest rage is Anna's insult to his masculinity: her claim that "men of our cast . . . cannot have the ardours that honest men have" (638), just as he is incited to the final act of violence by Mrs. Sinclair's "daughters," who "endeavoured to excite my vengeance, and my pride, by preaching to me eternally [Clarissa's] doubts, her want of love, and her contempt of me" (1482).

In Lovelace's promiscuous multiplicity, Richardson projects a complexly gendered subjectivity that he himself could barely control and that he could hardly have completely understood. In his sadism, Lovelace identifies with the power of the father, not only rejecting but punishing the mother in himself. In his peculiar deference to Mrs. Sinclair, however—especially in the rape, when he surrenders his will to hers—he accepts a masochistic subordination to the phallic mother that, in its regression, subverts the patriarchal order. It is as sadist *and* as masochist, therefore—from both masculine and feminine positions—that he initiates his own psychic destruction.[26] When he rapes Clarissa, he ruptures the fragile membrane that has connected, however tenuously, the fragments of his divided self. After the rape, as the fiction shifts back into the realistic mode, Mrs. Sinclair and Clarissa no longer enact aspects of his conflicted subjectivity but become autonomous figures in a morality play, while he is abandoned as an empty shell. When Clarissa flees after his first rape attempt, he asserts that "wanting *her*, I want my own soul, at least everything dear to it" (740); and after her death, he writes to Belford in desperation, "I am still, I am still, most miserably absent from myself! I shall never, never more be what I was" (1428). Losing Clarissa, he is not only deprived of a female object for his pornographic, male imaginings—he also loses the capacity he has had for empathic connection, however flawed and partial that capacity might have been. Cut off decisively from the ego ideal that she has represented for him, he is cut off as well from an internal source of goodness identified with the female and maternal.[27] After the rape, and for the remainder of the fiction, Lovelace is only a shadowy figure, repeating past gestures without energy, performing his ambivalence without conviction. Mrs. Sinclair's ghastly end is dissociated from him completely. Played out in moral terms that are colorfully gothicized, her death provides parodic justice for the phallic mother in the form of a metaphoric, gangrenous castration. Her leg, broken in a drunken fall, becomes mortified and is amputated before she "obscenely" dies. Categorically displacing her, Clarissa regains the center of the stage, this time as an embodiment of Christ.

The rape that marks the disintegration of Lovelace, then, signals the beginning of Clarissa's triumph. Her impenetrability penetrated, her narcissistic posture undermined, Clarissa feels at first without recourse, "when all my doors are fast, and nothing but the keyhole open, and the key of late put into that, to be where you are, in a manner without opening any of them. . . . Oh wretched, wretched Clarissa Harlowe" (894). Needing to close herself again, she must redeem and revise the dominant fiction of her life, which has been challenged by a brutal version of reality. The state of psychic fragmentation into which she falls initially is, in its extremity, madness and, in its expressivity, a kind of truth. The poetic fragments that she creates metaphorize both the instability and the receptivity of her mind. They map her progress as she struggles to renew and strengthen her reading of herself. A fallen Eve, she articulates in her "mad papers" the despair and guilt she feels that in loving Lovelace she has acted *"out* of nature, *out* of character, at least": acted as a "lady" who "took a great fancy" to a beast who, responding *"in* nature," has destroyed her "prospects of a happy life" (891–92). Knowing that "[w]hen honour's lost, 'tis a relief to die: / Death's but a sure retreat from infamy" (893), but recognizing that she cannot overtly kill herself, Clarissa seeks a Christian martyrdom that removes her from the vicissitudes of society while installing her irretrievably not just as exemplar, but as "divine example" (1306). Sleeping and eating little while withdrawing from those who would deprive her of autonomy, Clarissa rejects her "encumbering" body and eliminates the "keyhole" through which Lovelace and her family have tried to steal her self. Secured against incursion, she finds a voice powerful enough to silence even Lovelace, forcing him to ask,

"Whose the triumph now!—HERS, or MINE?" (901). Claiming the right to tell the story of the lady and the beast, she shapes a meta-narrative that suits her needs and redirects desire by rewriting the physical in spiritual terms.

With the last section of the novel, Richardson seeks to subject Lovelace's perspective to Clarissa's—and the fantastic to the realistic mode. It is not possible, however, for Clarissa to assert herself *realistically* against the patriarchal values that Richardson has both interrogated in defining her predicament and employed in representing her sense of self. For this reason, realism ultimately gives way to a regressive Christian allegory. Enacted socially and within the boundaries of the law, Clarissa's personal affairs remain matters for male negotiation. She has no power to retrieve her property from her father; she cannot hope for justice against Lovelace; she cannot even appoint a woman as executor of her "will." Now ruined, her body is not a marketable commodity. Her family would make its colonization explicit by deporting her, as a criminal, to Virginia. Psychologically, she cannot free herself from the force of the fathers' judgments until her character is demonstrated as superior to theirs but still unthreatening to the socioeconomic order.

Clarissa's embrace of a martyr's death superficially resolves the formal and moral dilemmas of the fiction. Shaping her narrative in the genre of the religious sublime, and projecting her into a world of spiritual rather than material value, Richardson is able to affirm female autonomy and moral transcendence without testing their pragmatic implications. From her position of moral unassailability, Clarissa's perspective is merged with Richardson's. She gathers the letters for publication, proselytizes actively for her interpretation, and fantasizes that Lovelace himself will be reformed when he reads the text that she is in the process of constructing (1177). Claiming authority to literalize secular metaphors as allegorical Christian truth, Clarissa deceives Lovelace by telling him that she is "setting out with all diligence for my father's house" (1233). With the ecstasy of "supreme love," she prepares herself as a "bride," for her "last house": the coffin that she purchases and uses temporarily as a desk. Overtly forgiving all and blaming none, she not only restores herself to but exceeds the position that she held at the beginning of the novel. She is a preferred child and the model for a now expanded and adoring community. In the letter she leaves for Lovelace to read after she has died, she suggests that the distance which has separated them only figuratively in the past—"I have long been greatly above you" (1427)—has now achieved its final, substantive meaning.

Still, the Christian sublime cannot conceal the contradictions that Richardson intends it to resolve. Although it appears to transcend the values of the dominant social fiction, Christian ideology in fact reflects, extends, and reinforces them. So, in willing her own death, Clarissa embraces with renewed determination the concept of an autonomous, unitary self. Defended against the incursions of others, she exposes the solipsism at the heart of affective individualism. A grandiose form of narcissism, her spiritual unassailability makes human reciprocity irrelevant and reveals her earlier vision of the human community as impossibly naive. Clarissa's martyrdom seems to free her from the encroachments of the patriarchal family, but the alternative she envisions functions to create a more potent version of that same structure. Always the "good girl," Clarissa identifies herself completely with the Father's judgment, as guilt and rage fuel her desire for death.[28] Wishing her virtue to be *seen* and recognized as it was before, her dying is a prolonged performance staged in all of its details. The body's exhibition proves to be a crucial aspect of physical denial.[29] Having played narcissist instead of masochist with Lovelace, Clarissa now reveals the interface of the two. As Christian martyr, she is masochist and narcissist simultaneously and displays the arrogance and pride of those positions.

Conceptualized both as an extension and a transcendence of the realistic mode, Clarissa's martyrdom strives for sublimity but realizes itself, through sentimentality, as ineffectual protest. Although Richardson seeks to define her death as the redemption of a fallen world, the Christian allegory confirms the radical social and sexual disjunctions of her situation and reinforces the status quo. So, while Clarissa's spiritual empowerment can be interpreted, on one level, as a rewriting of the psychic disintegration occasioned by the rape, it ends with a form of psychic dissolution that, in material terms, is more complete. Constructed by the gender arrangements that prevail, her sexuality remains oddly indeterminate, not only through her dying but in her death. Her rejection of her body reflects the definitional vacuum in which that body is suspended, caught as it is between virginal purity and possible maternity. The fact that the coffin is the only home that she can claim suggests the vacancy that

"woman" in the "real" world represents. The multiplicity of her fig-
ural roles—the Father's daughter, the bride of Christ, and Christ himself—only strengthens the ambiguous nature of her desexualized
androgyny. Sacralized first by Lovelace and then by Richardson in
his identification with her, Clarissa is projected as the mystical other
who holds the key to all meaning, while offering no meaning in
herself. To the fiction's end, she is a cipher to be read—by Lovelace,
by Richardson, and by generations of readers.

The text's desire for the sublime, then, reflects a desire also for the
dissolution of difference, particularly the differences that gender represents and structures. The ambivalence of that desire is reflected
within the modes through which it is projected: the positive sublime
of sentimental Christian allegory, which is ultimately associated with
Clarissa, and the negative sublime of the pornographic fantastic,
with which Lovelace is identified. The former is motivated by the
desire to achieve the oceanic experience of fusion; the latter is rooted
in a fear of fusion as erasure. Both articulate an urge to fill the space
left vacant by an increasingly secularized religion. Both mark a
doomed attempt to get beyond experience to the unconditioned: the
first, through an intensity of feeling posed to counter reason; the
second, in the negations of psychic appropriation.[30] Lovelace tries to
locate in Clarissa a significance that will allow him to transcend existential isolation, while Clarissa seeks to evade the necessity of relation altogether by locating her transcendence in death. Because
Clarissa has no space in which to express the subjectivity that she
wishes to affirm, and Lovelace cannot believe at all in a coherent
subjectivity, both stage performances of themselves that only enact
and exacerbate their alienation. Through his addiction to fantasy and
disguise, Lovelace obsessively replays the psychic and hermeneutic
instabilities that he wants to move beyond, while Clarissa literalizes
an allegorical version of the integrated self in a frozen figure that
refuses change. Mutually exclusive, their roles are also self-defeating.
Their futile repetition can only be halted in the physical deaths of
the protagonists.

In *Clarissa*, it is the relation of the socially constructed schisms of
sexual difference to the intrapsychic schisms imposed by psychic
differentiation that organizes realistic and fantastic narrative modes,
propelling them in the direction of the sublime. In the sentimental
form, sexual difference is absorbed in an androgynous Christian self

still stamped by impotent femininity. In the pornographic genre, the difference that originates within the male self is projected onto an objectified female other, and primal desires are then explored in the necessarily failed, eroticized relation. It is in the solipsistic self-referentiality of each narrative and, even more, in his disclosure of the radical disjunction between the two that Richardson achieves a vision more tragic than he could have understood. It is a vision that exceeds both the sentimental and the pornographic in its represen-tation of the fundamental incompatibility of men and women in his world. In the oddly truncated rape of Clarissa—both over-determined and only partially imagined—Richardson suggests the extremity of the effort that must be made if the two narratives—and the two worlds—are to be conjoined. At the same time, he reveals the failure even of textual and material violence to effect that impos-sible connection.

Where Richardson might have seen the possibilities of partial res-olution was where he most rejected it: in the refusal of his readers to conform to gender expectations. Women of his time refused to read exclusively like women; men—including Richardson himself—did not read simply like men. The truth that Richardson inadver-tently unearthed is one that readers both continue to reveal and, at the same time, continue to deny: that identifications and identifica-tory resistance take place at social and at psychological levels, across gender categories as well as within them. Like his society, his char-acters, and his narrative, Richardson was himself intellectually, ideo-logically, emotionally, and psychologically divided, a man who re-vealed at the level of fantasy what, at the level of realism, he strongly denied. In this, he was the protagonist of his own fantastic fiction, playing out through male and female aspects of himself desires that were not only male and female. The genuine complexity of gender relations can be traced in the dynamic process of his writing, and in those complex relations can be discovered the political possibilities of interpretation.

3

(W)holes and Noses

The Indeterminacies of Tristram Shandy

In the past, *Tristram Shandy* has been erased from origin stories told about the English novel or has required, within those stories, a Sternean digression of its own.[1] Although its affinities with the traditions of learned wit and Menippean satire have been noted, they have been used to justify arguments about the exceptional, rather than representative, character of the work. In a similar spirit, Sterne's rejection of linear time, and his obsession with a contradictory and internally divided self, have been viewed as remarkable in their anticipation of modernism. Now *Tristram Shandy* has come into fashion as a prophetically postmodern and even presciently Lacanian text, and while these claims have attracted readers to the fiction, they have made its position more anomalous than ever. It seems that every new appreciation of the work's complexity brings with it a renewed conviction of its aberrance.

While granting—even celebrating—*Tristram Shandy*'s eccentricity, I want to argue strongly against its critical marginalization. Despite the fact that it has been dismissed by theorists of realism and has not been considered at all by theorists of the fantastic,[2] I want to place the novel at the intersection of the two traditions, testing the limits of each in the context of their mutually constitutive dynamic. At the most basic level, the inclusion of Sterne's novel expands our understanding of the fantastic mode. It enables us to see how *Tristram Shandy*, which was published at the same time as *The Castle of Otranto*, shares the fundamental interests of "pure" fictions of gothic horror—with one important difference: its investigations are enacted through sentimental comedy that aspires to the sublime, while the gothic is played out in melodrama that struggles to transform itself in tragedy.[3]

Once placed in historical perspective, the impulses of the fantastic can be seen to structure a range of overlapping genres—the gothic novels of horror by Horace Walpole, Matthew Lewis, and Ann Radcliffe, for example; the nineteenth-century romance that includes *Wuthering Heights, Frankenstein,* and *Dracula,* as well as Freud's case studies; the comic absurd that begins with Sterne, moves through Lewis Carroll to Joyce and Beckett, and then extends to the novels of magical realism and the essays of Lacan. Although fictive and theoretical texts in this tradition are stamped differently by their differing historical moments, as we have seen, all depict a subjectivity that is internally divided; a desiring subjectivity that seeks to articulate the absence and loss by which it has been shaped: a subjectivity that resists societal forces that would appropriate it for family, class, and nation; for language and for reason; for the gendered division of labor and for forms of sexuality that are proscribed. Many fantastic fictions are contained largely by the interior landscape that the solipsistic mind projects, and most at least are dominated by it. While *Tristram Shandy* is not unique in its resistance to containment, it is certainly the first fiction to insist upon the necessary if partial engagement of the fantastic subject with its social context: the engagement of the fantastic with the realist mode.

At the center of *Tristram Shandy* is Sterne's ironic interrogation of Locke who, in *An Essay Concerning Human Understanding,* attempts to mediate between the old rationalism and the new empiricism, defining a subjectivity that functions in accordance with its own eccentric desires in a material world that still lies open to rational discovery. Sterne recognizes the paradoxical nature of Locke's search for incontrovertible truths hidden beneath inescapable relativities: absolute principles that could guarantee the relation of the idea to its reality, the name to its object, private to public meaning, and selfish interest to social need.[4] He sees the fragility of the bridges that Locke had built to connect rationalism's perspectives with those of empiricism: his deployment of a theory of error to close the gap between rational thought and the eccentricities of association, his presentation of the slippage of signifier and signified as an abuse of language, and his spasmodic appeal to a *deus ex machina* when other forms of regulation failed. Positioning himself on the side of radical empiricism, Sterne chooses to look directly into the chasm that marks the divergence of fantastic discourses from those of realism, not ultimately to connect them through some clever sleight of mind but rather to map the interaction of their constructive and deconstructive strategies. From this perspective, he prefigures modern epistemologies that insist knowledge is produced and not discovered and argue that what is known is inseparable from the subjectivity that knows.[5] But titling his book *The Life and Opinions of Tristram Shandy, Gentleman* Sterne also suggests that although knowledge relies on our personal constructions, the projections we call opinions are both privately referenced and socially embedded.

The point is that Sterne takes subjectivity as his subject. He does not conceptualize that subjectivity as coherent in the mode of realism, fully embodied and transparently available as character, if ultimately conflicted, still capable of integration. He conceptualizes it rather in fantastic terms as multiple and even pathologically divided, as mysterious to others and unknown even to itself. Following realism's familiar formula, Sterne has Tristram, his narrator, set out to tell the story of his life. In the process, he discovers that the single story he can write is "the history of what passes in a man's mind": an analysis of the way in which the self knows and constructs itself in language, and the way in which that construction marks him always as a character alienated from himself. This is a subjectivity that does uncannily anticipate those phrased, dissected, and debated by psychoanalytic theorists at later stages of the modern civilizing process. Once this subject's project is defined as self-retrieval it is inevitably doomed, since to know the self is also to recognize the self as other, and to recognize the self as other is to lose the self one seeks to know. As Sterne understood, the lost reclaimed is the loss denied: a farce of misrecognition that can never be resolved but is continually replayed as the telling—which is also the making—of a life.

But if Sterne took subjectivity as his subject, the form of subjectivity that he explored was clearly and distinctly male. For him—as, indeed, for Freud and later for Lacan—the central problem of this self-eluding and self-deluded subjectivity is concerned with the mystery of its engendering: the mystery of the origins of self, sexuality, and sexual difference.[6] The primal scene with which Tristram begins his inquiries, and to which he compulsively returns throughout the novel, is precisely the scene of origination—the scene in which he is conceived by a man and a woman as a male. Haunting, shaping, and prefiguring the text, it is a scene of interrupted coition that marks at once the irreconcilable differences between men and women, the incommensurability of passion and reason, the ultimate disjunction of the word and its referent, and the irrecoverable separation of desire from its object. Radically ambiguous, it is a scene of indeterminacy that is ultimately determining for its protagonist—as any scene of primal fantasy must be.

"The pitiful misadventures" that Tristram is doomed to suffer mentally and physically in a fundamentally unsympathetic world are rooted here, in the eccentric associations and radical differences of his parents: his father, the most "regular" of men, who "winds up" both his house clock and his wife on the first Sunday night of every month, and his mother who dares to speak as she is on the verge of being wound:

> Pray, my dear, quoth my mother, have you not forgot to wind up
> the clock?—Good G—! cried my father, making an exclamation,
> but taking care to moderate his voice at the same time,—Did ever
> woman, since the creation of the world, interrupt a man with such
> a silly question? Pray, what was your father saying?—Nothing.[7]

Whether Walter is able to continue doing what he was (or was not) doing before he was so literally interrupted can never be certain since Tristram is born a scant eight months later, "as near nine kalendar months as any husband could in reason have expected" (7). It is clear that Tristram's personal fate might indeed have been sealed on this occasion, along with the fortunes of the Shandy house, by the scattering of animal spirits "transfused" from father to son, "his muscular strength and virility worn down to a thread," and his melancholy disposition thereby established prematurely. But whatever the particular circumstances were of his conception, Tristram's fate as a man is necessarily determined by the anxiety of paternity that structures relations of reproduction in his eighteenth-century world.[8] With his fatalistic comment about the inevitable prematurity of infant births, Sterne suggests that a man's identity as father can never with certainty be fixed—although his name remains crucial to the cross-generational inheritance of property.[9] The male seed is alienated at coition, and the secrets of the enveloping womb are as final as the secrets of the grave. Man's stakes in the reproductive process are increased as he "discovers" his radical differences from woman, whose identity is inextricably bound to her strangely functioning body and her "essential" nature. So Walter sees that

from the very moment the mistress of the house is brought to bed,
every female in it, from my lady's gentlewoman down to the cinder-
wench becomes an inch taller for it; and give themselves more airs
upon that single inch, than all their other inches put together.
  "I think, rather," replied my uncle Toby, "that 'tis we who sink
an inch lower.—If I meet but a woman with child—I do it—." (213)

Walter's resentment and Toby's anxiety stamp the account that Tristram gives of his begetting. It is a story shaped by a masculinist
science that centers the father and all but erases the mother, casting
the prospective infant as a homunculus who resides, fully developed, in the sperm, requiring only safe delivery to the passive and
incidental womb, which is "the place destined for his reception."[10]
As Tristram ironically suggests, the erasure could only be improved
if after the ceremony of marriage and before that of consummation,
all the homunculi could be "baptized at once, slap-dash, by injec-
tion" (47).

  In Sterne's comic representation, the laws, scholarly treatises, and
medical practices that collude to help men establish women as un-
related to their children reflect the politics of reproduction, which
Mary O'Brien and other theorists have analyzed in a similar but
explicitly feminist mode. From this perspective, men bond together
seeking to repair their alienation in principles of continuity that lie
outside of nature. With their laws, they appropriate the children produced by female labor and substitute their own cultural productions
for women's reproductive creativity. But while Sterne ironically reveals the defensive nature of the impulse that makes a mere container
of the fertile womb, it is the fear of that container as a malign vacuum
that shapes, at conscious and unconscious levels, the fiction that he,
with Tristram, writes. It is all very well for Tristram, having abandoned his mother for several chapters just as she discovers his elder
brother's death, to bemoan the fact that, in rejecting her, he is acting
"like a Turk": "as if Nature had plaistered me up, and set me down
naked upon the banks of the river Nile, without one" (277). Despite
his protests, the novel does proceed as if it would be better for men
to be spawned spontaneously from river mud than to be born of
women. Like the psychoanalysts who succeed him, Sterne is trapped
in the terrain of male development that he also, with much precision,
maps. Mrs. Shandy moves through his text in the way that many

subtly maligned mothers move through Freud's case histories: initiating nothing, but vaguely responsible for everything unfortunate
that happens.[11] Never knowing "more than her backside" what anybody means, she is without intelligence, curiosity, or imagination.
Since a "temperate current of blood ran orderly through her veins
in all months of the year, and in all critical moments both of the day
and night" (451), she is without passion or desire, although Walter
refuses to see her as lacking in lust. Deprived of her own interior life
and disconnected from the interior lives of others, she cannot be
conceptualized in the mode of fantasy. Marginal to the social world
of family, she is barred from participation in the realistic mode as
well. Neither a "real" nor a spectral mother, she beckons toward
while veiling the places where those mothers should have been. As
an obstacle to narrative, she is refused all humane and humanizing
gestures by the text. Her long and difficult labor takes place offstage,
essentially unremarked by the Shandy men. We see her on the verge
of discovering the death of her elder son, but learn nothing of her
response to that discovery. As caregiver, she is similarly invisible:
we are told only that while Walter is writing his *Tristrapaedia*—the
educational theory intended to compensate for all of Tristram's
woes—Tristram himself remains uneducated, "totally neglected . . .
and abandonned to my mother" (283). Her breast—the sign and confirmation of her maternity—is evoked by Tristram only once, in the
context of a theory that associates the nursing breast's flaccidity or
firmness with the "length and goodness" of the infant's nose (174).
"My mother, you must know," he starts, but turns immediately from
description to digression. His mother remains clothed—the taboo in
place—but the few words he drops are adequate to seal his mother's
fate in the curious reader's mind. Given what we know of Tristram's
nose, and of his association of nose and penis, we conclude—as we
are meant to do—that hers is not the good breast, flaccid and nur-
turing, but the firm, bad breast complexly identified, in this context,
with castration.

   Already linked to Walter's possible impotence through her un-
timely inquiry about the winding of the clock, Mrs. Shandy becomes
a victim of the castration fear that floods the novel. She is associated
with the lascivious Widow Wadman, who unmans Uncle Toby with
her penetrating gaze, and with Susannah, the leaky vessel, who "cuts
off spouts" and destroys bridges—Tristram's significantly among

them. Throughout the text, the good mother—with the nourishing breast and sheltering, creative womb—is known only in her absence, an implied "other" of the women whose obstinate passivity or voracious sexuality causes the primary experience of differentiation to be displaced by fears of impotence and castration.[12] Unrepresented, the fantasy of that good mother is identified retrospectively with an originary loss experienced by the subject as a lack that, while displaced and veiled by language, persists as a desire that cannot be answered and a fear that cannot be calmed. Once the barely perceptible, oddly attenuated figure of Mrs. Shandy is placed at the center of Sterne's fiction with the elusive space that she both confirms and hides, the novel can be read as an effort on the part of the male subject—both Sterne and Tristram—to deny, embody, and appropriate this present absence in and for themselves, with all the traces of femininity by which it is stamped and with the promise of wholeness that it extends. Struggling to deny sexual difference by transforming it into a male sameness, the text attempts on one level to substitute father for mother, phallus for breast, word for thing, and integral self for multiple subjectivity, but the fetishizing gesture necessarily undoes the compromise that it is intended to effect. Desire is intensified by displacement. The threat of lack and the knowledge of difference are always present, and the need they arouse must continually be articulated in order to be allayed. Entombed within the self, the unrepresented aspects of the female other become the source of a perpetual mourning that seeks formal and thematic expression in the text, where it is most obviously suggested in the melancholy resonance of Tristram's name.[13]

While the idealized woman, who is the object not of fear but of desire, makes her appearance as the romantic other in both *A Sentimental Journey* and *Journal to Eliza*, she is largely excluded from *Tristram Shandy*, where she is (mis)represented by the fathers: primarily by Walter but also by Yorick, Uncle Toby, and Trim. Replacing the triangulated, competitive, heterosexual nuclear family of realism with an extended family that comprises a male homosocial community organized around the dyad of father and son, Sterne lovingly brings the emotional logic of his misogynistic world into fantastic focus. The occasion for relations between and among men, women become mere background for the enactment of male passion and the trading of male property. Central to the functioning of the private as well as of the public world, men perform their emotional and intellectual labor in the context of an ambiguous masculinity that completes the appropriation of the female role on all but the most grossly biological of levels. Without competition, Tristram's relation to the fathers—like their relations with one another—is erotic in its longing for an unmediated connection that resurrects the imagined primal bond: a desire not to be *like*, but to *be*. It is an empathic urge that makes each male project himself into the other in order to retrieve that other as a version of himself. Moreover, since each, with his ambiguously mutilated manhood, serves as a feminized other for the others, each confirms the others' masculinity in order to construct a phallic economy that is based, ironically, on lack.

In this way, Sterne fantasizes a cultural form of the preoedipal moment in which the identification with the mother is shattered and the male child identifies with what Freud calls the ideal father of personal history.[14] It is a moment between the fall from Edenic wholeness, retrospectively remembered, and entry into the conflictual world of hierarchical difference, in which women can be suppressed but not denied. It is a psychic moment that Sterne—with Tristram and all Shandyean males—seeks to concretize as social space. The primary lack, while not erased completely, is veiled by each man's attempt to connect empathically to other men who, projected as aspects of themselves, are also objects of desire. In the fantasy, homosociality supplants the ambisexuality of infancy and anticipates while suspending the engendering of culture. External objects in which the prospectively male body finds parts of itself symbolically reflected are often ambiguously male and rarely only female. The penis is everywhere and nowhere; the breast has no correlative; and cracks and holes and crevices have not only a vaginal but also an anal reference. Walter "engenders" his dissertations "in the womb of speculation" (78); and Toby, in rejecting the cold sexual fact of the Widow Wadman, need never learn "the right end of a Woman from the wrong" (463). Instead he founds his family with Corporal Trim, with whom he happily raises Le Fever's son.

But Sterne's fantasy of wholeness is belied by the complex nature of the subjectivity that he describes. The idealized identificatory relation that he portrays reaches for erotic connection but reveals solipsism as its other side. To lose altogether the boundary between self and other is to descend into the madness of a reflecting wall of mirrors, while to retrieve the self as other is to confront one's own ultimate strangeness. Either way—and both are the ways of the fantastic—the self is trapped, subverted, and destroyed by its own projective and introjective strategies. Sterne both acknowledges and partially averts these threats, refusing a tragic reading of the psychic side of individualism and bringing his fantasy into humorous conversation with realism. Attempting to retrieve his subjects from the brink of solipsism to which he carries them, he anchors them in society while revealing the full narcissism of their natures. In order to allow them to steer a course between their assimilation of and their accommodation to a reality that can be known only through linguistic representation, Sterne mounts the Shandy men on hobbyhorses, which they ride along an edge that divides the internal from the external world. "A secondary figure, and a kind of background to the whole" (13), the hobbyhorse is a comic double that expresses a man's eccentricity while defining the adaptive strategies that he employs in order to function in his social world. As Sterne explains:

> A man and his Hobby-Horse, tho' I cannot say that they act and react exactly after the same manner in which the soul and body do upon each other: yet doubtless there is a communication between them of some kind, and my opinion rather is, that there is something in it more of the manner of electrified bodies,—and that by means of the heated parts of the rider, which come immediately into contact with the back of the Hobby-Horse.—By long journies and much friction, it so happens that the body of the rider is at length fill'd as full of Hobby-Horsical matter as it can hold;—so that if you are able to give but a clear description of the nature of the one, you may form a pretty exact description of the genius and the character of the other. (57–58)

Functioning to mediate, initiate, and defend, the hobbyhorse seeks to modify claustral psychic structures in a performative process through which the self establishes its relation to itself.[15] Accomplishing the important work of sublimation, it allows the Shandy males to channel sexual energy into activities that have nothing to do with women and everything to do with other men. "Never did lover post down to a belov'd mistress with more heat and expectations than my uncle Toby did, to enjoy . . . in private" the war games that he plays with Corporal Trim. Walter, "hugely tickled" by an intellectual

concept, is wont to "clap . . . both his hands upon his cod-piece" and
Tristram flees the temptations of Nannette—repelled by the slit in
her petticoat—in order to write the story of Uncle Toby's courtship.
All the hobbyhorsical activities of the men—Toby's war games, Walter's theories, Tristram's autobiography, Yorick's wit, Trim's inventions—are forms of play that help the self to assimilate, instead of
accommodating to, the undeniable otherness of the real world. They
are transitional practices, in D. W. Winnicott's sense, which allow
inner and outer realities to be maintained as separate yet interre-
lated.[16] The balance is delicate, however, and the imaginative illusion,
with its productive compromise, can slip into a form of madness
when it is not shared by others. As Tristram suggests, "A man's
Hobby-Horse is as tender a part as he has about him" (87), and the
bridges it constructs between the psychic and the social are very
fragile. Anxieties of difference—the difference of man and woman,
self and other, word and thing—can cause the dynamic interactions
of symbolic play to be frozen into the hardened strategies of obsession. Because "it is the nature of an hypothesis, when once a man
has conceived it, that it assimilates every thing to itself" (114), the
hobbyhorse comes easily to exert a tyranny of its own. Attempting
to control the world through theoretical formulations that experience
belies, Walter's "whole life [becomes] a contradiction to his knowledge": "his rhetoric and conduct . . . at perpetual handicuffs" (150).
Toby, enamored of the game he plays with Trim, attributes to it more
reality than the reality it imitates. He condemns the Peace of Utrecht
and "grieves the war was not carried on a little longer," although he
would not wish more of his fellow creatures slain. Toby's horse
throws him "somewhat viciously" in this collision of fantasy with
reality, creating "a sort of shyness" between them that gives the
Widow Wadman her opening and allows her to initiate her own cam-
paign (352). In a similar way, Tristram is written by the autobiography that he seeks to write and Sterne is shaped by Tristram, the
persona he projects. And while they, like Yorick, are able to reflect
on the spaces they open in their attempts at self-retrieval, self-
reflexivity does not close the yawning gaps, even though it is responsible for the creative dynamism of their projects.

    Representing the uniqueness of a man's "character"—the way he
shapes the reality he lives—the hobbyhorse has no relevance to
women, who, according to Tristram, "have no character at all" (49).[17]

To have no hobbyhorse means to be deprived of the subjectivity that emerges with the splitting of the self and to experience not desire but need: in Sterne's women, in the form of lust. To be, in this sense, without an "other" is to be disengaged from culture and to be identified with nature: to exist as essence on the margins of language and to be literal rather than metaphorical in speech. Without self-consciousness, women in the Shandy world lack an awareness even of the lack they lack: the lack that is signaled and performed by the hobbyhorse itself.[18] An imitation horse's head mounted on a stick that fits between its rider's legs, the hobbyhorse enables children's mimicry of power. Seeking reparation for their anxiety of impotence, the Shandy males—like "the wisest of men in all ages" (10)—gallop childlike out into the world under the sign of this fantastic phallus. A fetish object, the hobbyhorse disguises and discloses the fear, if not the actuality, of castration. Identified with potency, it enables subjectivity to perform itself symbolically, at the same time that it reveals the inevitable impotence of that performance. To ride the hobbyhorse is to play the Other who is powerful. It is to take on what Lacan has called the Name of the Father and to participate, therefore, in the patriarchal order from a position presumed dominant in language.

In *Tristram Shandy,* Sterne explores the process through which the primal experiences of fragmentation, differentiation, and loss come to be experienced as castration through linguistic representation. Specifically, he describes how the male body is castrated by the cultural mind and suggests some of the ways (the hobbyhorse among them) in which men seek compensation for that symbolic mutilation. From the moment of conception, when the scattering of animal spirits wears the homunculus's "muscular strength and virility . . . down to a thread," Tristram's potency as a male is questioned. That question becomes more pressing with his birth, for while Dr. Slop in delivering him does not mistake his hip for his head and grasp it with his forceps, that substitution is implicitly suggested when it becomes clear that Tristram's nose, small already by heredity, has been flattened by the doctor's intervention. The circumcision performed later by a falling window sash further focuses the significant ambiguity. Encouraging Tristram to piss out of the window, without considering that "nothing . . . in our family . . . was well hung" (284), Susannah proclaims the "murder" of the child and announces that

"Nothing is left . . . nothing is left—for me, but to run my country" (284). For Walter, who perceives that Tristram "comes very hardly by all his religious rites," the problem that results from the catastrophe is rhetorical, not anatomical. The "world" will have formed its opinion of these events, as Walter knows, and is not likely to change it even if Tristram "is shewn publickly at the market cross" (329).[19] That opinion, formed on the basis of the community's own fears, is sealed irrevocably by the mishap of Tristram's naming. To compensate for all of his infant's woes, Walter intends to name his son "Trismegistus": the Greek name of the Egyptian god Thoth, regarded as the inventor of writing, the creator of languages, the scribe, interpreter, and adviser of the gods, and the representative on earth of Ra, the god who signifies fertility. Through the error of Susannah—who has as little understanding of mythology as she has sensitivity to words—the boy is named for sorrow and represents the lack that, while inherent in language, is experienced in the body. The difference between the name that Walter wishes for his son and the name that he is given measures the distance between the male's idealized and real power. Whatever the "reality"—and, in this sense, there is for Sterne no reality outside of language—Tristram is emasculated. Later he flees from the slit in Nannette's petticoat, and stands impotent before his Jenny's gaze, "reflecting upon what had *not* passed" (395). Describing himself as one "who shall never have a finger in the pye" (423), Tristram reflects that while a man "may be set on fire like a candle, at either end—provided there is a sufficient wick standing out," he himself prefers to be lit at the top rather than at the bottom, where the flame "has the misfortune generally to put out itself" (426). That is where Walter also chooses to be inflamed—at the source of his theories—and Toby as well, in the games that do not test his modesty. It is only through displacements such as these that the Shandy men can escape the gaze of women: the Widow Wadman who wishes to see Toby's wound, Susannah who sees that "all" is gone, Jenny who sees Tristram's impotence, and even Mrs. Shandy who sees in Walter the inept winder of the clock.

But while the Shandy males can avoid the female gaze that they experience as castrating, they cannot evade at all the castration that is imposed on them by language. Like Toby, "whose life was put in jeopardy by words" (67), all find, with Tristram, that the search for Truth is endless and that the path one follows to it is "a thorny and bewilder'd track,—intricate are the steps! intricate are the mazes of this labyrinth! intricate are the troubles which the pursuit of this bewitching phantom KNOWLEDGE, will bring upon thee" (69). An elusive object of desire, truth is always somewhere else, lost in the endless play of words by which it is projected: a testament, in its absence, to man's alienation from the society in which he lives and from the self which he inhabits. Refusing a realistic view of language that binds the word to its object, Sterne follows Locke in connecting words to ideas that are arbitrary and subjective. But while Locke identifies this relativity of meaning with abuses of language that are corrigible through careful definition, Sterne rejects the possibility that definitions can be anything but tautological. In his world, there is no way for individuals to move beyond the eccentricity of ideational associations to communication that is based upon shared meanings. As Walter recognizes, "the highest stretch of improvement a single word is capable of, is a high metaphor for which . . . the idea is generally the worse and not the better" (306). For this problem he has a formalist solution: the deployment of auxiliary verbs "to open new tracks of enquiry, and make every idea engender millions." But while his strategy enables him to produce endless variations on the theme of the white bear (Have I ever seen one? Might I ever have seen one? Am I ever to see one? Ought I ever to have seen one? Or can I ever see one? [307]), it can do nothing to prevent the slide in ordinary discourse from association to metaphor and from metaphor to metonymy. As Sterne suggests, each man either must remain mired, alone, in the path that his hobbyhorse has broken—risking collision if he dares even the most harmless of diversions—or, like Tristram, he can self-consciously exploit the excessiveness of language in an effort to transform paralysis into creativity. To the extent that communication is possible within the vicissitudes of language, it is based less on shared assumptions and common definitions than on culturally induced and reinforced obsessions.

Nowhere is the relation of personal to social signification more graphically demonstrated and more wittily explored than in the fiction's production of the meaning of "noses." Well might Tristram protest: "For by the word NOSE, throughout all this long chapter of noses, and in every other part of my work, where the word NOSE occurs,—I declare, by that word I mean a NOSE, and nothing more or less" (162). The fact is that, throughout the text, Sterne creates for his reader the association of nose with penis and, as part of that association, the identification of Shandy noses with inherited impotence and lack. We are told, for example, that Tristram's great-grandfather was forced to provide "an unconscionable jointure" for his wife in order to compensate for the size of his nose. While it is "little or no nose," according to his wife, "no more nose . . . than there is upon the back of my hand," according to his son, and "shaped like an ace of clubs" in Tristram's view, his nose was still— as his great-grandfather himself insists—"a full inch longer than my father's" (163). Walter does not "conceive how the greatest family in England could stand it out against an uninterrupted succession of six or seven short noses," and indeed Tristram with Toby—if not Walter himself—signals the end of the familial line by not conceiving at all. But the nosology of the Shandy family raises more questions than it answers since, according to the logic of the text, the mutilations that the Shandy males endure are more psychological than they are physical: fears of inadequacy that reflect a cultural imperative.

The anxiety about less and the desire for more are all-pervasive, as "Slawkenbergius's Tale" reveals. The sense of lack yields images of an idealized Nose which all men want, from which all benefit, and which no man can possess. Diego, the story's hero, has stopped in Strassburg as he travels from the Promontory of Noses, which he visits when his "dear Julia" rejects him because she has suspicions about the adequacies of his nose. What he has gotten there is everybody's business and anybody's guess. Clearly, he feels obliged to save himself for his beloved and defends his organ valiantly against the sight and touch of others, with a sword so massive that no scabbard is large enough to fit it. Everywhere and nowhere, reputed to be both on his face and in his breeches, his Nose is the subject of fantasy, the topic of gossip, the object of women's desires, the cause of men's anxiety, and, not least of all, the focus of scholarly theorizing and debate. Among the learned, disputes about the nose's nature and the possibility of its existence become so heated that the Nose itself is soon forgotten, having served "as a frigate to launch [the theorists] into the gulph of school divinity,—and then they all sailed before the wind" (198). "Macerated with expectations," the Strassburgers can do nothing but obsess about the veiled appurtenance of Diego. The men, women, and children who leave their city to wait for his return are "tossed to and fro . . . for three days and nights . . . with

the tempestuous fury of [their] passion." When they finally do reen-
ter the gates of Strassburg, no more the wiser, they discover themselves to have been undone by curiosity, for the French, "ever upon
the catch," have taken advantage of their absence and marched in.
"Alas! alas! cries Slawkenbergius—it is not the first—and I fear will
not be the last fortress that has been either won—or lost by Noses"
(203).

As Sterne's anatomy of the nose is, in fact, an anatomy of the
personal and cultural meanings of the penis, his allegory of the Nose
is an allegory of the penis's relation to the Phallus: an exploration of
the process through which the ideal concept is constructed and a
revelation of the fragility of that construction. Projected by castration
anxiety and the fear of impotence, the Phallus represents a penis
that, invincible in perpetual erection, signals both self-control and
power over others. Appropriately, Diego's codpiece does not permit
an unobstructed view of the reputedly impressive organ that it neither fully contains nor completely hides. Veiled, it becomes, with all
of its elusive allusivity, the social and individual object of desire that
marks the lack out of which desire emerges and which it reproduces.
But Sterne, unlike Lacan, does not present the Phallus as a transcen-
dental signifier—an originating idealization that generates significations but is not itself the effect of a prior signifying chain. On the
contrary, he demonstrates the Phallus's embeddedness in culture,
insisting that it cannot be detached from the penis on which it depends to symbolize its difference as a positive reconfiguration of the
negative term.[20] Further, by subjecting the idealized organ to the laws
that govern language, Sterne brings the paternal law, which pro-
motes this idealization, into the realm of relativity and desire, emphasizing the vulnerability of the Symbolic order itself. Truth,
knowledge, justice—and the father—are revealed by Sterne to fall
as far short of their ideal representations as penis does from Phallus.

From the beginning of his story, what it means to Tristram to
become a man is not only to accept the erasure of his mother but,
even more importantly, to assume his father's place. But the place of
the father, as Tristram learns, is not a place of personal power, however it might appear societally. At every crucial moment of Tristram's
development, Walter inadvertently undermines the masculinity of
his son, turning him into a version of himself. The pitiful misadventures of Tristram's conception, of his birthing, of his naming, and of

his education are all expressions of Walter's futile hobbyhorsical obsession. So, too, with Tristram's incapacities as a writer: his inability to narrativize his life in a coherent form. "'[T]is my father's fault," he defensively explains, "and whenever my brains come to be dissected, you will perceive, without spectacles, that he has left a large uneven thread, as you sometimes see in an unsaleable piece of cambrick, running along the whole length of the web" (351). It is this inherited irregularity that makes Tristram a writer in the fantastic mode: one who unwillingly turns the realistic narrative inside out in order to interrogate psychic integration, rationality, and social order. Had his vision been elaborated in a tragic register, its perversity would have projected disintegration and despair as appropriate responses to the entropic pull toward the vacuity of meaning that is death. But Sterne's register is comic, and it is through humor that Tristram actively engages the maddening disjunctions by which the other characters are paralyzed. Unlike the other Shandy men, he deploys his hobbyhorse to articulate his doubleness, producing an ironic form of autobiographical self-reflection that acknowledges while refusing psychic fragmentation. Recognizing that everyone's life is farcical, he believes that "it was ordained as a scourge upon the pride of human wisdom, that the wisest of us all should thus outwit ourselves, and eternally forego our purposes in the intemperate act of pursuing them" (284). The comic view that he enjoys of others is for him but a version of the pleasure he derives from the performance of himself: a performance in which he is both audience and actor. Proliferating roles, he achieves a fullness of self-expression that is experienced as subjective depth. And as subjectivity is for him performance, so reality seems to be a construction that he is easily able to revise.[21]

Representing subjectivity as performance, Sterne points to a radical indeterminacy that refuses gender difference and interrogates the misogynistic urge that largely motivates and anchors the precarious balances of his fiction. In his exploration of that sexual indeterminacy, Sterne moves his fantastic project—sporadically and ambivalently—beyond the merely comic into the self-transcendent space of the sublime. Collapsing the Phallus into the always already collapsed penis, Sterne, with Tristram, surrenders all claims to a universalized and mastering masculinity.[22] But at the same time that he renounces phallicism, he embraces a form of gendered subjectivity that seeks to obliterate the oppositions of sexual difference while paradoxically remaining male. The indeterminacy that he struggles to embody in his text is grounded in a place outside of the Symbolic order, in a supplementarity that is not controlled by reason, in an excess that is not subordinate to paternal law. It is an indeterminacy identified by some feminists (who share his focus, but not his perspective) with the suppressed body of the mother, with feminine space, therefore, and with an erotic connection that is thought to predate the primal rupture responsible for initiating difference and differentiation.[23] Julia Kristeva conceptualizes it as the semiotic (*le semiotique*): an affective dimension of human experience that disrupts the Symbolic, mediating between it and the primal experience of infantile mentation that Jacques Lacan calls the Real.

In *Tristram Shandy*, Sterne draws on that unrepresentable space both formally and thematically. He captures affectivity in the immediacy of color, shape, and sound: in black, white, mottled, and blank pages; in visual images of assorted kinds; in deletions, asterisks, and underlinings; and always in the omnipresent dash. Interrogating the denotative function of language, Sterne emphasizes the connotative richness of ironic ambiguity, of multiple references, and of jokes and puns. Refusing the illusion of public time—the time of the fathers, which is linear and death-directed—Sterne emphasizes the synchronicity of an interior present characterized by repetition, simultaneity, and cyclicality: a time that is for Kristeva women's time.[24] Like Uncle Toby's whistling, these are expressive strategies which suggest that "little knowledge is got by mere words" and that to achieve wisdom of a deeper sort it is necessary, as Tristram notes, "to go to the first springs" (479). These strategies are part of a fantastic discourse that, shaped by the eccentric consciousness of the writer and available also to transgressive forms of reading, strives to articulate the yearnings and frustrations of desire. When it is sounded in a tragic register, that discourse reveals pathological states of mind that lead to psychic disintegration and the destruction of the social self. When it is played in comic tones, as in *Tristram Shandy*, it is endlessly playful in its multiplicity and denial of hierarchical difference: it is a kind of exuberant speech that works to heal the wounds inflicted in the Symbolic. Whether comic or tragic, this discursive form rejects the complementarity of sexual and gender differences. So, while the tragic fantastic is rooted in the culturally carved depths of an oppositional psychosexual division, its comic counterpart—exemplified first by Sterne and later by Lacan—seeks to obliterate that difference altogether by returning to (or projecting) a prior psychic state. The urge to indeterminacy, which is expressed by this nostalgic desire for return, speaks vividly to the conflict between psychological and cultural imperatives, which is intensified under specific historical conditions. In Sterne's and Lacan's strikingly ingenuous, historically distanced, yet surprisingly similar interventions, the intransigence of the misogynistic construction of modern subjectivity is revealed with a force that is no less disquieting for all its comic energy and exuberance.

Although Sterne and Lacan position themselves quite differently in relation to the phallic order with which they are obsessed, both seek to define a subjectivity that has access to a self-transcendent and transformative world beyond the phallus. Trapped in the oppositional terms of the cultural symbolic, the two men describe the ungendered/gendered subjectivity of their fantasies both as fundamentally male and as shaped by structures of knowledge and feeling that they identify with, but paradoxically deny to, women. The elusive theory that Lacan formulates to mask and to exploit this paradox is similar to the fictive strategies that Sterne deploys on behalf of the same interests. Extending his comic fantasy into the register of the sublime, Lacan names as *jouissance* that state of self-transcendent being—excessive, suprasensible, intense—which is the object of his own heroic quest. The term is equally appropriate in suggesting the aspiration of the Shandean hero and the nature of the Sternean text.

Associated with the sexual moment that is always in excess, *jouissance* is the plenitude that can only be achieved outside of the cycle of desire that belongs to a phallic economy. Doomed always to be listening, like Mrs. Shandy, unheard, behind the door, women are said by Lacan to possess in their linguistic exclusion a supplementary *jouissance* that remains as mysterious to them as it is impenetrable to men.[25] In this, they are like the "good old God" to whom Lacan also refers: without substance, merely reflecting surfaces that project the (male) self back upon itself so that in loving God or women, men must always love themselves.[26] Searching for the integrity of transcendence, men must put aside the phallic function that divides one always into two and never reconstructs unity from division. "Short of castration," Lacan says, "man has no chance of enjoying the body of the woman, in other words, of making love."[27] For him, male *jouissance* cannot originate in the materiality of the body to which women are un-self-reflectively confined. It is discoverable rather in an erotics of immateriality which is the "outsidesex" (*hors-sexe*) represented by men's "love" of an idea, for example, or a poem, or a spiritual experience. For Lacan, those who go "beyond the phallus" are mystics who put themselves on the side of the "not-all." Their souls are conjured not out of the heterosexual relation but out of the *hommosexual*. They *speak* of love, which is a form of *jouissance*, and bond lovingly with other men since it is "by their courage in bearing this intolerable relation to the supreme being, that friends come to recognize and choose each other."[28] Finally, these poetic, self-transcending, mystical, and male-identified souls who appropriate the roles of the woman and the God whom they have lost are exemplified in the Master's work: "Add the *Ecrits* of Jacques Lacan, which is of the same order."[29]

Add also to that order the Shandean comedy of Laurence Sterne—with an important difference. Throughout *Tristram Shandy*, as we have seen, Sterne reduces women to barely perceptible presences in his text, placing them outside of language, denying them complex subjectivities, describing them as lustful but making them incapable of the *hors-sexe* to which he, with Lacan, assigns the highest value. Appropriating as much of women's reproductive function as he can, Sterne denies their capacity to create culture or to make ethical judgments based on empathic connection. And while women are more visible in his two later works than they are in *Tristram Shandy*, they exist in those works only as imaginary, idealized others, fueling but not moving beyond the regressive cycle of desire. In the maudlin *Journal to Eliza* and, with fuller consciousness, in *A Sentimental Journey*, Sterne reveals the solipsistic nature of the Imaginary phallic function through which the other is both projected by and worshipped as the self. Rejecting women's subject status, Sterne—like Lacan—seeks in the homosocial love of other men and, more centrally, in the narcissistic love of self, the route to erotic self-transcendence that defines the sublime in its comic fantastic form. It is a quest that releases him into the "love" of the idea, not as truth but as a form of self-creation; into art, as the exploitation of linguistic multiplicity; and, unlike Lacan, into the immediacy of prelinguistic space. Having said "no" to the idealized Phallus, having revealed

the fallacies of the phallic order and the finitude as well as the un-
knowability of the father's name, Sterne seeks his *jouissance* partially
in a form of Lacanian "castration" that belongs to the carnivalesque
order of the penis/breast: "the same order" as that which structures
the *Ecrits* of Jacques Lacan, despite his protests to the contrary.[30]

This order, which functions at social and psychic levels, is both
potentially radical and insistently conservative. For Lacan, the conservative impulse always dominates, binding him to linguistic meaning, the Phallus and, most importantly, the self. In the momentary
resolutions of his repetitious quest, the sublime urge is drawn back
into comedy, and mystical knowledge emerges from the ethereal
body of his work. For Sterne, the balance is more heavily weighted
by ambivalence, and the liberatory gesture is made continuously
available as excess. In the ambisexual aesthetic of his text,[31] in his
thematic addiction to the pure affectivity of tears, and in his celebra-
tion of sentimentality as the ground of an empathic *hommosexual* connection that undoes differentiation, Sterne unveils the Phallus as the
penis and hints at its symbolic relation to the maternal figure. In his
appropriation of the feminine, Sterne tries to transform the negations
of cultural and psychic loss into an impossible plenitude by releasing
the entombed body of the mother into the body of the text, by assuming as fantasist the function of the good and nourishing breast,
and by atoning for the reinscription of otherness by struggling to
magically undo the misogynistic knot. But the carnivalesque order
to which these strategies belong, while radical in its social critique
and its articulation of desire, is bound to the dominant discourse and
is limited, therefore, in its capacity for subversion. Social roles that
are playfully inverted still retain their symbolic cultural meaning.
The psychic fantasy of the penis/breast, as Melanie Klein suggests,
is not integrative but expressive of ambivalence. And while sentimentality encourages the expression of humane sympathy, it can also
maintain the social and psychological status quo, reinforcing the
feeling subject's difference by insisting upon his superior moral
stance. So, too, while empathy allows the boundary between subject
and object to be momentarily suspended, it does yield readily to the
mirroring dynamic that claims and celebrates the self in the other's
name: a form of solipsism exhibiting itself as virtue. Finally and fundamentally, while the androgynous performance, the sentimental

tear, and the erotics of empathic connection are all ultimately identified in Sterne's fiction with the exclusion of the female subject, it is her femininity that indelibly marks the male body, which is presented both as castrated and as polymorphously perverse. The ultimate irony is that this master of irony, like his equally masterful successor, should install the woman's body firmly in the space of indeterminacy, which the fantastic sublime must then strive to embody and achieve on the basis solely of her exclusion. The misogynistic text, like the form of feminist critique that is its mirror image, perpetually reenacts a displacement that becomes the inevitable condition of compulsive reassertion. Once the maternal body and the primal bond are identified specifically as originary points of loss and self-transcendence, the anxiety of indeterminacy restricts the power of the sublime motive along with its potential for subversive change. In Sterne's comic vision, women are the scapegoats who must be cast out if the male community is to be reproduced and reinforced. But in signaling the end of the Shandy line, his "cock and bull" story suggests, at the level of realism, the profoundly antisocial aspect of his comedy, which can then be no comedy at all.

It is in his repeated gesture toward the sublime that Sterne seeks, perhaps unconsciously, to halt the unraveling of his comic form. Unlike Lacan and very like Kristeva, Sterne continually emphasizes the significance of an erotic affectivity that, underlying and resisting language, is central to the construction of community. And although the community that he wishes to construct is male, the aspiration and the impulse are not gendered, and refuse the hierarchicalizations of social difference. They are conceptualized in the mode of the fantastic as lying at the core of a narcissistic subjectivity that, in its yearning for nondifferentiation, undermines the stereotyping function of the civilizing process.[32] In its tragic form, this sublime impulse accepts aggressivity and violence as its proper mode and looks toward death and dissolution. In its comic form, it answers to eros and responds profoundly to the promise of *jouissance*. Even as Sterne's skepticism about the purity of the empathic motive grew, his faith in its binding albeit fleeting power increased. In this, he was able to point beyond cultural and personal misogyny, which his text so intricately maps, to a space of indeterminacy that exists within the self. It is in that space that he imagines the generation of an ethics of connection that would not be restricted by the social law.[33] If such an erotic connection could be rewritten in the realistic mode, it would facilitate the transcendence of oppressions born of difference by linking the individual to what Sterne calls, in A Sentimental Journey, "the great Sensorium of the world."[34]

4

Horace Walpole and
the Nightmare of History

With the notable exception of *Moll Flanders,* the texts examined in the preceding chapters are structured through the interaction of realistic and fantastic narratives. Their diverse bimodal patterns reveal the complexities of modern consciousness in the process of definition—a consciousness stamped in part by the self's appropriative relation to others, in part by its uncanny haunting of itself. In *Robinson Crusoe, Roxana, Clarissa,* and *Tristram Shandy,* powerful subjectivist narratives suggest how the ideology of individualism constructs an internally divided, gendered subject, which is both oppressed by and resistant to determinant social forces. Because these narrative fragments are neither dominant nor sustained, they disrupt, without finally threatening, the hegemonic values of the texts. It was to the absence of an extended, interrogatory form that Horace Walpole responded when he wrote and published *The Castle of Otranto* in 1764. He was not interested in exploring both aspects of modern self-awareness, as Laurence Sterne was doing in *Tristram Shandy.* Instead, he wanted to shape an alternative kind of fiction that would refuse the "boring" and "insipid" conventions that he derided in the works of his contemporaries.[1] He had no difficulty in achieving that objective. Despite its glaring primitivity, his thoroughly eccentric "gothic story" was an immediate, and is a continuing, success.[2] The genre that it initiated dominated popular fiction for the next sixty years, anticipating Romantic, modern, and postmodern versions of the fantastic, all of which challenged the realistic narratives and dominant ideologies that collaborated in their construction.[3]

Although Walpole did produce an innovative interrogatory form, it was not—nor could it have been—separate from the narrative mode of which it provided a critique. As extreme as Walpole's formal strategies proved to be—and as bizarre as the story was that he

conceptualized—both strategies and story were necessarily molded
by the literary and cultural assumptions that they questioned. In
Walpole's gothic, as in the fantastic generally, the symptom is not
present without the shadow of its cause, and patterns of interiority
are etched by the pressures of a culture that reflects, while reproducing, the self's dis-ease. Although the fantastic text buries its realistic roots in much the same way that its realistic counterpart disguises its fantastic subtexts, Walpole's anti-hero—whose boundless
egotism it explores—can be seen to wear the face of realism's aspiring, heroic individual. In his perverted masculinity and incestuous
desire, in his false autonomy and outrageous greed, he is not different from the subject whom capitalism and the sex-gender system
have combined to form. He is, rather, its monstrous parody. I read
his story—which for Walpole is the story of the father—at the intersection of realistic and fantastic modes, where the self is constructed
through its relation to others.

There is also a second fantastic narrative in *The Castle of Otranto*
and it demands a different reading. Here the rejected realm of the
socially symbolic is transformed into a claustral intrapsychic world
where the self that takes itself as object experiences the depth of its
own isolation, alienation, and despair. An articulation of solipsistic
self-awareness, this is the story of the son, and it is buried deep inside
the father's story. It concerns the child's melancholic obsession with
a traumatic loss that, irremediable, can never be forgotten or
mourned. Dim figures of fantasy move through its scenarios. Gesturing toward Walpole—as they do toward one another—they suggest that their secrets belong, at the most profound level, to the authorial mind. To disinter the secrets to which the text compulsively
returns, I place *Otranto*'s intrapsychic narrative in conversation with
its author's biography, his fantastic tragedy—*The Mysterious Mother*—
and the gothic fictions of Nicolas Abraham and Maria Torok, psychoanalytic theorists whose writings this originary gothic novel
seems uncannily to anticipate. The place from which the second
reading emanates is a place at which fiction, autobiography, and
theory all converge.

Centering that which has been excluded from dominant myths of
the cultural symbolic, fantastic narratives deconstruct the boundaries

that separate legitimated elements of the hegemonic culture from their illegitimate others (e.g., the integrated from the fragmented self, sanity from madness, rationality from irrationality, social sameness from difference, and defined from indeterminate meanings). The gothic novel shares in this larger deconstructive project, mediating between an older romance tradition, whose metaphysical and social assumptions it cannot share, and an emergent tradition of the fantastic, which is overtly psychological in perspective. From that intermediary location, gothic texts portray the horrifying emptiness of a secularized world. Representing irrational impulses, they do not claim access to a higher integrative truth but attest to meanings that elude language and analysis. For a cosmos composed of interlocking segments hierarchically arranged, they substitute a disjunctive universe in which secrets of the past impose themselves upon a fearful and bewildered present. In the place of an open, permeable soul, which anchored an earlier analogical order, they insert a form of consciousness that is self-enclosed. Resisting the recognition of death's materiality, they reinvent immortality in the ghosts that stalk their pages, and their need to project and exorcise those apparitions reflects the deep ambivalence with which their effort is invested.

Supernatural presences in late-eighteenth-century texts reflect the remystifying urge of a demystified world. The inhabitants of that world sought a new form of transcendence in the intense experience of sublimity. When Burke theorized the sublime, identifying it simultaneously with the perceived object, the perceptual occurrence, the sensible body, and the perceiving mind, he signaled his assumption of a paradigm brought into being by modern self-awareness. It is a paradigm that places the self and its experience at the center of knowledge, a place that God had occupied before. Seeking to identify with a transcendent force, which the imagination projects and then discovers, the self dissolves the boundaries between signifier and signified, subject and object, and external and interior realities. In the positive moment of the sublime, the secular and alienated individual seeks and momentarily finds, in the power of the unconditioned, a compensation for vacuity and loss. When successful, the effort culminates in the experience that Kant described as a union of reason and imagination, and that Freud theorized as sublimation: the alliance of the superego and the ego.[4] When sublimation fails, the self—which is overwhelmed by the possibility of its own appropriation—turns back upon itself, discovering that the threatening vastness without mirrors a frightening absence within.[5] In defense against the anxiety aroused, the ideal of power is internalized as conscience, and the painful burden of modern self-awareness is increased.[6] Terror, guilt, and melancholy mark this negative moment of the sublime, as the torments of Crusoe, Roxana, Lovelace, and even Tristram testify. Experienced intrapsychically, the negative sublime shapes the past into fantastic narratives that concern unconstrained desire, the phantasmatic family, and the alienated self. Often focused on the secret of incest, those narratives subordinate the urge for transcendence to the lure of transgression, and place the demands of primitive narcissism over the family's social function.

Writing in the spirit of the negative sublime, Walpole established a specific link between the supernatural and the psychological when he explained in a letter to a friend that the inspiration for his fiction was given him in a dream:

> I waked one morning in the beginning of last June from a dream, of which all I could recover was that I had thought myself in an ancient castle (a very natural dream for a head like mine filled with Gothic story) and that on the uppermost bannister of a great staircase I saw a gigantic hand in armour. In the evening I sat down and began to write, without knowing in the least what I intended to say or relate. The work grew on my hands, and I grew fond of it—add that I was very glad to think of anything rather than politics—In short I was so engrossed with my tale, which I completed in less than two months, that one evening I wrote from the time I had drunk my tea, about six o'clock, till half an hour after one in the morning.[7]

As he recognized, the surreal dream image drew on his intense fantasies about the Middle Ages and referred specifically to a staircase at Strawberry Hill, the miniature, baroque castle he had constructed on the skeleton of a modest structure, which became his home and his obsession.[8] As Walpole describes it, the dream that transported him from the realities of his life moved him to a form of automatic writing that was neither consciously nor rationally motivated. In the creative process, he developed characters and themes that spoke to him of matters profoundly personal in nature. In this merging of dream, fantasy, and art, he established a model for those who would later write in and theorize the tradition he established.

At first glance, *The Castle of Otranto* seems anything but personal. Its complicated plot is the stuff of fairy tale, while the speech and behavior of its characters seem sufficiently mannered to be parodic. As in fairy tale, however, disturbing insights into the personal and social forces by which the subject is constructed are encoded into the naive conventions of the fiction. Crude motivations point beyond themselves to transgressive desires, and a disjunctive, associational structure suggests the illogic of fantasy and dream. Tragic in theme and often comic in effect, the fiction suggests an unrestrained pleasure in the primal and forbidden, which is reminiscent of the uncensored playfulness of a child. A summary of the story, while defying all attempts at brevity, is essential to an analysis of the fiction's underlying purposes and themes. The tale begins on the fifteenth birthday of Conrad, the son of Manfred, prince of Otranto. It is the day on which Conrad is to wed Isabella, and it proves also to be the day on which he is killed, crushed by a gigantic helmet that is topped by a "mountain of sable plumes." Without much ado—and with no sign of mourning—Manfred, who has always "doted" on his only son, decides to put aside his now-sterile wife Hippolita in order to take Isabella as his bride. His declared purpose is to ensure the continuation of his "race" through the production of other sons, thereby evading the mysterious prophesy by which he is haunted: "That the castle and lordship of Otranto should pass from the present family, whenever the real owner should be grown too large to inhabit it" (15–16).

Theodore, a young peasant, recognizes the deadly helmet as one that is missing from the statue of Alfonso the Good in the church of St. Nicholas. Outraged by the boy's claim, Manfred accuses Theodore of necromancy and orders that the helmet be transformed into the young man's prison. Through the inattention of the guards, Theodore escapes and is able to rescue Isabella as she flees from the lecherous prince. Isabella falls in love with Theodore who, in turn, falls in love with Mathilda, the daughter whom Manfred despises because she is merely a woman. When Manfred realizes that Theodore has helped Isabella to evade him, he condemns him to death. Father Jerome is summoned to perform the last rites and, seeing the mark of a bloody arrow on the boy's arm, recognizes him as the son who, kidnapped by corsairs at the age of five, had been taken to Algiers with his mother, who subsequently died (81). Manfred pardons

Theodore, expecting that Jerome will reciprocate by participating in his conspiracy against Hippolita and Isabella.

Meanwhile, amid much fanfare and bearing an enormous saber, Frederic, marquis of Vicenza, returns from a pilgrimage he had taken after the death in childbirth of his wife, Isabella's mother. It is Frederic's intention to reclaim his daughter, whom Manfred had bribed away from her guardians. As a relative of Alfonso the Good, Frederic wants also to wrench the principality of Otranto from Manfred, who had inherited it from his own father, the son of a chamberlain to whom Alfonso had bequeathed his estates when he died in the Holy Land. Although Manfred has been unsuccessful in his attempts to strengthen his position by marrying Isabella, his hopes are rekindled when Frederic becomes enamored of Mathilda. Those hopes are finally dashed when he inadvertently stabs and kills his daughter. The castle walls are then thrown down, revealing the immense form of Alfonso the Good at the center of the ruins. Ordering them all to "Behold in Theodore, the true heir of Alfonso," the specter ascends to heaven in a "blaze of glory" as the clouds part and St. Nicholas appears (108). The time has arrived for the full disclosure of secrets and the fulfillment of prophesies. Exclaiming that "I pay the price of usurpation for all" (109), Manfred admits that Alfonso had been poisoned by his grandfather, Ricardo, who had then drawn up a fictitious will. For his part, Jerome reveals that on the way to the Holy Land, Alfonso had fallen in love with and secretly married Victoria, with whom he had a daughter who ultimately became Jerome's wife. Theodore therefore inherits the principality of Otranto through the bloodline of his unnamed mother. The recognition of Theodore's nobility quiets the "long-restless Prince's shade," which had "grown too large to inhabit" the castle. Manfred abdicates, he and Hippolita join neighboring convents, and Isabella marries the melancholy Theodore, who seems terminally overwhelmed by Mathilda's loss.

The supernatural saturates the text, but its effects, while occasionally impressive, seem largely superficial and gratuitous. The enormous shade of Alfonso dominates, as it is assembled piece by piece throughout the story along with its baroque appurtenances. There is a helmet with black plumes waving in punctuation of events, a gigantic armored foot and leg, a huge saber, and finally an enormous armored hand that lies "upon the uppermost bannister of the great stairs": the vision that had initially haunted Walpole's dream. In addition to these fragmented, symbolic body parts, the text is filled with the supernatural's familiar visual and aural portents: mysterious sighs, disembodied groans, creaking door hinges, and wavering candles. A portrait of Ricardo falls off the wall, sighing and heaving its breast before "coming to life" as a ghost. There are the dark, subterranean passages of a sort that decades of frightened heroines will scurry along, and ubiquitous trapdoors that promise and even sometimes deliver escape. Perhaps most inventively, when it appears that Frederic will wed Mathilda and waive his claim to Otranto, three drops of blood fall gloomily from the nose of Alfonso's statue. Although the text's substantial labors ultimately produce the operatic scene of Alfonso's declaration and ascension, many of its omens (supernatural and otherwise) point nowhere. So, after climbing down from his portrait, the ghost of Ricardo disappears into a chamber of the castle, locking the door behind him so that the pursuing Manfred is left without a place to go. Isabella flees in terror through the labyrinthine passage, comes to no harm, and easily finds an exit. Theodore escapes imprisonment because the guards forget to guard him, and rumors of Hippolita's death prove both unfounded and irrelevant to the plot. The anticlimactic nature of these and other sequences call the fiction's seriousness of purpose into question at the same time that the story's often powerful, hallucinatory quality conveys a contradictory sense that significant meanings may lie in less obvious places.[9]

Walpole's statements of artistic purpose do not provide the desired clarification, since they contradict one another while contravening the actual practice of the novelist. Walpole insists on his fidelity to the tragic unities, for example, even though a mixture of tragic, comic, and romantic perspectives is reflected in the fiction's deployment of language, as well as in its representation of character and plot.[10] And although Walpole claims complete originality and imaginative freedom, he locates himself firmly in a Shakespearean tradition upon which he draws and which he also uses to justify his aesthetic choices. Additionally, he describes elements of style that seem to the reader primitive and naive as aspects of a sophisticated and self-conscious strategy. So while he intends "to blend the . . . ancient and the modern" in his novel, he leaves "the powers of fancy at liberty to expatiate through the boundless realms of invention" in the creation of situation, "conduct[ing] the mortal agents in [the] drama according to the rules of probability . . . mak[ing] them think, speak and act, as it might be supposed mere men and women would do in extraordinary positions."[11] His desire to achieve a defensible realistic effect in a fundamentally fantastic fiction is surprising enough, but even more surprising is the identification of his success with a bombastic, massively inconsistent anti-hero and a group of stereotypical and one-dimensional proper ladies. Indeed, the "typical" romance that Walpole disparages in his critical comments—one in which "an improbable event never fails to be attended by an absurd dialogue"[12] —is precisely the kind of romance that he manages, at least superficially, to reproduce.

Certainly Walpole was more ambivalent about the relative value of realistic and fantastic strategies than he confessed or might have recognized. But whatever the reasons for that ambivalence might have been, his preference for the fantastic was clearly governed by the exigencies of his psychic life. His approach to history illustrates the nature of his strong subjectivist urge. Although he was obsessed with things medieval, his obsession was rooted not in the records of antiquity that occupied him as a scholar, but in the political and cultural circumstances of his time and in the emotional weather by which he was buffeted. As the miniature gothic castle, which he converted from a coachman's cottage on the Thames, was an outrageously eccentric personal indulgence and an expression of the historical revivalism of members of his set, his representations of the Middle Ages—of class and gender relations, patriarchy, and the Catholic Church—were all stamped by a nostalgia configured in a desiring and disillusioned present. On one level, Walpole tried to negotiate the intrapsychic conflicts of his childhood through the interactions of the characters he projected. On another, he looked back with longing—although not without ambivalence—to continuities that were grounded in the linked hierarchical structures of a patriarchalism lost in 1688. Inconsistent in his politics, Walpole was a Whig who flaunted his hatred of authority. Although he kept copies of the Magna Carta and the warrant for the execution of Charles I beside his bed, he became a dedicated, even a fanatic royalist when the French Revolution brought radicalism too close to home. Unlike his father, Walpole did not accept the Enlightenment narrative that celebrated a progressive present that had broken with a retrograde past. In his novel, the sins of the fathers, which are visited on the sons, are eighteenth-century crimes against property and excesses of possessive individualism that lead to the instrumentalization and objectification of others. Walpole's was a conservative, Burkean view of society as materialistic, alienated, and individualistic. It could only redeem itself through the active recovery of traditions that it embodied but experienced as lost.[13] As Walpole struggled to work through personal and social dilemmas, he invented a version of the past that the present had surrealistically engraved. From this temporal hybrid emerged a nightmarish narrative that was simultaneously radical and conservative at the social level and, at the psychological level, was a projection of his own intense fantasies.

Because *The Castle of Otranto* was shaped by a strong subjectivist perspective, many of its strategies were anticipated by fantastic elements in the mixed-genre texts that have already been explored. So Walpole's novel might be seen to present a melodramatic version of the comic critique of Enlightenment values found in *Tristram Shandy*. Like Sterne's fiction, it denies the transparency of language and contextualizes it as style, which can be manipulated because it is conventional. Rejecting reason as the arbiter of artistic and social values, *Otranto*—like *Shandy*—propounds the superiority of the imagination and unveils the strength of obsession and desire. Although mind supplants society as the text's ultimate point of reference, the self is not master in its own house, as Freud would subsequently observe about the ego. The fragmented and conflicted psyche is held up by Walpole as the perverse mirror image of the consistent and coherent self; solipsism is revealed as the other side of individualism, and madness is a frightening specter hovering at one edge of sanity. Scattering the severed pieces of Alphonso's armored body through his text, Walpole—like Sterne and Richardson—reveals the infantile fear of dispersal, which threatens realism's myth of physical wholeness and impermeability. Substituting the supernatural for the religious, representing fathers as absent or impotent and the inheritance of power as corrupt, Walpole questions, as does Sterne, the root assumptions of a belief system that upholds patriarchal power and authority. Exploring the nature of male subjectivity, both inadvertently unmask the psychological costs imposed by the social system of gender difference. Finally, like Sterne's ironic narrative and

Richardson's epistolary novel, Walpole's gothic fiction demands an active reader who experiences the frustration of an open text and participates in the perpetual making and unmaking of its meaning.

In its depiction of Manfred, *The Castle of Otranto* follows in the fantastic tradition that was inaugurated by Defoe in *Robinson Crusoe* and elaborated by Richardson in *Clarissa*. Like Lovelace, Manfred is the possessive individual who is motivated by unbounded egotism and a false belief in his own autonomy. Trapped on the desert island of the self, he is paranoid in his relation to others, whom he attempts to use instrumentally. Since there is no elsewhere from which he can perceive himself, he is a narcissist, like Heinz Kohut's: hollow rather than self-satisfied. Like the fantastic Crusoe and Lovelace, Manfred is a cluster of responses and a chaos of feelings. Multiple and diffuse, he is also inconsistent. He doesn't mourn the death of Conrad, whom he is said to have loved dearly, for example, but seizes the event as an opportunity to claim his son's fiancée as the mother of his future sons. Telling Isabella that he "hope[s] in a few years to have reason to rejoice" at Conrad's demise, he reassures her that "[i]nstead of a sickly boy, you shall have a husband in the prime of his age" (22). Typically, when he feels "shame" and "returning love" at his wife's "tenderness and duty," he "curb[s] the yearnings of his heart" so that "[t]he next transition of his soul was to [an] exquisite villainy" (34), which makes him insist that Hippolita divorce him and pander with Isabella on his behalf. Walpole reassures the reader that "Manfred was not one of those savage tyrants who wanton in cruelty unprovoked. . . . [H]is temper . . . was naturally humane; and his virtues were always ready to operate, when his passion did not obscure his reason" (30). Since Manfred is always motivated by his passions, however, his humanity is little in evidence, and he functions through much of the novel at a high level of hysteria that serves to feminize him, as Lovelace is also feminized. Without boundaries, Manfred, like Lovelace, perceives others as aspects of himself—roles to be assumed and selves to be used and then discarded. Indeed, Walpole seems to have conceptualized his other characters from Manfred's perspective—and it is this that partially accounts for their apparent primitivity. With the exception of Walpole's anti-hero, who looms over the text, each of the central characters is interchangeable with others who occupy a similar relationship to Manfred's desire: Mathilda, Isabella, and Hippolita form one group; Theodore is increasingly identified with Alfonso; and the stories of Frederic and Jerome emerge as versions of one another, as they are also versions of Manfred's story, which contains them.

Although *The Castle of Otranto* is ostensibly a political fiction that advocates legitimate succession and the reinstatement of an older socioeconomic order, it is essentially concerned (like all gothic novels) with intrafamilial relations that determine the origins and development of the self.[14] For this reason, the succession crisis proves to be a problem of power between father and son, with Manfred's dilemma a variant of Crusoe's predicament. Driven to secure his place as patriarch, Manfred competes with Conrad, who will inevitably displace him but is also crucial to his immortality: the reproduction of his bloodline, his property, and his political authority. Like Defoe, Walpole poses an imaginary resolution to the father's quandary. If Manfred can marry Isabella after Conrad's death, he will symbolically become his own son, as well as a begetter of sons who can always be supplanted in the repetition of a deathly oedipal fantasy that is conceptualized from the paternal position. Like Lovelace, who wants to father Clarissa's child, whom he also wishes to *be*, Manfred seeks to consolidate the present, past, and future in himself. Because the patriarchal identities of father and prince have lost divine legitimacy in Walpole's eighteenth-century world, only futile parodies of authority are available. Everything that Manfred does to strengthen his position moves him further from control and deeper into chaotic forms of competition. The gap that has opened between men's idealized and real power (a gap implied by Richardson and made explicit by Sterne) is exemplified by the emptiness of Manfred's shifting social identities and by his tragic destruction of the family, which should guarantee the perpetuation of his "house."

Manfred perceives his family to be the site and instrument of his influence, its members valued in proportion to their advancement of his sexual, economic, and political ambitions. Because Conrad both blocks and facilitates his desires, he is at once threatening and precious. Because women are without significance in themselves, but can be used biologically and materially, they are completely interchangeable. So, when Hippolita no longer serves his needs, Manfred simply discards her. Because Mathilda cannot extend his bloodline, he treats her with cruel indifference. When he recognizes that he might be able to trade her to Frederic in exchange for Isabella and the security of his dynastic position, his interest in her flickers. When that plan fails, the small flame of his attention is extinguished. Although he kills her accidentally, the murder has a psychic logic that reveals the hostility with which his continual assertion of masculine difference is invested.

The women in Walpole's fiction emerge as proper ladies who have been flattened, even more than proper ladies usually are, by the weight of Manfred's misogyny. Without agency, they are—like Mrs. Shandy—deprived of distinguishing forms of subjectivity. Although Theodore believes himself to have fallen in love with Mathilda, he cannot distinguish her from Isabella; and when Manfred wants to murder Isabella because he is unable to claim her, he kills his daughter by mistake. In the social world of Otranto, the value of women is determined by their sexual function: as virgins, Mathilda and Isabella can be traded, sold and ravished; as a legitimate wife who has passed child-bearing age, Hippolita is a useless commodity. All three try to protect themselves from Manfred's rages, with Hippolita and Mathilda playing masochist to his sadist. Accepting the hierarchy that places him at the top and herself at the bottom, Hippolita insists that "our husbands and fathers must decide for us" (66), and deploys willed ignorance to reinforce a safe passivity. As wife and mother, she not only submits to male power but aligns herself with it, as Mrs. Harlowe does. She offers herself as "the first sacrifice" to Manfred's avariciousness and lust, agreeing to their divorce and vowing to withdraw to a monastery. At the same time, she collaborates with her husband, who "is dearer to me even than my children" (21), playing the pimp for him with Isabella as she also does, on his behalf, for Frederic with Mathilda. Her "delicacy of conscience" is the female counterpart of Manfred's moral evil; she turns it back upon herself as guilt and doesn't draw upon it as a catalyst for action. Like Clarissa's mother, Hippolita tries to socialize her daughter so that she will accept her own economic and sexual oppression. More malleable than Clarissa, Mathilda refuses to harbor a thought without her mother's permission, is the epitome of female respectability in her interactions with Theodore, and with her dying breath begs her murderous father's forgiveness. Like Clarissa, she wishes to escape patriarchal control by entering a convent, which mirrors the family's institutional structure but would exempt her from the exigencies of her body. Wisely, she falls in love not with a man but with an image:

the portrait of Alfonso, which anticipates, while avoiding, the material likeness of the prince. Of all the women in the novel, only Isabella (like Anna Howe) dares to acknowledge and act upon her own desire. Admitting that she "had conceived little affection" for the feminized Conrad, she is not sorry when he is killed (16). She gossips with Mathilda's maid about the attractions of young men, falls openly in love with Theodore, and persists in her flight from Manfred, even when her actions countermand her father's orders. Because Walpole, like Richardson, cannot accommodate this degree of independence, Isabella is finally folded into the respectable Mathilda, whose surrogate she becomes in the melancholy marriage with which the novel concludes.

Still, despite the clear hegemony of the gendered division of labor in the novel's realistic strain, the relation of private and public spheres emerges as more complicated than it might at first appear. The channels of intrafamilial power are revealed to run in more than one direction, and the libidinal energy that courses through them produces strong undercurrents of resistance. The force required to ensure hierarchical difference reflects the potency of a fact that the fiction cannot completely disguise: that men never reproduce themselves alone, but always require the mediation of women. This means that they cannot be certain of their own paternity and that their rights and obligations as fathers are never clear. This is the truth that is woven into the repetitious pattern of male anxiety that shapes *The Castle of Otranto*, as it also helps to shape *Tristram Shandy* and *Clarissa*. At the most obvious level, that anxiety is revealed in the shape of father-child relations. Aside from Manfred, whose fears produce the lethal connection to his son and daughter that is centered in the text, all of the paternal figures have fled the families they have founded, and all have lived as strangers to their offspring. The narratives of Jerome, Frederic, and Alfonso begin with conception and abandonment, and end with return only when the forsaken infants (or her descendent, in Alfonso's case) have reached maturity, and the mother is safely dead.

Manfred's tragic relation to his son has a comic variant in Jerome's relation to Theodore. Manfred indirectly causes Conrad's death, bringing destruction down upon his own house with the aggressive assertion of his illegitimate claim. More, in his wooing of Isabella he exposes the murderous depths of his competitive motive. In a partial mirroring of the Manfred plot, Jerome nearly causes Theodore's death when he "sows the seeds of jealousy" in the prince's mind, falsely confirming Manfred's belief in an amorous connection between the boy and Isabella (50–51). Because Jerome is represented as a good man rather than an anti-hero, his aggression, while acknowledged, is tempered by a comic resolution. Once he has recognized Theodore as his child, he persuades Manfred to spare the young man's life and establishes a filial connection to him that, rooted in psychological debt rather than biology, is similar to the bond that Crusoe establishes with Friday. Still, the fact that Jerome recognizes Theodore's birthmark and not Theodore himself suggests the extent of the distance that has separated the two.

If the alienation of fathers from their sons is associated, through Manfred and Jerome, with a deadly competition that erupts in the older man when the boy achieves maturity, the relation of fathers to their daughters is given a disturbing sexual reference. In the dynamic between Manfred and Frederic, on one side, with Mathilda and Isabella on the other, the text explores a structure of desire that is insistently—if obliquely—incestuous. The shifting perspectives of the text cause the two women to seem interchangeable so that the courtship of one appears to be a screen for the courtship of the other. At the most obvious level, Isabella is constructed as Manfred's daughter, both a sister and a substitute for Mathilda. So the prince's angry assertion to Jerome that "I am [Isabella's] parent . . . and demand her" (47) earns the monk's rejoinder that "by me thou art warned not to pursue the incestuous design on thy contracted daughter" (47–48). The fact that Isabella is chosen by Manfred to supplant Hippolita, her surrogate mother, further reinforces the intrafamilial reference, as does the similarity between Frederic's relation to Isabella, whom he has not seen since her birth, and his relation to Mathilda, who incites his lust at their first meeting. Finally, the way in which the marriage of Theodore and Isabella, which is a marriage of cousins, repeats the pattern established by Manfred and Hippolita, who are related "in the fourth degree," indicates the inevitably asocial and endogamous nature of the gothic family (47).

The structure of desire that shapes *The Castle of Otranto* replicates, in an exaggerated and simplified form, the configuration of longing that Richardson, in *Clarissa*, painstakingly explores. Pornographic in its construction of women as the objects of an aggressively controlling and even violent sexuality, Walpole's novel suggests the compulsory and misogynistic character of heterosexual relations under patriarchal capitalism. Without material resources, women have few alternatives to marriage and know—as Mathilda's maid suggests—"that a bad husband is better than no husband at all" (18). For men, who have legal and economic power over women, villainy incurs no costs. This form of erotic domination, which is rooted in the larger inequities of the sex-gender system, extends beyond the married couple to define the libidinal structure of the bourgeois family. Situated somewhere between Lovelace and the Harlowe males, Manfred is the possessive individual who, seeking to appropriate others as aspects of his monstrously inflated self, articulates his needs through the family he eroticizes. In him (as in the gothic generally) the urge for the libertine sublime takes an ironic turn that makes him search for the nihilistic energy and affective excesses of a transgressive sexuality at home.[15] Just as the competitive father who saves his son's life appropriates the maternal role while affirming his patriarchal power, so the incestuous father recuperates his tenuous relation to his daughter while he organizes that relation safely, in terms of his domination and her submission.

The need for recuperation that grows out of the alienation of fathers from their children can be seen to motivate the text's obsessive return to the incest theme. The reason for that alienation is repressed by the fiction until the last possible moment, when it becomes clear that Theodore has inherited the principality of Otranto from the unnamed daughter of Victoria and Alfonso. It is then that the ultimate authority of the maternal bloodline emerges as the foundational explanation of the patriarch's vulnerability and anxiety. It casts an ironic shadow on all of Manfred's machinations, explaining the virulence of his competition with Conrad and the intensity of his desire for Isabella. It suggests that the father seeks to legitimate his claim of paternity, which is never more than notional, through the arrogation of power in intrafamilial relations and the exhibition of social authority. It is because he cannot prove himself to be the father of any that Manfred wants to be the father and lover of all. To this end, he seeks (like Jerome) to displace his son and (with Frederic) tries to become the lover/husband of his daughter. Because he needs to control the female sexuality that can both legitimate and invalidate him, he struggles desperately to prevent the departure of Mathilda/

Isabella from the family. Killing his daughter, he unwittingly ends the repetitious cycle of illicit desire and enacts the destruction of his "house." Although his downfall leads to the restoration of the aristocracy, the novel's conclusion does little to affirm the renewed power of an authority inherited through the male. With Manfred withdrawn to a monastery; Alfonso, the benevolent despot, in heaven; and Theodore, the noble hero, in a state of psychic collapse, the fiction suggests that political authority cannot be legitimated in a desacralized society any more than the patriarch's supremacy within the family can be other than a screen for the hidden power of the mother.

This reading of *The Castle of Otranto* has emphasized the realistic strain within the fantastic narrative. It tells the story of the father: the lustful, ambitious, and also paranoid individual, whose misogyny reflects the culture's anxiety about the mother's reproductive power. It is only a partial reading, since the father's story veils a crucial second narrative: the narrative of the son who has been raised in the family shaped collaboratively by possessive individualism and the modern sex-gender system. Constructed through the strategies of fantasy and dream, the son's story tells of estrangement from an aggressive and competitive father and of separation from a mother who, in her difference, is both desired and feared. At the deepest level, the son's is a story of feelings that cannot be articulated in language and longings that society cannot contain. Fundamentally, it is a story of melancholic loss.

In its representation of pervasive melancholia, Walpole's narrative of the son speaks most provocatively to the relation of interpsychic to intrapsychic events: the transformation of the social individual into the psychological subject and of the realistic into the fantastic mode. In its metaphors and symbolic structures, that narrative prefigures and is illuminated by Abraham and Torok's speculations about the connection of desire to traumatic deprivation.[16] Like Walpole, Abraham and Torok employ gothic metaphors to describe states of affectivity that language cannot capture. They seek to name the unnameable secrets that block signification, and they read through ambiguous symptoms to identify disorders of individuals, collectivities, and cultures. Like Walpole, they write compelling fictions of multiple and "encrypted" selves and create ghost stories of "phantoms" that haunt families across generations and through history. Developing a fantastic discourse that preserves the mysteries that it struggles to investigate, Abraham and Torok implicitly suggest how the process of subjectification is related to narrative form.

In developing their far-reaching and multilayered conception of melancholia, Abraham and Torok respond to the contradictions that emerge from a comparative reading of Freud's "Mourning and Melancholia" with *The Ego and the Id*. In the earlier essay, Freud clearly distinguishes the normal, conscious process of mourning from the unconscious and pathological process of melancholia. He contends that in mourning, the ego detaches its libidinal energies from the love object it has lost so that, by redirecting those energies, it is able to love again. In melancholia, the ego cannot transfer desire to another, but identifies with the abandoned or abandoning object that— in a mimicry of primary narcissism—it *becomes*. In this way, the love object, which is introjected as a permanent structure of identity, is rescued from annihilation, and the subject does not have to confront its feelings of bereavement.[17] In *The Ego and the Id*, melancholia— which has been defined as pathological in the first essay—is redefined as normal. Here Freud argues that because it is the sole process through which the ego can survive the deprivation of its object choices, introjection is a fundamental strategy in the construction of the self.[18]

Abraham and Torok mediate between Freud's earlier and later positions. They differentiate sharply between mourning and melancholia, as Freud had done initially, but they reassign to incorporation many of the functions that he had assigned to introjection. At the same time, they identify the strategies belonging to both processes as central to subjectification. In their view, introjection enables the ego's continuous process of self-fashioning by advancing psychic growth, creativity, and symbolization. Its role is to transform "instinctual promptings into desires and fantasies of desire, making them fit to receive a name and the right to exist and to unfold in the objectal sphere."[19] For Abraham and Torok, it is introjection that facilitates mourning while incorporation blocks the introjective process and produces melancholia in its place. Essentially conservative and narcissistic, incorporation is considered to be not a process but a "specific kind of fantasy," which strives to preserve the psychic status quo by "transform[ing] the world rather than inflict[ing] injury on the subject."[20] The individual who enacts this fantastic form of "preservative repression" internalizes or "swallows" the love object, whom she or he is then doomed to "become."[21]

Rooted in infancy, introjection and incorporation mark and are marked by the vicissitudes associated with the earliest experiences of differentiation and primal loss. The model of introjection is established when the infant learns "to fill the emptiness of its mouth with words," which symbolize and transcend the absence of the mother's body—an act of naming that inaugurates the entry of the child into society.[22] When introjection is incomplete, however, or when deprivation is too traumatic to be acknowledged, language is refused and the empty space, which is the condition of speech and signification, becomes the tomb in which the lost object is encrypted. Thereafter, whenever the self is plunged into a state of "inexpressible mourning," it resorts to this same "magical" but dangerous resolution.

Rewriting Freud's theory of melancholic introjection as a theory of incorporation, Abraham and Torok revise the psychic topography that Freud had mapped. As Freud describes it, the unconscious "complex" of melancholia "behaves like an open wound drawing to itself cathected energy on all sides . . . and draining the ego until it is utterly depleted."[23] Appropriating Freud's powerful metaphor, Abraham and Torok find this to be "precisely . . . the wound the melancholic attempts to hide, wall in, and encrypt"; but they place both the wound and its "counter-investments" not in the unconscious but in the preconscious-conscious system. There it is isolated from the rest of the psyche, "especially from the memory of what had been torn from it."[24] Through this activity of "inclusion" or "preservative repression," a "supplemental topography" is formed: a cyst created that protects while signaling the secret of the haunted subject.

Abraham and Torok's theory of incorporation has significant implications for their own broader theorization of fantasy and for a larger theory of the melancholic text. Although in an early essay Torok argues that fantasies irrupt into consciousness as symptoms that seek expression through the introjective process, the fantasy of incorporation—which is both conscious and not conscious, articulated and unspeakable—has to be narrativized in quite a different way.[25] Indeed, it might be said that fantasies which stimulate adaptive introjection are represented in realism's narrative mode and genres, while the melancholic fantasy is encrypted into the enigmatic genres of the fantastic. The melancholic strain of the fantastic text functions to reproduce the structure and strategy of preservative repression, revealing the mysteries of illegitimate burial in coded terms. In *The Castle of Otranto*, the fantastic narrative contains just such an encrypted text: the story of the son, which is entombed within the father's story.

In his preface to the first edition of his fiction, Walpole writes: "Though the machinery is invention, and the names of the actors imaginary, I cannot but believe that the groundwork of the story is founded on truth. The scene is undoubtedly laid in some real castle" (5). The "truth" of his invention is the dream that he identifies as the fiction's origin, and the "real castle" is both his flamboyant home on the Thames and the psychic crypt that holds his secret. As W. S. Lewis has observed, by presenting himself as a melancholic dreamer, Walpole suggests that Theodore and Manfred represent diverse aspects of himself.[26] In this way, he denies the prince his autonomy as a character and recasts him as an intrapsychic projection. To the extent that he does conceptualize Manfred as the father played by the son, Walpole exposes as his *own* desire Manfred's wish to be both father and son and identifies a central strategy of the fantastic. By constructing a narrative that functions like a hall of mirrors, reflecting him back to himself in multiple, distorted, and elusive shapes, Walpole initiates a fantastic novelistic tradition that explores a divided subjectivity connected mysteriously, but unmistakably, to the unconscious of its author.[27]

Because Walpole reveals himself to be the ghost that haunts his text, he makes us want to pierce his shadowy presence, reading through the fantasist to the fantasy in order to identify the desires by which his various stage settings are configured. Although Walpole was a prodigious writer, the mass of his work does not betray the mysteries of his psychic life. Conceiving himself to be a chronicler of his time, he translated personal into social history in memoirs, histories, notebooks, essays, and thousands of letters, all of which were narrated in the realistic mode.[28] For evidence of the catalytic traumas that shaped his gothic vision, one must look to accounts of Walpole's life and to *The Mysterious Mother*, his fantastic blank verse tragedy.

One learns from the biographies, for example, that Horace's birth was surrounded by rumors of illegitimacy.[29] His powerful and famous father, Robert Walpole, was a notorious womanizer who was alienated from his wife long before her youngest son was born. He lived publicly with his mistress, Maria Skerritt, during the boy's childhood and adolescence and married her six months after Lady Walpole's death. Because Lady Walpole's "occasional gallantries" were well-known, and Sir Robert was generally observed to pay very little attention to his son, Horace's physical and temperamental resemblance to Carr Lord Hervey, his mother's friend, was often noted, and Hervey was named by many as the boy's real father.[30]

Whatever the facts and rumors about Horace's legitimacy might have been, and whatever the boy's response was to them, it does seem that Sir Robert existed as a distant if tantalizing figure for his son. W. S. Lewis speculates that Horace had profoundly ambivalent feelings for this charismatic, forceful, and ruthless man who, indifferent to him, also scorned the mother to whom he was devoted.[31] In Manfred, at the level of realism, Horace seems to have sketched a scathing, almost parodic portrait of the prime minister: lustful, cruel, and incapable of domestic loyalty in his private life; intemperate, dismissive of tradition, and abusive of his own authority and power in the public world. Although Horace ultimately defended his father against those who forced him from office, the life that he himself chose to live was shaped by its divergences from the life of Robert Walpole. An aesthete rather than a politician, and a writer rather than an activist, Horace held a seat in Parliament for twenty-seven years, but he neither sought nor attained office, never initiated legislation, and spoke publicly only half a dozen times.[32] He prided himself on working behind the scenes (often on behalf of his cousin, Henry Conway), but because he—like Manfred—was insecure and emotionally excessive, he never won the confidence of his colleagues.[33] Even Conway, who benefited substantially from Walpole's support, did nothing to repay his cousin's favors when, in 1765, he became secretary of state and leader of the House of Commons, an omission that injured Walpole painfully.[34]

At the time that Walpole dreamed of his ancient castle, he was in the midst of a political squabble that concerned his cousin. The events reverberated with echoes of his father's defeat and, possibly, with reminders of his own impotence before it. Having voted in Parliament against the policy of the Court party, Conway had been dismissed from the king's bedchamber and his regiment's command. Enraged, Walpole wrote an indignant reply to a pamphlet in which his cousin had been attacked. He also quarreled bitterly with his neighbor, Thomas Pitt, the man who had been Robert Walpole's chief antagonist and who was his triumphant heir.[35] The pain of the past was etched into the turmoil of the present moment, and the dream that irrupted just after he concluded Conway's defense presented him a coded version of the original trauma. "[G]lad to think of anything rather than politics," Walpole rewrote the social conflicts in which he was embroiled as the intrafamilial and therefore intrapsychic events that provided them their deepest meanings. Specifically identified with Theodore and Manfred, Horace was clearly also Conrad, the fragile son who, never legitimated by his father, was crushed beneath the accouterments of the patriarch's power and his own feelings of inadequacy. That is the perspective from which the fantastic narrative seems to have been conceptualized and the mind from which a variety of other personae are projected.

If Horace narrativized his ambivalent relation to Sir Robert in *The Castle of Otranto*, it was in *The Mysterious Mother* that he revealed the complexly erotic nature of his connection to Lady Walpole. Weak and delicate as a child, and substantially younger than his siblings, Walpole had been his mother's constant and adored companion. His deep love for her clearly dominated his psychic life.[36] They shared an appreciation of art and a taste for the ridiculous. She died when he was twenty, and his mourning was so protracted that his friends feared that he would not survive it.[37] He claimed that he was paying an emotional debt to her by maintaining a close association with Conway, to whom he twice offered a substantial portion of his fortune and on whose behalf he tirelessly worked.[38] The most libidinally invested relationships that he had outside the family reproduced the structure of his relationship with his mother. He never married and, despite the prevalence of what one of his biographers has called "the queer feminine element" in his personality, there are no indisputable signs of explicitly homosexual behavior.[39] Rather, it was his association with women much older than himself that was remarked by his contemporaries and emphasized in writings about him.[40] The most important of those intimacies was the one he conducted with Madame Du Deffand, whom he met in 1865 during a trip to France that followed the debacle with Conway. Walpole was forty-eight and she was sixty-nine. Fascinated by the stories she told of the Regency elite to which she had belonged, he frequently visited her well-known salon, commencing an odd but important relationship that lasted for more than fourteen years. Although it is her emotional neediness that has been emphasized in the writings about him, it is evident that their friendship satisfied some crucial need in him as well.[41] They corresponded weekly until her death and, despite his gout, he made five difficult journeys to Paris to see her. Here again, his feelings are a matter of speculation since few of the 800 letters written by each of them remain. Apparently embarrassed by the relationship, Walpole uncharacteristically asked her to destroy all the letters he had written to her (only seven survive), while he destroyed most that she had written to him. Notably, it was within a year of the time that they met that he began to write *The Mysterious Mother,* a daring and powerful play that takes mother-son incest as its theme.

Walpole did not write his five-act, blank verse tragedy with the inspired ease with which he had written *The Castle of Otranto.* He began it on Christmas Day in 1766 and finished it fifteen months later, after many stops and starts. He printed only fifty copies, most of which he kept for himself, a few of which he circulated among close friends. When he finally published it after thirteen years, it was with great reluctance and only to avoid the publication of a pirated version. In his preface to the 1781 edition, he says that he is "sensible that the subject is disgusting, and by no means compensated by the execution," and he adds: "All the favour the Author solicits or expects, is, to be believed how unwillingly he has submitted to its appearance: he cannot be more blam'd than he blames himself for having undertaken so disagreeable a story, and for having hazarded the publicity by letting it out of his own hands."[42] Because of the subject, he never expected the play to be performed and, indeed, there is no record that it has been, either in England or in the United States.[43] In general, those of his contemporaries who read it found it shocking, although Byron (not surprisingly) admired and praised it as a "tragedy of the highest order."[44] If the text itself does not speak adequately to the nature of its author's concerns, one has only to consider the fact that when Walpole arranged his works for post-humous publication, he decided to print his celebratory "Epitaph on Lady Walpole" following the play.[45]

The plot of *The Mysterious Mother* was suggested to Walpole by a report he had heard in childhood about a woman whose guilty conscience had driven her to an interview with Archbishop Tillotson. According to this account, she had taken the place of her maid in a planned assignation with her son and had given birth to a daughter with whom, in ignorance, her son had fallen in love and whom ultimately he married.[46] Setting his play in the Middle Ages, Walpole begins with the secret return from exile of Edmund, the Countess of Narbonne's son. Ostensibly banished by his mother for impiously having sex with her maid, Beatrice, on the night of his father's death, Edmund—who is described as his "father's very image" (I, 2, 160)—courts Adeliza who, unbeknownst to him, is both his daughter and his sister. As the "melancholy" Countess, who can neither confess nor forget her secret sin, reveals to Edmund at the very end of the play:

> Grief, disappointment, opportunity,
> Rais'd such a tumult in my maddening blood,
> I took the damsel's place; and while thy arms
> Twin'd, to thy thinking, round another's waist,
> Hear, hell, and tremble!—thou did'st clasp thy mother! (V, 6, 247)

Motivated by what she calls her "disappointed passions," the Countess had substituted herself for Beatrice when her husband returned as a corpse from an eighteen-month absence. Born after Edmund's banishment, Adeliza has been raised by the Duchess as her orphaned ward, and she is now encouraged by her mother to marry Florian, Edmund's friend, who will take her away from the city. The Duchess wants to protect her daughter from Benedict, the monk who suspects her secret and resents the fact that she is a "thinking heretic" who resists his efforts to control her (IV, 1, 212). Plotting to destroy the Countess, the monk urges and executes the marriage of Adeliza and Edmund on the sixteenth anniversary of Edmund's father's death. The "House of Narbonne" perishes through the Countess's suicide; the supposed death of Edmund, who goes off to war; and the retreat of Adeliza to a convent.

In *The Mysterious Mother*, as in *The Castle of Otranto*, Walpole reveals his own family secrets that, previously unnamed, return to demand signification when external events threaten his psychic balance. Those secrets saturate the narratives with incestuous longing and melancholic regret. Transcending differences among characters, they direct the reader's attention to Walpole and to his projection of himself as the son in fantasies about parents, with whom he also identifies.[47] Playing both Theodore and Conrad in *The Castle of Otranto,* Walpole is the object of Manfred's murderous, competitive ambition and, as we have seen, the lustful father. In the tragic drama, he is similarly the son literally called upon to replace the absent father sexually, and he is the transgressively desiring mother. Further, since he does identify with the mother in that drama, he must identify also with Adeliza, who substitutes for and veils her as the object of Edmund's desire. Reading back, then, from the multiple identifications of *The Mysterious Mother* to those of *The Castle of Otranto,* one can speculate that since Manfred's craving for Isabella displaces his mourning for Conrad, Isabella and her double, Mathilda, stand in for Walpole as versions of the fragile, feminized son. All are indeed experienced by the reader as aspects of the authorial consciousness, which is then centered in the fiction, at the same time that each is called upon to play a specific role within the complexly plotted scenario. As the characters merge with one another, and authorial identifications multiply and change, the distinctions among characters—and between them and the authorial mind—are deconstructed and erased. Patterns of meaning come in and out of focus, demanding articulation while refusing exclusivity. This is the nature of the fantastic narrative.

Shaped by the unconscious, but given conscious form, these meanings have a quality that Freud theorizes as "uncanny": "that class of the terrifying which leads back to something long known to us."[48] In the irrational mind, which Freud identifies as the source of the strange and familiar effect, that which has been banished to the unconscious returns to consciousness. Spawned by traumas that occurred early in the developmental history of the individual and the social group, shadowy feelings associated with partially exhumed memories reflect fears of the self's fragility, the primal chaos of undifferentiation and dependence, and transgressive desire and sexual otherness. Drawing in part on E. T. A. Hoffmann's "Sandman," Freud describes the uncanny effect of strategies that the self evolves in order to cope with its own anxieties and ambivalence. All of these appear in Walpole's novel, and some are found in the verse tragedy as well: the projection by the son of an imaginary father, for example, and the splitting of that father into good and bad personae; the son's homoerotic projection of himself as a daughter whose relation to the father is both loving and passive; the self's fantasized divisions, multiplications, and projections of itself as defenses against psychic fragmentation, alienation, and extinction; the invention of the supernatural as a reflection of the wishful fear that death will not be final after all; the fantasy of the body shattered into pieces as the retrospective reproduction of a primal, infantile experience; and the postulation that the body of the mother is the foundational uncanny object, at once desired, lost, and feared.[49]

Intended to expose anxieties associated with preoedipal and oedipal traumas that are routinely inflicted by the bourgeois family, Freud's developmental narrative is relevant to Walpole's fictions, which seem powerfully to prefigure it. Still, the emphases (even, perhaps, the obsessions) of Walpole's texts are more narrow than those that shape Freud's theoretical essay. In Walpole's world, as in the world that Abraham and Torok fabricate, the uncanny effect is always linked to melancholia. From their fantastic perspectives, the three describe reality as the burial ground of secrets formed as a result of traumatic loss: a spectral graveyard in which corpses, like memory, have a way of surfacing. In this context, men and women are, like Walpole's Duchess, perpetual mourners who live in a past that cannot be laid to rest. Traces of the catastrophes that have befallen them emerge from the depths to subvert the process of "self-fashioning," which is the driving force of psychic life.

In *The Castle of Otranto* and *The Mysterious Mother*, characters and plot unfold through an elaboration of those phenomena that Abraham and Torok describe as obstacles to the introjective process: incorporation and preservative repression, the burial of family secrets, and the experience of traumatic loss. Placing his narratives in a present saturated with an unmourned but never forgotten past, Walpole gives a melancholic structure to his uncanny fictions. The presence of the supernatural; the splitting, multiplication, and projection of the self; and the irruption of transgressive desire all seem to be responses to irretrievable deprivation. They reveal the ways in which incorporation shapes the child's experience of parents who are forfeited in the internalizing processes of his development and lost again (although not with finality) in death. Further, although the transgenerational phantoms that haunt these texts are social as well as personal, the collective secrets that they have to tell are presented always as individual traumas. (It is a blind spot of gothic fiction as it is of psychoanalytic theory.) So the mystery that the specter of Alfonso represents can be interpreted at several levels. Most obviously, it concerns an illegitimate succession that was enabled by his murder. At the historical level, his is the story of the shameful regicide that haunted eighteenth-century England with its twinned themes of parricide and class rebellion. Considered biographically, it is the story of the upstart Robert Walpole, who stood against traditional values and an ensconced aristocratic order. Psychologically, it is the story of the illegitimacy of the son, the painful secret that Horace inherited from and saw buried with his father. It represents paternal alienation through a filter of filial desire and rage. Woven together, the narrative threads create the fiction's melancholic affect, focusing the traumatic loss of social and personal possibilities in the ghost of a prince who is described nostalgically as "adorned with every virtue; the father of his people! the delight of mankind" (91).

The inextricable connection of loss and incestuous desire that suffuses Walpole's fictions produces the deepest if most elusive meanings of the texts. In both *The Castle of Otranto* and *The Mysterious Mother,* the death of a loved one is immediately followed by a transgressive form of sexual desire. So after Conrad has been crushed into "bleeding mangled remains," Manfred is concerned neither for the "disfigured corpse" of his son nor for the "unhappy princesses his wife and daughter." Instead, the first words that he speaks—"Take care of the Lady Isabella" (127)—betray his lust for his almost-daughter, Conrad's fiancée. Similarly, the death of the Count unleashes the Countess's desire for her son (whom she mistakes, upon his return, for the "phantom" of her husband) and Edmund's desire for Beatrice, who is a substitute for his mother. Walpole's seemingly odd conjunction of heightened sexual desire with loss anticipates Torok's theorization of the "illness of mourning." In the gothic fiction that she constructs, an individual experiences this strange malaise when a substantial libidinal investment in an object is doomed to inadequate introjection by premature bereavement. Because the subject needs to sustain an unrealistic hope that its desires will be fulfilled at some point in the future, the ego preserves the object's imago, "substituting fantasy for the real thing; magic and instantaneous incorporation for the introjective process."[50] Although the hallucinatory, even orgasmic fulfillment that is experienced with this sudden act of incorporation is immediately condemned and re-pressed, the ego continues to preserve its wish "as an 'exquisite corpse' lying somewhere inside it; [it] looks for this exquisite corpse continually in the hope of one day reviving it."[51]

While traces of this illness of mourning can be identified with Manfred, the Duchess, and Edmund, as we have seen, it is Theodore who seems most nearly to exemplify Torok's theory, as her theory helps to explain a necrophilic tendency in fantastic fiction that begins with Walpole and reaches its apogee with Poe. Seeking to "make [Mathilda] mine in death," Theodore "threaten[s] destruction to all who attempt to remove him from [the corpse]," as he "print[s] a thousand kisses on her clay-cold hands" (107–8). Because "he was persuaded that he could know no happiness but in the society of one with whom he could forever indulge the melancholy that had taken possession of his soul" (110), Theodore marries Isabella. The vaguely incestuous marriage to his cousin serves as a substitute for the marriage to the dead Mathilda, which he had previously sought. And although Isabella enables him to remain fixated on the encrypted, exquisite corpse, he also *becomes* that lost object in his ultimate de-sexualization and passivity. He is represented as being without de-sire for Isabella because she is not an other, but the same. As the feminized, melancholic prince, whose paralysis is sexual and social as well as psychological, he reveals the despair that lies at the very heart of Walpole's project.

In the palimpsest of Theodore's story, still another level of mean-ing can be detected. Immediately after Mathilda's death the castle walls are "thrown down with a mighty force," and Alfonso appears in order to provide an account of Theodore's birth. Here another of Abraham and Torok's metaphors seems apt. Melancholia does not appear, they observe, as long as "the crypt" that protects the re-pressed memory holds fast. Memory erupts "when the walls are shaken, often as a result of the loss of some secondary love-object, which had buttressed them. Faced with the danger of seeing the crypt crumble, the whole of the ego becomes one with the crypt, showing the concealed object of love in its own guise."[52] As in the reading of the father's story, the unmourned mother is revealed to be the secret love object in the novel, but in the fantastic narrative it is the death of Mathilda that releases her from her tomb. In his desire to be united with his beloved's corpse, the feminized Theodore assumes the persona of the nameless woman for whom Mathilda is a substitute. Motivating the fiction from a place outside of language, that woman is the mother who has been encrypted in the authorial unconscious, a place beneath the dream/fantasy from which *The Castle of Otranto* explicitly emerged. In the context of this reading, it is Harry Conway's defection and loss that shook the sepulcher in which Walpole's own exquisite corpse was buried. As the probable object of Walpole's homoerotic love, the faithless Conway was, at the more conscious level of fantasy, a substitute for Walpole's father, whom Horace conceptualized ambivalently as Manfred. But sharing the bloodline of Horace's mother—the bloodline that determines identity in the novel—Conway is, at a still deeper level, a surrogate for Lady Walpole, the unnamed maternal figure to whom the son owes a psychological debt that he will never be able to repay. At a later stage of Walpole's life, it is Madame Du Deffand who shakes the walls of the crypt in which the mysterious mother is buried. And while the concealed love object is shown "in its own guise" in both of Walpole's fictions (more explicitly in his drama than in his novel), the deep reference of the fantasy is protected by the narrative structure. The son is only secondarily represented as loving and losing, after all; it is the parents who are the tragic protagonists. As Abraham and Torok explain, "The 'shadow of the object' strays endlessly about the crypt until it is finally reincarnated in the person of the subject."[53] It is he who "lends his own flesh to the phantom object of love."[54] The subject fantasizes the imaginary suffering of the one who is incarcerated within himself, but it is "a fantasy that only serves to mask the real suffering, this one unavowed, caused by a wound the subject does not know how to heal."[55] Manfred desires Isabella and suffers for the deaths of Conrad and Mathilda, while the Duchess endures the guilt and pain of her incestuous love for and sacrifice of Edmund. Representing his loss as theirs, the son perpetually buries his dead at the same time that he perpetually disinters them.

In his preface to the first edition of *The Castle of Otranto*, Walpole interprets his narrative of the negative sublime as a superegoic story. The "moral" of his regressive psychological fiction is "that *the sins of fathers are visited on their children to the third and fourth generation*" (5). This is also his conception of *The Mysterious Mother*, with Adeliza suffering for the guilt of the Duchess. In Walpole's life, the "sins" that he had attributed to fictive parental figures are enacted in his own relation to a young woman who seems to have functioned in his fantasy as mother-daughter-wife. At the age of seventy, ten years before his death, Walpole met and—in the words of one of his biographers—"bec[a]me the helpless victim of a love which he could neither deflect nor overcome."[56] Mary Berry, the object of that love, was twenty-five, and she refers to Walpole in her correspondence as her "second father."[57] Visiting with her every day for the remainder of his life, he formed a relationship that seems to have been haunted by the phantom that had animated his fictions.

It appears, then, that while Walpole's writing allowed him to explore his melancholia, it did not enable him to transcend it. Because the need to master produces the compulsion to repeat, fantastic fictions tend to resist the resolution that they also crave. The specters that they summon are tethered to corpses of memory that, never more than partially exhumed, are also never finally buried. Conscious and unconscious, familiar and strange, they testify to the immeasurable and tragic power of loss. So, as Abraham and Torok describe it: "Sometimes in the dead of the night, when libidinal fulfillments have their way, the ghost of the crypt comes back to haunt the cemetery guard, giving him strange and incomprehensible signals, making him perform bizarre acts, or subjecting him to unexpected sensations."[58] The fantastic mode is the mode of nightmare: its narratives awaken the fearful dreamer to consciousness, but the script is doomed to be ceaselessly replayed.

Conclusion

The Relation of Fiction and Theory

It might be said that I have used my theory of the bimodal narrative to interpret eighteenth-century fictions and their traditions retrospectively, conceptualizing the past to conform to and anticipate a version of the present. To some extent, this seems to me inevitable. It is, after all, the way in which we read ourselves, revising memory as current patterns of experience provide access to conscious and unconscious material that has been inaccessible before.[1] Texts written in the past achieve importance for us because we find them eloquent in the present moment. Their resonance is cultural as well as personal: a sign of collective and individual inheritance. The subject does seem familiar to us in these early novels, as does the narrative structure through which its doubled form of consciousness is articulated. We recognize both, as we recognize the trauma of gender imposition, which these texts simultaneously disclose and struggle to conceal.

The subject that emerges from these chapters is one that is painfully divided. Clinging to an illusion of autonomy, it is estranged from others, whom it seeks to dominate and control. Plagued by an obsessive self-awareness—and beset by guilt and shame—it is alienated also from itself. In its developmental process, it is thwarted inevitably by a sex-gender system that allows expression of some identifications while suppressing others. When it is represented in the realist mode, it labors to achieve a normative identity, performing—as if it were autonomous—roles that the society has scripted. Experiencing ideological contradictions as signs of personal rather than systemic failure, it struggles for self-mastery and psychic wholeness: disguises that social accommodation wears. Although the story of the realist subject is ostensibly about fulfillment, it is motivated by denial. When that story is written in the fantastic mode, the veil of ideology is pierced. Psychic pain and developmental deformations are exposed, and the traumas of individuation and gender acquisition are laid bare.

The dominance of realist narratives in the early, experimental novel suggests that the eighteenth century was more concerned with social transformations that were taking place than it was with subtle shifts in forms of consciousness that we can now identify. As consciousness itself became an object of intense scrutiny, however, and as conventions of the novel started to cohere, the two modes were increasingly differentiated, although they continued to be mutually constitutive. The depth model of consciousness (which could already be detected in *Roxana*) was presupposed by the great realist novelists of the nineteenth century and provided the formal and thematic focus of Romantic texts.[2] The Romantic self was essentially the self that Freud inherited. It was the self that he interpreted for modernism and is the one that psychoanalytic theorists have continued to dissect. In the preceding chapters, it is the self I have assumed.

The continuity that aligns the subject of the eighteenth-century novel with the subject of psychoanalytic theory makes each effective in considering the other. Beginning with Freud, psychoanalytic theory invented a language to describe the deeply alienated self, which the bimodal novel represents perceptively but without full consciousness. The insights that fictions offer with sensuous immediacy, psychoanalytic theory has helped to integrate, order, and refine. Freud mapped interior space, gave names to intrapsychic functions, and tracked the negotiations of an embattled self between its own lawless impulses and its disciplining conscience. Although he understood the self he studied to be partially hidden and disguised, he recognized its channels of communication in the symbolic codes of dreams, reveries, and works of the imagination. For this reason, he could chart the mysterious domain from which fantastic narratives draw their substance, and he could relate it to the superegoic realm, which determines the contours of realistic texts. Freud also told a developmental story about the molding and deformation of the child's desire in the crucible of the bourgeois family. That story can be detected in the doubled narratives of bimodal fictions, where its importance is signaled by repetition and where the threat of its power is acknowledged through realistic disguise and fantastic hyperbole.

Although Freud illuminated the shadowy landscape of the unconscious mind, his specific blind spots produced their own distortions and omissions. Taking the male subject as his model and describing a psychological dynamic that was predominantly intrapsychic, he overlooked aspects of the sex-gender system that were crucial for his theory, as they were crucial also to the novel. The issues which Freud overlooked, and upon which many eighteenth-century fictions focus, were precisely the issues with which feminist psychoanalytic theorists have been most concerned. Studying the transformation of the natural order of biological difference into social structures of gender inequity and domination, these theorists have continued the revolution that Freud initiated, but they have dramatically changed its direction.[3] They have identified the divergences of female from male development as pivotal, and they have argued for the inextricable connection of the intrapsychic and the intersubjective. In Freud's own theoretical emphases, they have found examples of personal and cultural bias; in his oversights, they have read signs of individual and collective repression.

One of the most striking of these oversights concerns the mother. Throughout his career, Freud ignored the preoedipal phase of childhood development and focused on the oedipal triangle, over which the father looms. When he ultimately acknowledged the significance of that early moment (which he did only in the case of girls), he compared it to an ancient civilization, too deeply buried to be exhumed.[4] In contrast, object-relations theory (which has attracted feminists with its relational focus) insists on the decisiveness of the preoedipal stage for male as well as female children and gives to the mother a critical formative function.[5] Identifying her as the first object in the infant's psychosocial world, object-relations theorists center her in the primal struggle for separation and individuation. Conceptualizing her as a bridge from intrapsychic to intersubjective experience, they represent her as the motivating impulse of the transformational process through which the child discovers and creates itself.[6] In the United States, psychoanalytically inclined feminists who accept the object-relations perspective understand that the linking of psychic power to social impotence has made the mother extremely problematic for her children. At the deepest level, the primal maternal figure inspires desire and fear, promising wholeness and integration while also threatening engulfment. She survives in bodily memory as a powerful, if inchoate, core of affectivity, but she is

demeaned and devalued in culture. Late-twentieth-century psychoanalytic theorists have explicitly investigated the legacy of ambivalence that she bequeaths, and we can see that ambivalence reflected
in eighteenth-century fiction. In *Roxana,* for example, Defoe unknow-
ingly exposed contradictions that separate the mother from the thriv-
ing individualist. In *Clarissa,* Richardson articulated an early version
of the claustral modern family in which the mother is psychologically omnipotent but socially despised, while in *Tristram Shandy* and
The Castle of Otranto, the excluded maternal body produces the melancholic text. In the twentieth century, theories of abjection, the
semiotic, the uncanny, and *jouissance* continued to enact—even as
they analyzed—the individual's desire to retrieve the intense affectivity that is identified with the frightening maternal presence.

Feminist psychoanalytic theorists have examined the culture's
ambivalent obsession with the mother as a crucial symptom of the
illness that the modern sex-gender system creates. They have shown
how that system polarizes identification and object choice, prohib-
iting identification with the other who is different, while proscribing
desire for the other whom one is like.[7] Because prohibited identifications are as powerful as prohibited desires, the sexual order produces a tragic gender melancholia and an equally tragic gender
complementarity. In the eighteenth-century novels I examine, the
obsessive erasure of Mrs. Shandy and the nightmare figure of Mrs.
Sinclair expose misogyny's melancholic aspect. At the same time, the
poignancy of Tristram's narrative transvestism and the intensity of
Lovelace's fantasies of gender mutation show how fear and rejection
of the other can lead to its incorporation and perpetual acting out.
In *Clarissa,* this same suspicion of difference is expressed through the
production of polarized gender categories that block the possibility
of mutual recognition.[8] As Lovelace and Clarissa search desperately
and unproductively for the reflection of themselves in one another's
eyes, they encounter the conundrum of complementary heterosexuality. Because they are not able to identify with the other whom
they desire, they can experience mutuality only where desire is
banned. They long for empathic connection, which depends upon
the recognition of likeness in difference, but from their categorically
opposed positions they are never able to achieve it.

In the context of feminist theory, the pornographic imagination—
which is displayed in many eighteenth-century texts—can be seen

to perform the work of gender melancholia. Its central function is to create fantasies of omnipotence that deny primal loss and psychic deprivation. In its scenarios, the self refuses recognition to others, melancholically reproducing the struggle of differentiation, which it also seeks to avoid. So, Lovelace's desire for Clarissa is inseparable from his urge to appropriate her otherness. If he were successful in his efforts, he would effectively destroy her. Failing, he believes himself to be destroyed. His inability to resolve the vacillation between desire and rage results in the compulsive repetition of his assault. In Richardson's novel—as in Walpole's—the pornographic fantasy shows itself to be a sadistic hallucination: cruelly violative and crudely unreal. Although it may be fundamentally infantile and narcissistic, it is dangerously enacted in adult relations of erotic domination.[9] Lovelace and Manfred relentlessly pursue the emotional and social logic of their positions. Their goal is psychic appropriation. Their strategy is rape. Their hidden motive is retaliation against the maternal figure that haunts their fantasies.

Because of the modern sex-gender system's economy of desire and identification, these eighteenth-century novels inevitably make mutual recognition in heterosexual relationships seem impossible to achieve. To the extent that empathic connection can take place at all, it does so in eroticized same-sex friendships. The romantic idyll of Friday and Crusoe, the intimacy of Amy and Roxana, the homosociality of the Shandy males, and the yearning companionship of Clarissa and Anna Howe offer the possibility of affiliation and reciprocity. That the first two should be enabled and disguised by class inequity, and that the last should be controlled by the limitations of epistolary communication, suggests the power of the prohibition against homosocial intimacy. That power prevents the centering of intense homosocial relationships in realistic narratives and saturates with paranoia the predominantly fantastic novels that do extensively explore them.[10] In these fictions, the gesture toward mutuality is finally utopian: a promise that palliates the anguish of melancholia without awakening the consciousness that is essential to mourning.

Tristram Shandy is a notable exception among the novels I examine and, for this reason, it serves as a valuable test case. Its account of the male subject's response to primal loss and sexual difference is not merely expansive and complex. As it is incorporated into Sterne's

comic vision, it is also marvelously subversive. The novels of Richardson, Defoe, and Walpole expose the connection of melancholia to
the denial and incorporation of the maternal, and they show how
the failure of recognition, which that denial creates, makes other
forms of recognition impossible. Sterne begins where they do, but
in his novel the paralysis of melancholia is converted into creative
forms of play. Although the conversion is partial and fleeting, it allows for moments of intersubjective reciprocity among men.

In *Tristram Shandy* the mother is banished from the story of the
son, but while the son rejects her, he usurps many of her defining
qualities for his own imaginative purposes. Swallowing her, in Abraham and Torok's sense, Tristram becomes her. Becoming her, he constructs the text in her image. In Tristram, as in his fiction, gender
melancholia yields to a gender indeterminacy that resists the boundaries and hierarchies that systems of difference establish. At times
appropriated and at times appropriating, oscillating between the assertion of himself and the recognition of others, Tristram struggles
tenaciously for empathic connection. Although his imagination is
salacious, it is not pornographic. Drawing on sensations of the preoedipal moment and the polymorphously perverse body, it reinvents
a maternal world that is partially outside of language. This is a space
of symbolic play and intersubjective relation, where the desire for
recognition reveals itself to be at the core of narcissistic subjectivity.
In this place, the Shandy males share versions of the precious auratic
gaze. It is the fully empathic gaze that Clarissa and Lovelace long
for but cannot find in one another. That its origin should be the
mother who is rejected and scorned speaks to the limited awareness
of the fiction, which intuits more than it consciously comprehends.

Sterne's novel shows us that through the innovations of hobbyhorsical play, through the embrace of gender indeterminacy, and
through the empathic gaze that resonates with the profound intimacy of the moment before splitting, the self saves itself from tragic
isolation: the fate that the illusion of autonomy imposes. At every
level, intentionally and unintentionally, *Tristram Shandy* exposes the
falsity and danger of the commitment to autonomy. Explicitly, it
shows how Tristram has been shaped and marked by the paternal
figures with whom he identifies and whom he loves. When he attempts to explore himself, he finds their images engraved where he
had thought to find his own. Setting out to tell his own story, it is

their stories that he is doomed to tell.[11] Implicitly, through Tristram's usurpation of the maternal mind and body, the text also reveals the indissolubility and power of the primal bond, which underlies all other connections. The story of that bond cannot be told, because having no place in consciousness, it cannot be represented in language. Instead, it speaks through the creative energy that enables Tristram to convert sadness to laughter as he claims his individuality.

Substituting eccentricity for autonomy as an organizing principle of character, *Tristram Shandy* constructs a subject that is emphatically social but always unique: contradictory, ambivalent but also, in some sense, coherent. Although gendered, that subject is feminine as well as masculine. Even though it is constrained within a system of compulsory heterosexuality, its desires are undeniably homosocial. Rejecting a fixed boundary between itself and others, it insists on the possibility of empathic connection. Committed to psychic struggle, it conceives relationships that can be, however fitfully, generous and humane. In these ways, this subject is remarkably similar to one that feminist psychoanalytic theorists have conceptualized and projected in a utopian spirit[12] —but there is a crucial difference.

Despite *Tristram Shandy*'s wonderful liberatory impulses, it remains a deeply misogynistic and heterophobic text. Despite its commitment to self-consciousness and its efforts of psychic reparation, it remains also profoundly melancholic. In its misogyny and melancholia, *Tristram Shandy* is more like than unlike the other eighteenth-century fictions that this study has explored. And although the confluence of its realistic and fantastic narratives does reflect a more complex vision of the relation between social and psychological forces than theirs, it is the gap between the text's extraordinary self-awareness and its persistent disavowal that signals the intransigence of deprivations that it cannot verbalize. Ultimately, there is not more comprehension of institutionalized gender arrangements in the wise playfulness of Sterne's fiction than there is in the insouciant denials of *Robinson Crusoe*, the conceptual contradictions of *Roxana*, the pornographic fantasies of *Clarissa*, or the overwrought melodrama of *The Castle of Otranto*. All of these bimodal novels are doubly dark because the secrets of subjectivity and sexuality that their narratives protect remain unspoken and unrecognized. Pain is palpable in the texts, but its causes are unclear.

Over the last twenty years, feminist theorists have provided concepts for understanding and a language for naming what is—from a fantastic perspective—the catastrophe that has so largely shaped our fictions and influenced our lives. At once natural and unnatural, pervasive and invisible, the disaster they describe did not take place in a single discernible moment but emerged slowly, across three centuries, creating an incalculable number of victims without producing witnesses. The novel emerged to manage the effects of the trauma of gender. Its bimodal narratives stunningly revealed the misfortunes that men and women have suffered, but these same narratives also concealed them from consciousness. Melancholia grows out of a paralysis of memory, which is marked by the abandonment of words. Mourning begins with recollection and the return of speech. To read these fictions through the lens of feminist theory is to remember what they gestured toward and disavowed. We cannot cure them of their melancholia, of course, but understanding the causes of their incurable sadness, we can begin to know and heal our own.

But I do not wish to end this book with a simple privileging of theoretical analysis over fictional representation. To read today's theoretical texts in relation to the richest of our fictions is to grasp the ways in which this first form of knowledge, while crucially insightful, is also inevitably schematic and, in some sensuous, experiential sense, thin. It is understandable, in other words, why theory—including the feminist theory that I so highly value—*needs* fiction to complete it. Fictions *perform* their experiences of multiplicity, ambiguity, and contradiction in ways that enable identification. They bind us with the threads of their desire, their rage, their joy, their alienation, and their despair. They establish a circuit that connects us, through our minds and our senses, to the expressive perplexity of their authors. They clear a transitional space for creative collaboration and empathic recognition. Through the structures of their narratives, they teach us about the relation of psychic resistance to social accommodation. They remind us of the place outside that is the place within. It is the place in which difference originates and in which it is, however briefly, overcome. To read these eighteenth-century novels from a feminist and psychoanalytic perspective is to understand that men and women have struggled within and against the modern sex-gender system for three hundred years. They have struggled for more capacious identities and for fuller expressions of their need and ability to love. They have undertaken this struggle without being able to name what precisely they are fighting for and what specifically they are fighting against. Enlightened by their doubled narratives, and by the theory that these narratives prefigure, we join the hopeful if interminable effort to transform melancholia to mourning and then to convert mourning to social and psychological change.

Notes

INTRODUCTION

1. Of course, it is Ian Watt who, in *The Rise of the Novel*, provided the most influential and provocative form of the argument that links the formal specificities of early fictions to middle-class values of individualism, rationalism, and empiricism. Naming Defoe, Richardson, and Fielding as representatives of the governing tradition, Watt also established the core of an eighteenth-century canon that represented the novel as a single categorical genre. (In "The Importance of Ian Watt's *The Rise of the Novel*," Daniel R. Schwartz describes the reception of Watt's book.) While more recent books about the development of the English novel have had different emphases, they have not challenged Watt's fundamental thesis. I note specifically John Bender, *Imagining the Penitentiary*; Lennard J. Davis, *Factual Fictions* and *Resisting Novels*; and Michael McKeon, *The Origins of the English Novel, 1600–1740*.

2. Obviously, many critics have come to recognize the importance of the sex-gender system as it is reflected in the novel's themes and treatment of character, and many feminists have participated in the recuperation and examination of women's fictions. (Ros Ballaster, Catherine Gallagher, Jane Spencer, and Janet Todd have been most important in reassessing the status of eighteenth-century romances and their female authors. Ballaster's book *Seductive Forms: Amatory Fiction from 1684–1740* is particularly notable; it complicates the structure of women's romances and attempts to bring female and male traditions of the novel into conversation.) Only Nancy Armstrong has defined her project in terms similar to mine, however. In *Desire and Domestic Fiction: A Political History of the Novel*, Armstrong indicates her intention to provide a feminist analysis of the ways in which the English novel managed the relations of gender as well as class. She defines the novel as a modern discourse of gendered subjectivity that makes its appearance in seventeenth-century conduct books and then shapes and is shaped by what she categorizes as domestic fiction: the genre begins with *Pamela* and includes all novels with female protagonists and an emphasis on sexuality and the marriage plot. In fact, Armstrong's concerns are neither predominantly feminist nor psychological, as her emphasis on subjectivity would lead us initially to believe. She wishes to demonstrate that the novel sought to disentangle sexual relations from the language of political power in order to mask socioeconomic interests by representing them *as* psychological and by iden-

tifying that psychological discourse with women. Hypothesizing the textual restructuring by men of women's sexuality and subjectivity, she subjects sexual to class relations, as do McKeon and Watt, and a textualized female subjectivity to a male materiality conceptualized in oppositional and hierarchized terms. Despite her allegiance to Foucault, she reads the history of the novel positioned, albeit uneasily, with the formal realists: positioned, that is, within the masculinist and materialist discourse that she wishes to interrogate. I examine Armstrong's argument at greater length in an essay, "The Anxieties of Indeterminacy: Towards a Feminist Theory of the Novel."

3. The reader will note that I have used the term "fantastic" instead of the terms "romance" and "gothic," which have also been employed to characterize eighteenth-century texts in this tradition. My choice of terms derives from my conceptualization of narrative modes and literary genres. As I theorize it, a narrative mode defines and connects texts across historical periods through its articulation of linked epistemological, ideological, and psychological perspectives, and through its employment of specific formal strategies. A narrative mode is elaborated through historically specific genres, which are themselves governed by particular formal and thematic conventions. In the modern period, the mentality of capitalism found direct expression in realist genres, while the fantastic (which that same mentality produced) interrogated the normative concepts and psychological constraints that realism represented. So, although the novel was shaped by the contestation of realism's bourgeois values with the earlier aristocratic values of romance, the fantastic absorbed and altered romance impulses that survived capitalism's social transformations. The eighteenth-century novel charted this modal evolution, as my analysis of *Robinson Crusoe* will suggest. In early modern fictions, romance often coexists with realism (this is true of *Tom Jones* and *Joseph Andrews*, for example) and both are sometimes accompanied by incipient strains of the fantastic (Elizabeth Inchbald's *A Simple Story* provides a late-eighteenth-century example of such a trimodal collaboration). In the gothic novel, which is the first of the fully formed fantastic genres, romance elements are given a psychological as well as a supernatural reference. It is precisely this psychological emphasis that defines nineteenth- and twentieth-century fantastic genres, as it also distinguishes more fragmentary fantastic narratives found in eighteenth-century fictions.

4. Sir Robert Filmer's *Patriarcha* is generally cited as the representative statement about patriarchalism. Written in the 1630s or '40s, it was published in 1680 and refuted by Locke in his *Two Treatises of Government*, published in 1690. Significantly, Filmer was a committed royalist who wanted to refute the claims of popular rights and popular sovereignty that were made by parliamentarians against the king in the 1640s. He argued on behalf of the king's unlimited power to rule England by insisting that all government derives not from consent but from a father's natural and unlimited authority over his family. Because a father's power was unlimited, Filmer concludes, the power of kings must be acknowledged to be unlimited. Locke argued against Filmer that the customary interactions of the family were quite dif-

ferent from the contractual relations of the state. By defining women in terms of their roles as wives and mothers, Locke restricted the rights and responsibilities of contractual relations to men.

5. In an important essay that traces the shift from patriarchalism to modern patriarchy, Michael McKeon argues that class and gender reverse their functions in the eighteenth century, with each appearing to undertake the work that had previously been performed by the other. Gender is associated with biological essence, he points out, while class is seen as socially variable and historically contingent ("Historicizing Patriarchy: The Emergence of Gender Difference in England, 1660–1760," 303). McKeon also argues that "the emergence of modern patriarchy is coextensive with the emergence of gender difference, which is therefore historically specific to the modern era" (300).

6. In her classic book *Working Life of Women in the Seventeenth Century*, Alice Clark observes that while wives of emergent capitalists became idle, wives of skilled laborers lost their economic independence and became unpaid domestic servants, and wives of wage earners were driven into sweatshops. The lives of poorer women became lives of ceaseless labor, exploited as they were at work, paid lower wages than men, and responsible for domestic work at home. More recent books qualify and moderate Clark's more general claims, emphasizing the different kinds and rates of change that took place in England at this time, depending upon class status and geographical location. Still, while the historical details of the account have been modified and nuanced, its basic outline remains intact. For example, see Susan Amussen, *An Ordered Society: Gender and Class in Early Modern England;* Susan Cahn, *Industry of Devotion: The Transformation of Women's Work in England, 1500–1660;* Bridget Hill, *Women, Work, and Sexual Politics in Eighteenth-Century England;* and Amanda Vickery, *The Gentleman's Daughter: Women's Lives in Georgian England.*

7. In *The Culture of Sensibility: Sex and Society in Eighteenth-Century Britain,* G. J. Barker-Benfield maps the debate that took place around the gendering of sensibility in eighteenth-century England. On one side, the subordination of women was rationalized on the basis of women's finer sensibility, which was thought to derive from a more delicate nervous system and which was associated with moral and imaginative power, and physical and mental fragility. Alternatively, sensibility was seen as fundamental to the reformation of men's manners: a process intended to bridge the growing gap between male and female, making men similar to women in those qualities upon which moral behavior and affective relationships were thought to depend. At the heart of the reform movement, however, was the contradiction between masculinity and sensibility: the fear that "sensible" men were also effeminate. In the nineteenth century, essentialism ultimately triumphed over reform and sensibility became a largely feminine attribute.

8. In *Making Sex: Body and Gender from the Greeks to Freud,* Thomas Laqueur argues that "sex as we know it was invented in the eighteenth century." In his view, the rethinking of the body was intrinsic to and not the

result of evangelical religion, Enlightenment political theory, and the invention of new public spaces (149). Laqueur's influential argument runs counter to Edmund Leites's earlier contention that changes in attitudes about the strength and nature of women's sexuality *followed* changes in attitudes concerning women's stronger moral character: attitudes that, in his judgment, "freed men from the demand for moral constancy and the threat of moral failure" (Leites, *The Puritan Conscience and Modern Sexuality*, 121).

9. See Mary Poovey, *The Proper Lady and the Woman Writer: Ideology as Style in the Works of Mary Wollstonecraft, Mary Shelley, and Jane Austen*.

10. See Thomas Laqueur, *Making Sex: Body and Gender from the Greeks to Freud*.

11. See Felicity Nussbaum, *Torrid Zones: Maternity, Sexuality, and Empire in Eighteenth-Century English Narratives*.

12. See Randolph Trumbach, "Sex, Gender, and Social Identity in Modern Culture: Male Sodomy and Female Prostitution in Enlightenment London."

13. In *The Civilizing Process*, Norbert Elias analyzes changes in attitudes and manners that begin to be perceived in the sixteenth century. He maps the social and psychological transformations that accompanied "the civilizing process" through which the lives of human beings were increasingly divided between intimate and public spheres, between permissible and prohibited behaviors. Examining the ways in which increasing social prohibitions come to be internalized as self-control, he also explores the construction, in this period, of a self divided against itself—the self that Freud would ultimately study.

14. In "The Unconscious," Freud writes, "By the medium of consciousness each one of us becomes aware only of his own states of mind: that another man possesses consciousness is a conclusion drawn by analogy from the utterances and actions we perceive him to make, and it is drawn in order that this behavior of his may become intelligible to us" (101–2). In the same essay, he describes the unconscious as a "second consciousness"—"a consciousness of which its own possessor knows nothing" (103).

15. In *The Unconscious before Freud*, Lancelot Law Whyte argues that in the seventeenth century, the individual's experience of "self-consciousness" was isolated for the first time and treated not as a moment of "self-elimination, but as a primary concept or value." He contends that by 1700, when the incipient movements of individualism, liberalism, democracy, rationalism, and scientific skepticism take self-consciousness for granted, the existence of the unconscious begins to be inferred from immediate conscious experience. Elias also attributes this perception of interior fragmentation to the civilizing process:

> The pronounced division of the "ego" or consciousness characteristic of man in our phase of civilization, which finds expression in such terms as "superego" and "unconscious," corresponds to the specific split in the behavior which civilized society demands of its members. It matches the degree of regulation and restraint imposed upon the expression of drives and impulses. Tendencies

in this direction may develop in any form of human society, even in those which we call "primitive." But the strength attained in societies such as ours by this differentiation and the form in which it appears are reflections of a particular historical development, the results of a civilizing process. (*Civilizing Process*, 190–91)

16. This specular self is theorized by Jacques Lacan in "The Mirror Stage as Formative of the I." I will be arguing throughout the following chapters that this experience of specularity is at the heart of the fantastic tradition.

17. Although I focus on male writers in this book, it does seem important to note here that eighteenth- and early-nineteenth-century realistic and fantastic fictions that are female-authored generally have female protagonists (Mary Shelley's *Frankenstein* is, of course, a notable exception). While male-authored realistic fictions also commonly have female protagonists, male-authored fantastic narratives ordinarily center on male characters. I would speculate that in the case of realistic narratives, the gendered division of labor made it difficult, as well as unseemly, for women to describe the psychological lives of men, while female subjectivity provided male writers, who were less constrained, with the opportunity to explore a wider affective range in their fiction. In the case of predominantly fantastic fictions, it would have been all the more inappropriate for female writers to represent male desire (one recalls the opprobrium directed at Emily and Charlotte Brontë for their inventions of Heathcliff and Rochester, for example). While male writers obviously felt no such prohibition about depicting female desire (with which they were acknowledged to be familiar), the form of the fantastic authorized a more quasi-autobiographical form of writing (as I discuss at some length in my chapter on Walpole), which made male authors more likely to center male protagonists.

18. Ann Radcliffe's novels *The Mysteries of Udolpho* and *The Italian* are the classic female gothic fictions. It is particularly interesting to compare *The Italian* with Matthew Lewis's *The Monk*, which it attempts to rewrite. The comparison makes clear the extent to which Radcliffe felt it necessary to represent obliquely the male and female desires that Lewis is able to openly explore.

19. In her book *In the Name of Love: Women, Masochism, and the Gothic*, Michelle A. Masse traces the construction of female masochism in the female gothic and in psychoanalytic theory. It is her view that these texts show the ways in which women in Western culture act as both victims and accomplices who incorporate social expectations and ultimately hurt others as they have been hurt (5).

20. In an essay that ingeniously unravels the complexities of *The Mysteries of Udolpho*, Claudia L. Johnson points out that in the novel, "every household conceals the dead body of its mistress" ("The Sex of Suffering: *The Mysteries of Udolpho*," 112).

21. It is interesting to compare Ann Radcliffe's fictions *The Mysteries of Udolpho* and *The Italian* with Charlotte Brontë's *Jane Eyre* and *Villette*. While

Radcliffe's complexly ambivalent novels are stamped by the wish fulfillment of the romance tradition, to which I allude here, Brontë provides a critique of romantic resolutions of female gothic in Rochester's maiming and in M. Paul's death. M. Paul is a compelling mixture of the feminized gothic hero and the sadistic anti-hero: a nurturant feminized male and a forbidding father figure.

22. The anti-hero is analyzed at some length in my study of *The Castle of Otranto* in chapter 4.

23. In *Between Men: English Literature and Male Homosocial Desire*, Eve Kosofsky Sedgwick argues, "The Gothic novel crystallized for English audiences the terms of a dialectic between male homosexuality and homophobia, in which homophobia appeared thematically in paranoid plots" (92). Her specific reference is to a late-eighteenth- and early-nineteenth-century subgroup of the gothic novel, which includes William Godwin's *Caleb Williams*, Mary Shelley's *Frankenstein*, James Hogg's *Confessions of a Justified Sinner*, and Charles Maturin's *Melmouth the Wanderer*.

24. In his book *The Fantastic: A Structural Approach to a Literary Genre*, Tzvetan Todorov defines the fantastic as a genre and analyzes it in terms of the hesitation experienced by a person who is familiar with the laws of nature when he or she encounters a supernatural event. The feeling of hesitation that is experienced can be resolved at the level of the uncanny (the supernatural explained) or the marvelous (the supernatural accepted), but in the case of the pure fantastic—as in Henry James's "The Turn of the Screw"—it is not resolved at all. Texts that induce this last form of hesitation are, for Todorov, genuinely subversive because they offer a sense of the transgression of boundaries, a shocking experience of limits. I follow Rosemary Jackson, rather than Todorov, in defining the fantastic not as a genre but, like realism, as a literary mode productive of a range of genres that themselves produce, regulate, and structure desire. With Jackson, I explore the psychoanalytic implications of the fantastic; but unlike her, I read fantastic and realistic genres of fiction and theory reciprocally in order to explore the processes through which gendered subjectivities are both constructed and deconstructed. None of those who have written on the fantastic—in addition to Todorov and Jackson, I would cite David Punter, William Patrick Day, Franco Moretti, and, most recently, Eugenia DeLaMotte, Michelle Masse, and Anne Williams—have studied the interactions of these two modes with their respective genres. In her chapter "Fantastic Realism" in *Fantasy: The Literature of Subversion*, Jackson moves in this direction, examining fantastic elements in nineteenth-century realistic novels.

25. Peter Stallybrass and Allon White observe that "whilst the 'free' democratic individual appeared to be contentless, a point of judgment and rational evaluation which was purely formal and perspectival, in fact it was constituted through and by the clamour of particular voices to which it tried to be universally superior. It is on this account that the very blandness and transparency of bourgeois reason is in fact nothing other than the critical negation of a social 'colourfulness' of a heterogeneous diversity of specific

contents, upon which it is, nonetheless, completely dependent" (*The Politics and Poetics of Transgression*, 199). Stallybrass and White extend and link Bakhtin's analysis of the carnivalesque and Elias's account of the civilizing process.

26. I would include in a list of early gothic texts, for example, Horace Walpole's *Castle of Otranto* (discussed at length in chapter 4), Matthew Lewis's *The Monk*, William Godwin's *Caleb Williams*, and Ann Radcliffe's *Mysteries of Udolpho* and *The Italian*. Mary Shelley's *Frankenstein*, Sheridan Lefanu's *Carmilla*, Robert Louis Stevenson's *Dr. Jekyll and Mr. Hyde*, Bram Stoker's *Dracula*, and Oscar Wilde's *Picture of Dorian Gray* would all represent the more psychologically developed, predominantly fantastic fiction of the later nineteenth century. Emily Brontë's *Wuthering Heights*, Charlotte Brontë's *Jane Eyre* and *Villette*, and many novels by Charles Dickens and Wilkie Collins would stand as examples of fantastic realism, a form in which neither mode is primary. Finally, to see the shift in the work of specific authors from Victorian realism to modernist subjectivism, one has only to compare D. H. Lawrence's early *Sons and Lovers* with *Women in Love*, Thomas Hardy's *Return of the Native* with *Jude the Obscure*, and Virginia Woolf's *Voyage Out* with *The Waves*.

27. One can see how this opposition functions, for example, in *Desire and Domestic Fiction*, where Armstrong, perceiving interiority to be a mere "strategy" of social discourse, appropriates the novel of female interiority for one that is shaped by socioeconomic interests. In this way, she erases the psychological determinants of subjectivity and sociality.

28. In the introductory chapter to *Literature and Psychoanalysis*, Shoshana Felman, the collection's editor, argues for the interdependent relation of the literary critic and the psychoanalyst, and of the literary text and the analysand. "In much the same way as literature falls within the realm of psychoanalysis (with its competence and its knowledge), psychoanalysis itself falls in the realm of literature, and its specific logic and rhetoric" (27). As the critic interprets and establishes a transferential relation with literary texts, the analyst establishes an interpretive and transferential relation with the analysand. Summarizing the privileged relation that literature and psychoanalysis share, Felman argues that "[f]rom the very beginning, literature has been for psychoanalysis not only a contiguous field of external verification in which to test its hypotheses and to confirm its findings, but also the constitutive texture of its *conceptual* framework, of its theoretical body. . . . Since literature and psychoanalysis are *different* from each other, but at the same time, they are also 'enfolded within' each other, since they are, as it were, at the same time outside and inside each other, we might say that they compromise, each in its turn, the interiority of the other" (9). I share Felman's view of the relation between literature and psychoanalysis, and that view guides my critical strategy.

29. I do not attempt to use psychoanalytic theory symmetrically in the chapters that follow, although all of my readings are psychoanalytically informed. The nature of my theoretical interventions varies from chapter to

chapter, as I try to respond to the interpretive requirements of the texts. Like Felman, I consider the boundary between fiction and psychoanalysis to be permeable, and I readily cross it, in the interpretive interests of both discourses.

30. While the narrative schema I propose is applicable to women's narratives, the historical development of modes and genres is different in female-authored texts, as are the specificities of their interaction. I plan to continue this project by studying eighteenth-century novels written by women, as well as male- and female-authored novels of the nineteenth and twentieth centuries. Essays that I have already published on the novels of Dickens and on Toni Morrison's *Beloved* can be seen as part of this larger effort. Of course, I also hope that others will be interested in pursuing lines of inquiry similar to those that I set out in the following chapters.

CHAPTER 1. DANIEL DEFOE AND THE GENDERED SUBJECT OF INDIVIDUALISM

1. See Joel Reed, "Nationalism and Geoculture in Defoe's History of Writing."

2. James Foster sees Defoe as "a traditionalist who is losing contact with his tradition and who must improvise in order to accommodate his faith to his Mandevillian fascination with the hubristic energy of commercialism" ("*Robinson Crusoe* and the Uses of the Imagination," 179).

3. For an elaboration of this argument, see particularly Richard Braverman, "Crusoe's Legacy," and Michael Seidel, *Robinson Crusoe, Island Myths, and the Novel.*

4. *Moll Flanders* is also shaped as spiritual autobiography, but the religious impulse seems more vestigial in that novel than it does in *Robinson Crusoe*. Because Moll reads her life in spiritual terms very rarely and only when she is in serious trouble, that tendency in her appears to be regressive. This third modal form seems all but absent from *Roxana*.

5. Defoe, *Robinson Crusoe of York*, 3. All subsequent references are to this edition, which will hereafter be cited in the text.

6. This sequence marks a development essential to the early economies of English and French islands. See Peter Hulme, *Colonial Encounters: Europe and the Native Caribbean, 1492–1797*, 185.

7. Foster makes a persuasive case for the double narration in his essay focusing on the importance of changing conceptualizations of the imagination, "*Robinson Crusoe* and the Uses of the Imagination."

8. Walter Benjamin discusses the way in which the "messianic time" of allegory is superseded by what he calls "homogeneous empty time": time with a presentness that is marked by calendar and clock (*Illuminations*, 261). Benedict Anderson analyzes the ways in which this shift in the conception of time is essential to the development of the mentality that enabled the "imagined political communities" of nations. He argues that the novel was a device for presenting simultaneity in homogeneous empty time (*Imagined*

Communities, 24–26). My argument is that *Robinson Crusoe* reflects just such a shift.

9. Crusoe's claim that he stops keeping his journal when he runs out of ink (69, 133) is apparently meant to disguise Defoe's change of narrative strategy, which emerges from the shift in perspective that I have described.

10. In this context, it is significant to note that for many years Crusoe's parrot is the sole "other" with whom he actively communicates and, trained as it is to call his name, it reflects Crusoe back to himself without affirming its own difference. On the one occasion when Crusoe does not recognize its voice, the momentary experience of its otherness threatens to overwhelm him.

11. The encounter of Crusoe and Friday is a paradigmatic scene of colonial discourse, as Hulme has indicated in *Colonial Encounters*. There, Hulme defines colonial discourse as "an ensemble of linguistically-based practices unified by their common deployment in the management of colonial relationships" and further explains: "Underlying the idea of colonial discourse is the presumption that during the colonial period large parts of the non-European world were produced for Europe through a discourse that imbricated sets of questions and assumptions, methods of procedure and analysis, and kinds of writing and imagery, normally separated out into the discrete areas of military strategy, political order, social reform, imaginative literature, personal memoir and so on" (2). He adds, "The Caribbean is particularly important in this discourse because of the encounter there between Europe and America, between civilization and savagery, and because it has been seen as the site of cannibalism: 'the mark of unregenerate savagery' " (3).

12. In *The Colonizer's Model of the World: Geographical Diffusionism and Eurocentric History*, J. M. Blaut defines "diffusionism" as the colonizer's model of the world, which projects both a permanent geographical center and a permanent periphery: a progressive and innovative Inside that is Europe, and a lagging and imitative Outside that is Africa, Asia, and America. Blaut argues that while diffusionism assumes Europe to have been more advanced and progressive both prior to and after 1492, it was Europe's geographical location that gave it primacy in the process of colonization before 1492. Its geographical location was also responsible for its success in the colonial period after 1492, which led to the selective modernization and development of Europe and the underdevelopment of Africa, Asia, and Latin America.

13. Psychoanalytic theorists have analyzed the construction of racial identities in terms similar to those implied by Defoe's representation of Crusoe and Friday's relationship. For example, Franz Fanon insists upon the connection between psychic development and cultural psychosis and grounds the "massive psychoexistential complex" of racism in the "subjective insecurity" of separation anxiety and the radical experience of fragmentation (*Black Skin, White Masks*, 55). Citing Lacan, Fanon argues that the white man is threatened by the black man with the destructuration of his bodily image, while the black man rejects the black Imaginary for a white ego ideal

and is doomed to seek from his white Other the fundamental recognition that is inevitably withheld (161). Homi Bhabha changes the site of othering in his extension of Fanon's Lacanian argument, but he does not disrupt the mirroring dynamic ("The Other Question: Difference, Discrimination, and the Discourse of Colonialism," 148–72). Insisting upon the ways in which stereotypical relations are based, for both the colonizer and the colonized, on an alienation *within* identity, he emphasizes not the relation of self and other, but the otherness of the self. The native subject, whom the colonizer defines as both harmlessly primitive and terrifyingly savage, serves in his judgment as a fetish object, which allows the assertion and disavowal of difference that threatens psychic wholeness. Both Fanon and Bhabha posit a racial dynamic that is universal and inevitable in its developmental grounding, while I try to make its historical context visible through my reading of its articulation in *Robinson Crusoe.* I discuss these issues in the context of an analysis of gender as well as race relations in "Redeeming History: Toni Morrison's *Beloved.*"

14. The substitution is made explicit when Friday chooses to accompany Crusoe to England instead of returning to his "nation" with his biological father.

15. Braverman argues in "Crusoe's Legacy" that in *Robinson Crusoe,* Defoe justifies the position that is taken by Locke and enacted in the legal settlement of 1688: that the son could not be deprived by the political father of the political sovereignty he has as a result of his inalienable rights and his possession of property. In Braverman's judgment, the novel shows how Crusoe creates and reproduces his political will through property gained independently of the father—through the accumulation of grain, which provides the foundation of natural sovereignty.

16. Anderson points out that the concept of the nation as sovereign emerged in an age when the Enlightenment and revolution were destroying the legitimacy of the divinely ordained, hierarchical dynastic realm (*Imagined Communities,* 6). In his judgment, the idea of nation became possible when three ideas lost their axiomatic grip on men's minds: that "a particular script-language offers privileged access to ontological truth precisely because it was an inseparable part of that truth"; that society was organized around huge centers, with monarchs who were distinguishable from other humans and who ruled through divine dispensation; and, finally, that cosmology and history were indistinguishable, with the origins of men and the world seen as identical (36).

17. This is the dilemma that Freud, writing from the perspective of the son, represents ahistorically as the Oedipus complex.

18. Christopher Flint points out that Defoe uses the conjugal family to establish normative models by which his characters differentiate themselves, and that he reinscribes—in the process—the domestic ideal which his characters flee. He argues, as I do, that Defoe's urge to define his characters required family background, at the same time that his desire to fantasize about the unbounded potential of the individual demanded the suppression

of familial discourse ("Orphaning the Family: The Role of Kinship in *Robinson Crusoe*," 382).

19. In "Matriarchal Mirror: Women and Capital in *Moll Flanders*," Lois Chabor approaches *Moll Flanders* from a Marxist, feminist perspective, examining the ways in which the novel reveals the problematic situation of women under capitalism. In a more recent Marxist essay, "Monstrous Generation: The Birth of Capital in Defoe's *Moll Flanders* and *Roxana*," Ann Louise Kibbie explores ways in which biological reproduction is bound up with the increase of capital in the two Defoe fictions that take women as their protagonists.

20. Juliet Mitchell argues that "In economically advanced societies, though the kinship exchange system still operates in a residual way, other forms of economic exchange—i.e. commodity exchange—dominate and class, not kinship structures prevail. It would seem that it is against a background of the *remoteness* of a kinship system that the ideology of the biological family comes into its own" (*Psychoanalysis and Feminism*, 378). Mitchell points out that while kinship relations were preserved among the aristocracy, the cult of the bourgeois family, which developed within the middle classes, was imposed upon the working classes in order to ensure the reproduction of the workforce through a higher birth and survival rate (379).

21. Defoe, *Moll Flanders*, 51. All subsequent references are to this edition, which will hereafter be cited in the text.

22. *Moll Flanders* provides a particular insight into the relation of the consciousness of individualism to this incest anxiety. In chapter 4, I examine the intrapsychic expression of this same anxiety.

23. Mitchell observes that if the family were not to be preserved in industrial society, the incest prohibition—with the compulsory exchange of women—would be unnecessary. "Under capitalism, the mass of mankind, propertyless and working socially together *en masse* for the first time in the history of civilization would be unlikely, *were it not for the preservation of the family*, to come into proximity with their kin and if they did, it wouldn't matter" (*Psychoanalysis and Feminism*, 380).

24. In *Eros and Civilization*, Marcuse coins the phrase "repressive desublimation," which seems appropriately to characterize the process that Defoe describes in both *Moll Flanders* and *Roxana*.

I propose in this book the notion of a "non-repressive sublimation": the sexual impulses, without losing their erotic energy, transcend their immediate object and eroticize normally non- and anti-erotic relationships between the individuals and between them and their environment. Conversely, one can speak of "repressive de-sublimation": release of sexuality in modes and forms which reduce and weaken erotic energy. In this process too, sexuality spreads into formerly tabooed dimensions and relations. However, instead of recreating these dimensions and relations in the images of the Pleasure Principle, the opposite tendency asserts itself: The Reality Principle extends its hold over Eros. The most telling illustration is provided by the methodical introduction of sexiness into business, politics, propaganda, etc. To the degree to which sexuality obtains a definite sales value or becomes a token of prestige and of playing according to the rules of the game, it is itself transformed into an instrument of social cohesion. Emphasis of this familiar trend may illuminate the depth of the gap which separates even the possibilities of liberation from the established state of affairs. (ix–x)

Of course, in *Moll Flanders* we see the early formation of "the state of affairs" that Marcuse perceives as fully developed.

25. In "Reification and the Consciousness of the Proletariat," Georg Lukács writes: "*Subjectively*—where the market economy has been fully developed—a man's activity becomes estranged from himself, it turns into a commodity which, subject to the non-human objectivity of the natural laws of society, must go its own way independently of man just like any consumer article" (87).

26. Again, to quote Lukács on the nature of the process of reification: "The essence of commodity-structure has often been pointed out. Its basis is that a relation between people takes on the character of a thing and thus acquires a 'phantom objectivity,' an autonomy that seems so strictly rational and all-embracing as to conceal every trace of its fundamental nature: the relation between people" ("Reification," 83). Lukács argues what Defoe seems to demonstrate: that the commodity structure penetrates all aspects of society and re-creates society in its own image. It effects the constitution of subjectivity, making the acquisition of value the primary aim of an ego that mediates between an external reality, which is composed of exploitable and quantifiable objects, and an internal reality, which must itself be instrumentalized in order to be productive. In the reifying process, wants are reencoded as needs, affectivity is crushed by rationality, and sexual desire is made to seek a material aim. Disengaged from the larger community, individuals define self-preservation as their primary goal, and they attempt to achieve it through their appropriation of nature and their unrelenting competition with others. Paradoxically, they also endeavor to preserve themselves through efforts of self-discipline and renunciation that "freeze the subject," as John Brenkman has pointed out, "in a self-domination that ideologically, and in practice, appears as freedom, self-sufficiency, and autonomy" (*Culture and Domination*, 182). The process of reification is especially difficult for women to sustain because it so deeply undermines normative roles that are fundamentally self-defining.

27. Defoe, *Roxana*, 40. All subsequent references are to this edition, which will hereafter be cited in the text.

28. Most recent feminist critics have seen Roxana's views (and therefore Defoe's) as protofeminist, while other critics have interpreted Roxana's feminist argument as proof of Defoe's condemnation of his protagonist. Robyn Wiegman points out an interesting irony of Roxana's position: as she tries to escape slave status, she solidifies her bondage to the patriarchal system through the masquerade of femininity that is implied by the commodification of her body ("Economies of the Body: Gendered Sites in *Robinson Crusoe* and *Roxana*," 38).

29. Particularly interesting in this context are the discussions of Roxana's

relation to Amy in Leo Braudy, "Daniel Defoe and the Anxieties of Auto-biography"; David Durant, "Roxana's Fictions," 167–68; Gary Hentzi, "Holes in the Heart: *Moll Flanders, Roxana,* and 'Agreeable Crime' "; and, most persuasively, Terry Castle, "Amy, Who Knew My Disease: A Psycho-sexual Pattern in Defoe's *Roxana.*"

30. One thinks, for example, of Richardson's *Clarissa,* with the split con-sciousness of Clarissa and Mrs. Sinclair (discussed later in the chapter), and of the madwoman in Jane Eyre's attic. The strategy of the double, introduced here by Defoe, pervades Romantic and Victorian literature, typifying the work of such diverse writers as Mary Shelley, Charlotte Brontë, Charles Dickens, Wilkie Collins, Robert Louis Stevenson, Bram Stoker, Edgar Allan Poe, and Nathaniel Hawthorne.

31. Braudy ("Daniel Defoe and the Anxieties of Autobiography"), Hentzi ("Holes in the Heart"), and Foster ("*Robinson Crusoe* and the Uses of the Imagination," 179) comment interestingly on the postmodern nature of De-foe's protagonists.

32. Raymond Williams distinguishes structures of feeling from ideology, finding in them "meanings and values as they are actually lived and felt" and "characteristic elements of impulse, restraint and tone: specifically ele-ments of consciousness and relationship" (*Marxism and Literature,* 132). Al-though the psychological resonance of this concept seems obvious, Williams himself never acknowledges or pursues it. In his essay "Forms of English Fiction in 1848," Williams discusses the ways in which dominant, residual, and emergent institutions and practices are discernible in the literary text.

33. In support, or at least in explanation, of my method, I quote Walter Benjamin: "Historicism contents itself with establishing a causal connection between various moments in history. But no fact that is a cause is for that very reason historical. It became historical posthumously, as it were, through events that may be separated from it by thousands of years. A historian who takes this as his point of departure stops telling the sequence of events like the beads of a rosary. Instead, he grasps the constellation which his own era has formed with a definite earlier one. Thus he establishes a conception of the present as 'the time of the now' which is shot through with chips of Messianic time" (*Illuminations,* 263).

34. In *The Analysis of the Self,* Kohut describes his theory as a revision of Freud's; but six years later, in *The Restoration of the Self,* he reduces Freudian theory to a simple theory of drives and represents his break with Freud as decisive.

35. Lacan and Lacanians have attacked American object-relations theory for its own entrapment in narcissistic fictions of the autonomous self, which are generated by the mirror stage.

36. Kohut, *The Analysis of the Self,* xv.

37. In Kohut's theory, the term "prepsychological" takes the place of "re-pression," and regressive experiences that are not conscious can be brought readily into consciousness.

38. The grandiose personality emerges at the end of the seventeenth

century with the tradition of the libertine, who seeks the freedom of the asocial, unconditioned, and, in this sense, the sublime experience. He is elaborated (as I argue in later chapters) in Richardson's Lovelace and in the gothic hero, beginning with Walpole's Manfred and Matthew Lewis's Ambrosio. In the nineteenth century, the tradition is broadened to include the Romantic hero—Heathcliff and Rochester, for example—and even resonates in such a late Victorian figure as George Eliot's Grandcourt. In Kohut's narcissistic individual, who can also be located in this historical lineage, the sublime experience, which seeks the impossible object of desire, takes the form of unconditioned, archaic merging.

39. Kohut lays out the analyst's role in this way in *The Analysis of the Self,* and then develops it extensively in *The Restoration of the Self.*

40. Kohut's good analyst effectively takes the place of the bad mother, repairing the narcissistic injuries that she has inflicted on the child by being inadequately empathic. Although Kohut sees empathy as central to the therapeutic process, he bases it in the empirical and analytic skills of the scientist and divorces it mainly from intuition and imaginative projection (e.g., *The Analysis of the Self,* 165, 175, 176, 191, 197). Further, although Kohut defines the empathic process as interactive, it is clear from his writings that it depends for its success upon the analyst's conceptualization and manipulation of materials presented by a directed patient.

41. Kohut, *The Analysis of the Self,* 3.

42. In *The Restoration of the Self,* Kohut argues, contradictorily, that the self-psychologist needs to blur self-other boundaries in the interests of achieving greater objectivity. He explains that Freud's theories, as opposed to his own, are not adequate to examine "phenomena that require for their observation and explanation a more broad-based scientific objectivity than that of the nineteenth-century scientist—an objectivity that includes the introspective-empathic observation and theoretical conceptualization of the participating self" (68).

43. Kohut is remarkably unconcerned about the extent to which his patient needs to become the therapist's "other" in order to be "cured." In his judgment, the therapist is readily able to control the countertransference through a "subtlety of understanding" (*The Analysis of the Self,* 176). Of course, the projection of readers onto fictive characters is similar to the countertransference of analysts, and it is an aspect of the fantastic mirroring dynamic.

44. Although I see Kohut as extreme in this regard, I will try to show how Freud and Lacan allow social assumptions to appropriate their radical insights—particularly in their treatments of gender difference.

CHAPTER 2. *CLARISSA* AND
THE PORNOGRAPHIC IMAGINATION

1. The odd contradictions that emerge from Watt's reading of *Clarissa* in *The Rise of the Novel* reflect the inadequacy of his model to account for the

fundamental relation that exists between the realistic and fantastic dimensions of the fiction. For example, without acknowledging the discrepancies, Watt represents Clarissa both as pathological and as the unwitting and innocent victim of a pathological culture, as ontologically unfettered and as hopelessly bound. He describes her as perversely playing masochist to Lovelace's sadist (unconsciously courting sexual violation as well as death [232]), at the same time that he affirms her as "the heroic representation of all that is free and positive in the new individualism" (222). And although he recognizes that issues of sexuality are absolutely central to the text, he observes that Clarissa's "triumph is one in which her sex is irrelevant and looks forward to the new and inward ethical sanction which an individualistic society requires" (225). Finally, because Watt does not wish to align a novel said to articulate "the highest moral and literary standards of its day" (219) with the "degraded" sensationalist, minor fictions of the time, he elides the formal differences that distinguish *Clarissa* from *Pamela*, and names both novels as realistic even though he identifies in Richardson's "sado-masochistic" text the theme of the persecuted maiden that both Sade and the Romantic tradition inherit (231).

2. See Terry Castle, *Clarissa's Ciphers: Meaning and Disruption in Richardson's* Clarissa; William Warner, *Reading* Clarissa: *The Struggles of Interpretation;* and Terry Eagleton, *The Rape of* Clarissa: *Writing, Sexuality, and Class Struggle in Samuel Richardson.*

3. Edmund Leites believes that the sexual division of labor that allowed women, with their purity and absence of animality, to take over the responsibility of moral constancy and enabled men to claim the power of often aggressive sexual initiation was mutually and equally beneficial to both parties (*The Puritan Conscience and Modern Sexuality,* 121). In *Hard Core: Power, Pleasure and the Frenzy of the Visible,* Linda Williams rejects the idea that this dynamic denotes a simple, complicitous balance of power in contemporary society. Examining sadomasochistic pornography in which women pretend to be coerced into sex by the phallic dominator, Williams points out that although the woman who plays at being the good girl in order to get the bad girl's pleasure does defeat the system that condemns women for acting out their desire, she cannot ultimately defeat the power of the phallus (209). I argue that despite itself, *Clarissa* suggests just such a conclusion.

4. In *Reading* Clarissa, Warner provides both a useful summary of the revisions that Richardson made in response to the interpretations of contemporary readers and an overview of subsequent contestations over the novel's meanings.

5. The two first significant deconstructive readings of *Clarissa* placed the novel in its own historical and literary context: John Preston, in a chapter of *The Created Self: The Reader's Role in Eighteenth-Century Fiction,* and Leo Braudy, in "Penetration and Impenetrability in *Clarissa.*" The books that Warner, Eagleton, and Castle wrote on the novel themselves became part of a discourse within academic feminism about gendered reading and writing. So, for example, Warner—who thanks Frances Ferguson in his acknowledgments

"for helping me to see the meaning of my harshness and injustice to Clarissa" (xiii)—is viewed by both Eagleton and Castle as unabashedly belonging to the rapist's party. Eagleton describes himself as feminist in his approach, but Elaine Showalter characterizes his as a "phallic feminism" that "seems like another raid on the resources of the feminine in order to modernize male dominance" ("Critical Cross-Dressing: Male Feminists and the Woman of the Year," 146).

6. Not psychoanalytically oriented but wanting a concept that suggested the interaction of the social and the personal or affective, Raymond Williams defined structures of feeling as "meanings and values as they are actively lived and felt[,] . . . characteristic elements of consciousness and relationships: not feeling against thought, but thought as felt and feeling as thought: practical consciousness of a present kind, in a living and inter-relating continuity. We are then defining these elements as a 'structure': as a set, with specific internal relations, at once interlocking and in tension" (*Marxism and Literature*, 132). In a similar vein, Franz Fanon insists on the connection between psychic development and cultural psychosis when he writes of the "massive psychoexistential complex" of racism that is grounded in the "subjective insecurity of separation anxiety and the radical experience of fragmentation (*Black Skin, White Masks*, 55). In *Difference and Pathology,* Sander Gilman also gives pathological attitudes toward difference a developmental root. He argues that the deep structure of the stereotype originates in the individuation process when the child projects a good and a bad self in order to reflect its own sense of control or lack of control over the external world. These crude mental representations "perpetuate a needed sense of the difference between the 'self' and the 'object,' which becomes the 'other.' " The complexity of the stereotype derives from the social context in which it is elaborated (18).

7. Although I am describing the pornographic imagination here as violent and sadistic, I mean to suggest not that pornography inevitably takes this form in the realistic mode, but rather that this was the dominant form of the pornographic narrative at this specific historical moment. The pornographic imagination changes as the narrative modes of realism and the fantastic change, all in response to shifting social norms. Our own reconceptualizations of pornographic genres—and, indeed, changes in pornography itself—are an obvious part of this dynamic.

8. Although the prosecution and repression of books for obscenity began in England in the seventeenth century, the term "pornography" does not appear until 1857. Michael Ganner argues for the overlapping constitutive histories of the genres of pornography and gothic beginning with the public's response to Matthew Lewis's novel *The Monk* at the end of the eighteenth century (see "Genres for the Prosecution: Pornography and the Gothic").

9. In his classic essay in *Puritanism and Revolution*, "Clarissa Harlowe and Her Times," Christopher Hill details the ways in which Richardson's presentation of the relationships within the Harlowe family is faithful to historical circumstances. Exploring the inherent contradiction between the Pu-

ritan belief in the integrity of the individual and the male-centered ideology of possessive individualism, Hill observes that "respect for Clarissa's integrity led [Richardson] to push the Puritan code forward to the point at which its flaw was completely revealed, at which it broke down as a standard of conduct for this world" (388).

10. Richardson, *Clarissa or The History of a Young Lady*, 48. All subsequent references are to this edition, which will hereafter be cited in the text.

11. Of course, these are the same alternatives that Freud defines for women who are to be seen by his society as respectable.

12. In his essay on *Clarissa*, Leo Braudy analyzed the polarization of Clarissa's and Lovelace's values in terms of Richardson's frequent use of the terms "impenetrable" and "penetrability": "Poles of penetration and impenetrability express Richardson's main theme—the efforts of individuals to discover and define themselves by their efforts to penetrate, control and even destroy others, while remaining unreachable themselves" ("Penetration and Impenetrability in *Clarissa*," 6).

13. It is interesting to note that while Leslie Fiedler (in *Love and Death in the American Novel*, 62) and Mario Praz (in *The Romantic Agony*, 97–109) both identified *Clarissa* as *the* foundational gothic text, they did so by centering Clarissa as the masochistic gothic heroine. This is the same argument that Michelle A. Masse has much more recently made in her study *In the Name of Love: Women, Masochism, and the Gothic*. My argument is that Lovelace's narrative is conceptualized predominantly in the fantastic mode while Clarissa is represented primarily in the mode of realism.

14. The paradoxical struggle of the self to achieve both independence and recognition was conceptualized in its fantastic form by Hegel in *Phenomenology of Spirit*. Here, the self that struggles to know itself as a separate and autonomous entity needs to be affirmed through the recognition of an other whom it must also negate if its own integrity is to be maintained. The conflictual dynamic resists mutuality and moves toward domination and what Hegel describes as the master-slave relation. This solipsistic project of self-consciousness is elaborated as a developmental process in psychoanalytic theory with its emphasis on intrapsychic rather than intersubjective development; on issues of separation, individuation, and autonomy; and on the self that poses as omnipotent in order to defend against its fears of powerlessness. Whether theoretical narratives of this sort refer to the child's difficult disentanglement from the mother, or to the endless repetition of the self-alienation of the mirror-stage; whether they are couched in the language of introjection and projection, or in one of appropriation and accommodation, they all emphasize the necessary precariousness of boundaries that separate inside from outside and self from other, and they all address the inevitable slippage of balanced connectedness into the imbalances of the power relation. While various psychoanalytic accounts of this dynamic have presented themselves as gender-neutral, Jessica Benjamin has provided a rereading of the Hegelian dialectic through a feminist extension of object-relations theory. She first developed her reinterpretation of the master-slave

relation in "The Bonds of Love: Rational Violence and Erotic Domination," and then significantly elaborated on her theory of erotic domination in *The Bonds of Love: Psychoanalysis, Feminism, and the Problem of Domination*, a book that has been important to the conceptualization of my argument in this chapter.

15. In *In the Name of Love*, Masse contends that the gothic woman inevitably plays masochist to the male sadist. Building her argument from a close reading of "A Child Is Being Beaten" and other of Freud's essays, she provides the most detailed reading to date of gothic fiction in this context. While extremely useful, her argument does inadvertently suggest the limitations that a strict Freudian interpretation of this dynamic imposes on the texts and the society that it is used to read. For one thing, Masse tends to collapse social and fictive "realities"; for another, her definition of female masochism necessarily cuts quite different texts to fit the same pattern. And finally, through my reading of Lovelace, I want to disagree with Masse's strict identification of masochism with femininity and of sadism with masculinity.

16. My discussion of the deep structure of gender complementarity that is suggested by *Clarissa* in its realist narrative is similar in its broadest outlines to the structure that Jessica Benjamin describes in *The Bonds of Love*. It is the differences in male and female patterns of differentiation that, in Benjamin's judgment, associate sadism with masculinity and masochism with femininity, producing relationships of erotic domination. In her narrative, male individuality is produced in a context of "false differentiation" that results from the boy's rejection of the mother and his subsequent perception of the other as object rather than subject. This complements the girl's inability to accept her own agency—a result of her father's disidentification from her in the rapprochement stage, which replays his disidentification from his own mother—and her subsequent willingness to offer recognition without expecting it in return (78). Benjamin observes, "As long as the father stands for subjectivity and desire at the level of culture, woman's desire will always have to contend with his monopoly and the devaluation of femininity it implies" (123).

17. Throughout this analysis of Lovelace, I am dependent on Jessica Benjamin's discussion of aggression, fantasy, and sexuality in "Sympathy for the Devil: Notes on Sexuality and Aggression, with Special Reference to Pornography" in *Like Subjects, Love Objects: Essays on Recognition and Sexual Difference* (175–211).

18. In *The Rise of the Egalitarian Family*, Randolph Trumbach discusses the ways in which child-rearing practices of this period created a division between boys and girls that had far-reaching implications for adult heterosexual relations. "The extent to which any man could associate closely with women and children was severely limited by the means by which masculine identity was forged. For separation from, and denigration of, women and children were crucial to the formation of a boy's gender identity in childhood and to the development of heterosexual behavior and the internalization of the homosexual taboo in adolescence" (238). He indicates that the competi-

tion of public schools "no doubt produced men of independent self-assurance but . . . men of impoverished hearts" (259). Finally, he argues that "independence and aggression, rather than tenderness and attachment were the bases on which men built their identities as males and through which they channelled their sexual behavior" (282–83).

19. In 1910, in "A Special Type of Object Choice Made by Men," Freud commented on the result of this form of socialization: "A restriction has thus been laid upon the object-choice. The sensual feeling that has remained active seeks only objects evoking no reminder of the incestuous persons forbidden to it; the impression made by someone who seems deserving of high estimation leads, not to a sensual excitation, but to feelings of tenderness which remain erotically ineffectual. . . . Where such men love they have no desire and where they desire they cannot love" (62).

20. In *Hard Core*, Linda Williams writes about film pornography that has traditionally offered a myth of sexual pleasure from the perspective of men who have the power to exploit and objectify the sexuality of women (22). She suggests that hard-core films seek to overcome the invisibility of the site of women's pleasure by identifying the involuntary paroxysm of female orgasm as the "thing" itself, reading it as the sign both of sexual pleasure and of sexual difference. At the same time, she argues, this effort of identification can be seen as a way of asserting the fundamental sameness of male and female pleasure in the progression to climax (49–50). In "The Blind Spot of an Old Dream of Symmetry," Luce Irigaray writes: "like the scientific, gynecological speculum, this camera probes the hidden secrets of the female body and female pleasure, and like the mirror-speculum, it ends up staring at its own reflection, frustrated in the 'nothing to see' of women" (54).

21. Linda Williams observes, "Pornography as a genre wants to be about sex. On close inspection, however, it always proves to be more about gender" (*Hard Core*, 267). Later she explains that pornography is not just one thing but "sexual fantasy, genre, culture, and erotic visibility all operating together" (270).

22. James Grantham Turner has written about this multifaceted aspect of the libertine tradition in "The Libertine Sublime: Love and Death in Restoration England" and "Lovelace and the Paradoxes of Libertinism," as has Peter Hughes, in "War within Doors: Erotic Heroism and the Implosion of Texts." I also found useful Richard S. Randall's discussion of the infantile nature of the pornographic imagination in *Freedom and Taboo: Pornography and the Politics of a Self Divided*. In her essay "Don Juan or Loving to Be Able To," in *Powers of Horror*, Julia Kristeva observes, "Indeed, nothing is ever said about Don Juan's mother, and one may surmise that the absolute of the beauty that excites him continually is finally none but SHE: primal, inaccessible, prohibited" (201).

23. Jessica Benjamin writes: "Like the oedipal symbolization of the mother as either a lost paradise or a dangerous siren, the denial of her sexual organs makes her always either more or less than human" (*Bonds of Love*, 166–67).

24. Judith Wilt, in "He Could Go No Farther: A Modest Proposal about Lovelace and Clarissa," was the first to analyze the centrality of Mrs. Sinclair in this scene. Although she suggests the way in which Mrs. Sinclair works as a "double" for Lovelace, she does not explore the maternal resonance of that relationship.

25. In "The Dread of Woman: Observations on a Specific Difference in the Dread Felt by Men and Women Respectively for the Opposite Sex," Karen Horney observes: "In sexual life itself we see how the simple craving of love which drives men to women is often overshadowed by their overwhelming inner compulsion to prove their manhood again and again to themselves and others. A man of this type in its more extreme form has therefore one interest only: to conquer" (359).

26. In *Masochism: An Interpretation of Coldness and Cruelty*, Gilles Deleuze explores the roles of the male sadist and the male masochist. Seeing them as separate, he describes the male sadist as seeking the repudiation of the mother, from whom he wishes to differentiate himself, and acceptance by the father and the phallic law. The male masochist, on the other hand, seeks fusion with the mother and subversion of the phallic law (109–10). In her discussion of Deleuze, Linda Williams disagrees that these are separate roles, either in practice or in fantasy. Instead, she suggests, sexual identity is an oscillation between male and female subject positions, held simultaneously. According to her argument, male and female subjects experience identificatory relations with both the father and the mother, and those gender-inflected forms of desire interrelate in one individual in both the sadist's control and the masochist's abandon (*Hard Core*, 215). It seems to me that without full consciousness, Richardson projects Lovelace's character in this bisexual mode, encouraging an unusual degree of oscillation between male and female positions in the reader's identification with him. It is this that so frustrated Richardson in his attempts to make Lovelace an unsympathetic villain, particularly to his large, even predominantly female audience.

27. Jessica Benjamin observes that "In breaking the identification with and dependency on mother, the boy is in danger of losing his capacity for mutual recognition altogether. The emotional attunement and bodily harmony that characterized his infantile exchange with mother now threaten his identity. He is, of course, able cognitively to accept the principle that the other is separate, but without the experience of empathy and shared feeling that can unite separate subjectivities. Instead the other, especially the female other, is related to as object. When this relationship with the other as object is generalized, rationality substitutes for affective exchange with the other" (*Bonds of Love*, 76). It is my contention that the novel maps Lovelace's effort to retain this connection at the same time that he continually undercuts it with his efforts at an erotic domination that marks the intensification of male anxiety and defensiveness against the mother. With Clarissa's withdrawal— with his destruction of the possibility of mutuality—there is no longer an object for his sadism, as there is no longer hope for his affective life.

28. In *The Ego and the Id*, Freud explores the way in which the superego,

becoming "super-moral," "become[s] as cruel as only the id can be" (56), when it turns against the ego. Under certain circumstances of melancholia, "[w]hat is now holding sway in the super-ego is, as it were, a pure culture of the death instinct, and in fact it often enough succeeds in driving the ego into death, if the latter does not fend off its tyrant in time by the change round into mania" (54–55).

29. In *Masochism in Sex and Society,* Theodor Reich observes that an external audience is "a structural necessity" if the exhibitionism of the Christian martyr is to be satisfied (197). He also suggests that the identification of the masochistic martyr with the suffering Christ implies "an utter negation of all phallic values" (198). While this would appear to be true of the male martyr, the dephallicizing gesture seems to be more ambiguous in the case of the female. Although Clarissa might be said to be androgynous in her identification with Christ, she is, as the bride of Christ and the Father's daughter, clearly marked as secondary in the divine hierarchy.

30. In his important book *The Romantic Sublime: Studies in the Structure and Psychology of Transcendence,* Thomas Weiskel observes that "In the history of literary consciousness, the sublime revives as God withdraws from an immediate participation in the experience of men. The secondary or problematic sublime is pervaded by the nostalgia and the uncertainty of minds involuntarily secular—minds whose primary experience is shaped by their knowledge and perception of secondary causes" (3–4). Noting that "the sublime was an antidote to the boredom that increased so astonishingly in the eighteenth century," Weiskel adds: "Boredom masks uneasiness, and intense boredom exhibits the signs of the most basic of modern anxieties, the anxiety of nothingness, or absence. In its more energetic renditions, the sublime is a kind of homeopathic therapy, a cure of uneasiness by means of the stronger, more concentrated—but momentary—anxiety involved in astonishment and terror" (18).

CHAPTER 3. (W)HOLES AND NOSES

An earlier version of this chapter was published in *Literature and Psychology: A Journal of Psychoanalytic and Cultural Criticism* 41.3 (1995): 44–79.

1. Again, Ian Watt's view is significant, since it has been extremely influential. Watt did not want to group *Tristram Shandy* with the "degraded sentimental or gothic fictions" of its day, but was firm in his belief that despite his marginality, Sterne was a master of realism, uniquely capable of reconciling Richardson's "realism of presentation" with Fielding's "realism of assessment." Watt insisted that if Sterne had applied his skills "to the usual purposes of the novel, [he] would probably have been the supreme figure among eighteenth-century novelists." Because he "turned his irony against many of the narrative methods which the new genre had so lately developed," however, he produced only a parody of the novel, excluding himself from the great tradition while becoming a chance precursor of modernism through his subversive treatment of time (*The Rise of the Novel,* 291–92).

Following Watt, Michael McKeon finds Sterne irrelevant to the dialectical construction of the realistic novel that originates, in his judgment, with Richardson's *Pamela* and Fielding's *Joseph Andrews*. McKeon refers to *Tristram Shandy* only once in *The Origins of the English Novel, 1600–1740*, when he observes, with interesting ambiguity: "The implications of the formal breakthrough of the 1740s are pursued with such feverish intensity over the next two decades that after *Tristram Shandy* . . . the young genre settles down to a more deliberate and studious recapitulation of the same ground, this time for the next two centuries" (410).

2. In *Problems of Dostoevsky's Poetics*, Bakhtin importantly links the fantastic narrative to the tradition of Menippean satire that extends backward to the Socratic dialogue. That tradition achieves a kind of apogee with the dominance of the carnivalesque tradition in the Renaissance and, although it loses its communal base in the seventeenth century, it goes on to become a dominant influence on the novel: on Swift and Fielding in the eighteenth century and then on such writers as Dickens, Dostoevsky, and Gogol. But although he mentions the connection of Menippean satire to Sterne, Bakhtin does not explore the relation further (156–59).

3. *The Castle of Otranto* was published in 1764; *Tristram Shandy* was published over the years 1759 to 1767.

4. In the first chapter of *The Philosophical Irony of Laurence Sterne*—my book about *Tristram Shandy*—I examine the ways in which the novel provides a critique of Locke's epistemology.

5. For Jurgen Klein ("Laurence Sterne's Novel of Consciousness"), Sterne marks a turning point in the English novel from a subject/object opposition to a subjectivist epistemology that connects "selves," "identities," and "world construction." According to Klein, "Our contemporary definition of 'identity' in philosophy and sociology cannot attain Sterne's intellectual level" (1544).

6. Writing of the primal fantasies that Freud described, J. Laplanche and J. B. Pontalis observe:

> If we consider the themes which can be recognized in primal phantasies (primal scene, castration, seduction), the striking thing is that they have one trait in common: they are all related to the origins. Like collective myths, they claim to provide a representation of and a "solution" to whatever constitutes a major enigma for the child. Whatever appears to the subject as a reality of such a type as to require an explanation or "theory," these phantasies dramatise into the primal moment or original point of departure of a history. In the "primal scene," it is the origin of the subject that is represented; in seduction phantasies, it is the origin or emergence of sexuality; in castration phantasies, the origin of the distinction between the sexes. ("Primal Phantasies," 332)

7. Sterne, *Tristram Shandy*, 4. All subsequent references are to this edition, which will hereafter be cited in the text.

8. It is fascinating that John Paul Hunter ("Clocks, Calendars, and Names: The Troubles of Tristram and the Aesthetics of Uncertainty") and Richard Macksey (" 'Alas, Poor Yorick': Sterne Thoughts") assiduously pursue this

issue of Tristram's conception and premature birth by trying to figure out who Tristram's "real" father might have been, without seeing the gender implications of the problem that Sterne sets. Only Calvin Thomas ("*Tristram Shandy's* Consent to Incompleteness: Discourse, Disavowal, Disruption"), in his fine Lacanian reading of the novel, understands that the question is as unimportant for Sterne as it is for Lacan. While Thomas recognizes that it is the main project of the Shandy males to deny the place of women in procreation, and therefore in the production of the male subject, he sharply distinguishes Sterne as a protofeminist from the misogynistic Tristram. In this, his position is diametrically opposed to that of Ruth Perry ("Words for Sex: The Verbal-Sexual Continuum in *Tristram Shandy*"), who provides an early and preliminary feminist Lacanian reading of the novel (see note 11). While I agree with Thomas that Sterne represents the Shandy males as misogynistic, I don't agree that Sterne's own views are completely different from those he represents. Rather, I find Sterne himself participating in and therefore justifying—at conscious and unconscious levels, both formally and thematically—positions that he also attempts to soften through irony and humor.

9. Sterne humorously supports the hint of Tristram's illegitimacy by having a *bend sinister*—"this vile mark of illegitimacy"—drawn across the coat of arms on his coach, instead of the respectable *bend dexter* (237).

10. The homunculus theory, which had some adherents in the seventeenth century, was as outdated at the time that Sterne wrote *Tristram Shandy* as was Robert Filmer's theory of patriarchalism, to which Walter also subscribes. Although Sterne's use of the theory obviously serves a comic purpose in this context, and is used to support Sterne's view of Walter's misogyny, it is also consonant with the gender anxiety that saturates the text on unconscious as well as on conscious levels.

11. In their feminist readings of the text, Leigh A. Ehlers ("Mrs. Shandy's 'Lint and Basilicon': The Importance of Women in *Tristram Shandy*") and Ruth Faurot ("Mrs. Shandy Observed") have attempted to save Sterne from accusations of misogyny by reading Mrs. Shandy as a strong presence and a viable alternative to the Shandy males. Clearly, I do not find their arguments persuasive. Perry ("Words for Sex") and Thomas ("*Tristram Shandy's* Consent to Incompleteness") also place the question of Sterne's attitude toward gender in the context of his being or not being a misogynist. For Perry, the answer is yes—for Thomas, no. Perry emphasizes the fact that all the women in *Tristram Shandy* are characterized by their desire for the phallus; Thomas reads Sterne as comprehending the way in which men displace their anxiety onto women and, for this reason, distinguishes him sharply from Tristram. I argue that Sterne participates, with Lacan and Freud, in the displacement of anxiety that he is able also to describe with real acuteness.

12. In "The Bodily Encounter with the Mother," Luce Irigaray writes eloquently of the way in which castration fear and the oedipal myth conceal the severance of the umbilical cord, and "[a] hole in the texture of language corresponds to the forgetting of the scar of the navel" (41).

13. In "Mourning and Melancholia," Freud distinguishes between the conscious process of mourning, in which the libido is slowly detached from the lost love object until the ego is free and uninhibited, and the unconscious process of melancholia, which marks not the withdrawal of libido but rather an identification of the ego with the abandoned object. In "A Poetics of Psychoanalysis: The Lost Object—Me," Nicolas Abraham and Maria Torok develop Freud's theory of melancholia, describing an "encryptment" of the lost object that ultimately supplants the subject and "carries the ego as its mask" (5). Finally, in *Black Sun: Depression and Melancholia*, Julia Kristeva describes melancholia as "an archaic expression of an unsymbolizeable, unnameable, narcissistic wound, so precocious that no outside agent can be used as referent" (12). I discuss melancholia at length in chapter 4 on Walpole.

14. It is interesting to consider the way in which Freud writes a "Sternean" version of the rapprochement period—a version without women—even as he attempts to understand the full gender complexity of this moment of psychic development. In *The Ego and the Id*, he suggests that behind the ego-ideal "there lies hidden an individual's first and most important identification with the father in his own personal pre-history." He then adds: "Perhaps it would be better to say 'with the parents'; for before a child has arrived at definite knowledge of the difference between the sexes, *the lack of a penis*, it does not distinguish in value between its father and its mother." But he swerves again as he adds: "In order to simplify my presentation I shall discuss only identification with the father" (31). This, of course, is what he goes on to do, and the mother, like Tristram's mother, is erased again.

15. In *The Ego and the Id*, Freud describes the relation of the ego to the id with a similar metaphor: "like a man on horseback, who has to hold in check the superior strength of the horse. . . . Often a rider, if he is not to be parted from his horse, is obliged to guide it where it wants to go; so in the same way the ego is in the habit of transforming the id's will into action as if it were its own" (19). One can also define the hobbyhorsical function as one that mediates between Lacan's Symbolic and his Imaginary.

16. In *Tristram Shandy*, Wolfgang Iser interestingly develops his discussion of the hobbyhorse in terms of game theory, referring both to Richard Lanham's early study, *Tristram Shandy: The Games of Pleasure*, and to Roger Caillois's *Man, Play, and Games*. Here I draw on the work of D. W. Winnicott, who explores the centrality of transitional phenomena in helping the infant to accomplish the primary process of individuation and the adult to continue the endless project of mediation between interior and exterior realities. "This intermediate area of experience, unchallenged in respect of its belonging to inner or external (shared) reality, constitutes the greater part of the infant's experience, and throughout life is retained in the intense experiencing that belongs to the arts and to religion and to imaginative living, and to creative scientific work" (*Playing and Reality*, 14). As Winnicott points out, the illusion that represents the compromise of this transitional state "becomes the hallmark of madness when an adult puts too powerful a claim on the credulity

of others, forcing them to acknowledge a sharing of illusion that is not their own" (13). This is, of course, the problem posed by the hobbyhorse.

17. The exception in his family, according to Tristram, is his great-aunt Dinah, "who, about sixty years ago, was married and got with child by the coachman" (49). Thumbing her nose at class difference and rejecting a central mandate of gender difference by following the urgings of her own desire, Dinah stands as a kind of phallic woman in the text.

18. The Lacanian resonance is made all the more appropriate by Macksey's report both of Lacan's own statement that *"Tristram Shandy* est le roman le plus analytique de la litterature universelle" and of his appreciation "of the peculiar way in which all of the 'characters' in the novel constitute themselves as 'modes of discourse' and the equally peculiar way in which the novel constitutes itself around a notorious 'lack' " (" 'Alas, Poor Yorick,' " 1007). Neither Macksey nor other Lacanian critics of Sterne have noted or discussed the specifically phallic nature of the hobbyhorse.

19. Interestingly, Lacan seems to share the opinion of the "world" in viewing circumcision as a form of castration: "Feminine sexuality appears as the effort of a *jouissance* wrapped in its own contiguity (for which all circumcision might represent the symbolic rupture) to be *realized in the envy* of desire, which castration releases in the male by giving him its signifier in the phallus" ("Guiding Remarks for a Congress on Feminine Sexuality," 97).

20. My reading of Lacan (through Sterne) is similar to the feminist readings of the phallus-penis relation in Jane Gallop's "Beyond the Phallus" and Judith Butler's "Lesbian Phallus and the Morphological Imaginary." In "The Lacanian Phallus," Kaja Silverman offers the most impressively detailed feminist critique of Lacan's position, explaining that whether the phallus functions in its idealized Imaginary capacity, holding out the possibility of a jubilant *méconnaisance* to the male subject, or in its veiled symbolic function, signifying what every subject has surrendered to language, it is dependent upon the erect penis. "As should be evident by now, there is a good deal of slippage in Lacan not only between the phallus and the penis, but between the phallus in its symbolic capacity and the phallus in its imaginary capacity. The erect penis seems to represent both, in the one case as that which no fully constituted subject can any longer 'be,' and which is consequently 'veiled' or lacking, and in the other as that which only the male subject can 'have' " (97). I hope it will be obvious from this and subsequent sections of my argument that while I wish to make explicit the connection between a Sternian perspective of Lacanian theory and some feminist readings of the same material, I am not suggesting that Sterne is himself a protofeminist. I am interested in deconstructing the differences between theory and fiction, as well as strict definitions of the meaning of gendered writing and reading.

21. Freud's observation in "Humour," that narcissism triumphs in humor, is relevant here: "The ego refuses to be distressed by the provocation of reality, to let itself be compelled to suffer. It insists that it cannot be affected

by the traumas of the external world; it shows, in fact, that such traumas are no more than occasions for it to gain pleasure." He also points out: "In humour, the super-ego repudiates reality and serves an illusion. Its liberating gesture means 'Look! Here is the world, which seems so dangerous! It is nothing but a game for children . . . just worth making a jest about' " (162, 160).

22. In this Sterne is clearly to be distinguished from Lacan. As Gallop suggests, in "Beyond the Phallus," "The Lacanians' desire clearly to separate *phallus* from *penis*, to control the meaning of the signifier *phallus*, is precisely symptomatic of their desire to have the phallus, that is, their desire to be at the center of language, at its origin. And their inability to control the meaning of the word *phallus* is evidence of what Lacan calls symbolic castration" (127).

23. A dominant aspect of Julia Kristeva's project has been to define, conceptualize, and foreground preoedipal and prelinguistic space. For example, in "Revolution in Poetic Language," she deploys her concepts of the maternal chora, the semiotic, and the thetic to explore the ways in which language resists intelligibility and signification in a dynamic interaction of symbolic and presymbolic stages. In "The Bodily Encounter with the Mother," Irigaray explores the ways in which we can connect, through the nonmeanings of prosody, rhythm, and polyvalency, to the meaning of what she calls "the Thing": the lost body of the mother whom we have killed in order to annul a debt that allows no reciprocity.

24. Julia Kristeva, "Woman's Time."

25. "What gives some likelihood to what I am arguing, that is, that the woman knows nothing of this *jouissance*, is that ever since we've been begging them—last time I mentioned women analysts—begging them on our knees to try to tell us about it, well, not a word! We've never managed to get anything out of them" (Lacan, "God and the Jouissance of the Woman," 146).

26. Lacan, "God and the Jouissance of the Woman," 142.

27. Lacan, "God and the Jouissance of the Woman," 143.

28. Lacan, "A Love Letter," 155.

29. Lacan, "God and the Jouissance of the Woman," 147.

30. Interestingly, Lacan condemns Melanie Klein's description of the child's fantasy of the penis/breast as "monstrous" and vehemently rejects her attribution of the power of the phallus to the maternal body, scornfully referring, for example, to her "persistent failure to acknowledge that the Oedipal fantasies which she locates in the maternal body originate from the reality presupposed by the Name of the Father" ("Guiding Remarks for a Congress," 90). At the same time, as Silverman points out, Lacan suggests in "Four Fundamental Concepts" that the phallus may not always be the primary or even the earliest signifier of desire; and in "Seminaire X," he confers foundational status upon the breast as a part object also suggesting the primal significance of the gaze and the voice, both experienced initially within the maternal domain ("The Lacanian Phallus," 112–13).

31. Dennis W. Allen ("Sexuality/Textuality in *Tristram Shandy*") argues that Sterne invaginates his text, but it will be clear that in my view the text, like its author, is ambisexual and complexly gendered.

32. Hans Loewald writes, "The more we understand about primitive mentality—which constitutes a deeper layer of advanced mentality—the harder it becomes to escape the idea that its implicit sense of and quest for irrational nondifferentiation of subject and object contains a truth of its own, granted that this other truth fits badly with our relational view and quest for objectivity" ("The Waning of the Oedipus Complex," 772).

33. Julia Kristeva suggests a "reformulation of the moral imperative . . . lead[ing] to an ethics which would not be one of repression," in the context of the narcissistic subject whom she calls "the-subject-in-process": "The subject-in-process is always in a state of contesting the law, either with the force of violence, of aggressivity, of the death-drive, or with the other side of this force: pleasure and jouissance" ("An Interview with Julia Kristeva," 8).

34. Sterne, *A Sentimental Journey*, 117.

CHAPTER 4. HORACE WALPOLE
AND THE NIGHTMARE OF HISTORY

1. According to W. S. Lewis, Walpole, who saw his century as wanting only cold reason, was "bored" with the "insipidity" of Richardson and the coarseness of both Fielding and Smollett (*Horace Walpole*, 161). In *The Life of Horace Walpole*, Stephen Gwynn, another of Walpole's biographers, observes that "Walpole valued Shakespeare, recognized the greatness of his friend, Thomas Gray, and considered Pope to have set the standard of his time. All the rest of what was greatest in the literature of his age, he either ridiculed or tolerated. Fielding pleased him; but he condescended to Fielding much as he condescended to Garrick; Sterne he chose to despise" (145). For Walpole, Gwynn adds, "the natural" had been exhausted—and none was guiltier of the crime than Richardson, whose writing he found "insupportable" (192).

2. Because Walpole feared the critical response to his fiction, he published its first edition anonymously, presenting himself in its preface as the translator of an Italian text that—"discovered in the library of an ancient catholic family in the north of England" and printed in Naples in 1529—described events that happened in Italy between 1095 and 1243 (*The Castle of Otranto*, 3). All subsequent references to the novel are to this edition, which will hereafter be cited in the text. It is worth noting that by now, Walpole's fiction has passed through more than 115 printings.

3. The publication of Charles Maturin's *Melmouth the Wanderer* in 1820 is generally seen as marking the end of the gothic tradition. Issues of classification have been much complicated by the use of the term "gothic" by various critics to include not simply this late-eighteenth- and early-nineteenth-century genre, with its significant use of the supernatural, but all fictions and even films that share a predominantly psychological and subjectivist

focus. Among the more influential of these critics are William Patrick Day, *In the Circles of Fear and Desire: A Study of Gothic Fantasy;* Eugenia C. De-Lamotte, *Perils of the Night: A Feminist Study of Nineteenth-Century Gothic;* Maggie Kilgour, *The Rise of the Gothic Novel;* Michelle A. Masse, *In the Name of Love: Women, Masochism, and the Gothic;* David Punter, *The Literature of Terror: A History of Gothic Fictions from 1765 to the Present Day;* and Anne Williams, *Art of Darkness: A Poetics of Gothic.* Throughout this book—as elsewhere in my writing—I follow Rosemary Jackson (*Fantasy: The Literature of Subversion*) in defining the gothic as a historically shaped genre within the fantastic mode: a mode that is narrated through a range of genres that produce, regulate, and structure desire.

4. Sublimation is a process "postulated by Freud to account for human activities which have no apparent connection with sexuality but which are assumed to be motivated by the force of the sexual instinct. The main types of activity described by Freud as sublimated are artistic creation and intellectual inquiry. The instinct is said to be sublimated in so far as it is diverted towards a new, non-sexual aim and in so far as its objects are socially valued ones" (J. Laplanche and J. B. Pontalis, "Sublimation," 431).

5. In his book *The Romantic Sublime: Studies in the Structure and Psychology of Transcendence,* Thomas Weiskel points out that in addition to centering the senses (which motivated the natural sublime), Locke detached the soul from the hierarchy of relations in which it had been installed and effectively emptied it out. "The soul is a vacancy, whose extent is discovered as it is filled. Inner space, the infinitude of the Romantic mind, is born as a massive and more or less unconscious emptiness, an absence" (15).

6. Weiskel writes compellingly of the ways in which the negative sublime is characterized by obsessional neurosis and melancholia as responses to guilt. He observes that "The sublime appears as a remedy for the languid melancholy, the vague boredom that increased so astonishingly during the eighteenth century; it transformed this state into the firmer, more morally sanctioned melancholy of the gloomy egoist. Consequently, the sublime of terror may be characterized as an *episode in melancholy.* In terms of the history of sensibility, this suggests that the prestige and attractiveness of the sublime is a direct function of the prevalence or predisposition to melancholy" (*The Romantic Sublime,* 97).

7. Walpole to the Reverend William Cole, March 9, 1765. Quoted by W. S. Lewis in his introduction to the Oxford edition of *The Castle of Otranto,* ix.

8. Walpole, who was an antiquarian, purchased Strawberry Hill in 1747 and made it the center of his life. After he reconstructed it with pinnacles and battlements, galleries and cloisters, he stuffed it full of precious objects he had collected; and he continued, over many years, to improve its grounds. He wanted to create an illusion of barbarism and gloom, while enjoying "modern refinements in luxury" (Robert Wyndham Ketton-Cremer, *Horace Walpole: A Biography,* 156). Although Strawberry Hill clearly served as the inspiration for Manfred's castle in the novel, Ketton-Cremer points out that Trinity College at Cambridge—which Walpole had visited the year before

he wrote his fiction—supplied the great hall, the courtyard, and "some other things" (217).

9. In "The Unguarded Prison: Reception Theory, Structural Marxism, and the History of the Gothic Novel," David H. Richter argues that the phenomenon of "the unguarded door"—the ways in which unfreedom turns inexplicably into freedom in gothic texts—suggests that the prisons were unreal in the first place: they are "prisons of the mind from which one finds oneself freed when one no longer feels oneself bound" (12). This argument seems to apply extremely well to the fictions of Ann Radcliffe, where repeated anticlimaxes are used to emphasize the psychological nature of the heroine's susceptibility to the supernatural, and where her changing responses to the supernatural suggest her development from excessive sensibility to rational good sense. The argument seems less compelling here, where there is no sustained development of the protagonist and no movement from ignorance to self-knowledge.

10. Walpole, "Preface to the First Edition," 4.

11. Walpole, "Preface to the Second Edition," 7–8.

12. Walpole, "Preface to the Second Edition," 8.

13. In *The Rise of the Gothic Novel*, Maggie Kilgour usefully analyzes the ways in which the term "gothic" was used in the eighteenth century both to demonize feudal tyranny and to idealize it as a golden age of liberty. She argues that Robert Walpole inhabited the first position, identifying with the middle-class forces of enlightened progress, while his son identified with Burke and the latter position, seeing the British tradition of freedom as lost in 1066 through the invasion by Britain of France, and then regained through the Magna Carta and the Revolution of 1688. For Burke, and also for Walpole, England's Revolution provided an evolutionary model of organic change in which older traditions and systems of relations could be rediscovered and reproduced (13).

14. Certainly it is possible to read in the political theme of the novel Walpole's concern with the succession crisis that dominated Restoration politics and to see in his novel's resolution a characteristic ambivalence toward the principles of dynastic inheritance and patriarchalism, which the Hanoverian Settlement of 1689 called radically into question.

15. Peter Hughes discusses the ways in which the "erotic heroism" of the late seventeenth and eighteenth centuries pushes the sexual and amorous "beyond itself into the language of power, of masters and victims, of self-consciousness that turns into the sacrifice and even the destruction of the self" ("Wars within Doors: Erotic Heroism and the Implosion of Texts," 403). James Grantham Turner examines the development in the Restoration of a discourse that linked erotic love to the sublime. In what he calls the "libertine sublime," sexuality is heroized and associated with quasi-religious pleasure, emotional and physical excess, amoral individualism, and creative genius ("The Libertine Sublime: Love and Death in Restoration England"). I would define the libertine sublime as a form of the negative sublime, which characterizes the fantastic mode.

16. My references in this chapter are to the essays by Nicolas Abraham and Maria Torok that are collected in *The Shell and the Kernel*. Throughout this chapter, I refer to Abraham and Torok as collaborative theorists at the same time that, in the footnotes and occasionally in the text, I specify the author of individual essays. While possibly confusing, this approach seems to me to be responsive to the larger intention of their work.

17. Freud points out that in the case of melancholic introjection, where the initial attachment of self to other was ambivalent, the anger that was once directed at the object is turned back against the self, and the ego is punished by the judging superego. The result can be sadistic self-destruction that, calling on the "primal animosity" of the ego, can even lead to suicide ("Mourning and Melancholia," 163).

18. Reflecting on his discussion of introjection in "Mourning and Melancholia," Freud writes: "Since then we have come to understand that this kind of substitution has a great share in determining the form taken by the ego and that it makes an essential contribution towards building up what is called its 'character.'" He adds: "It may be that this identification is the sole condition under which the id can give up its objects. At any rate the process, especially in the early phases of development, is a very frequent one, and it makes it possible to suppose that the character of the ego is a precipitate of abandoned object-cathexes and that it contains the history of those object-choices" (*The Ego and the Id*, 23, 24). In *The Psychic Life of Power: Theories in Subjection*, Judith Butler draws on Freud's reassessment of the role of introjection in *The Ego and the Id* and on Abraham and Torok's revision of Freud's theory of melancholia in order to develop her own influential theory of the melancholic structure of gender identity (57–72).

19. Maria Torok, "The Illness of Mourning and the Fantasy of the Exquisite Corpse," 113.

20. Nicolas Abraham and Maria Torok, "Mourning or Melancholia: Introjection versus Incorporation," 125.

21. Abraham and Torok, "Mourning or Melancholia," 125–26.

22. Abraham and Torok, "Mourning or Melancholia," 127.

23. Freud, "Mourning and Melancholia," 163.

24. Abraham and Torok, "Mourning or Melancholia," 135.

25. In "Fantasy: An Attempt to Define Its Structure and Operations," Maria Torok writes against such theorists of unconscious fantasy as Freud, Melanie Klein, and Susan Isaacs who, she believes, strip fantasy of its specificity and operational value by identifying it with "the whole expanse of mental life." Torok suggests that the production of fantasy is an essentially conscious process in which the ego, feeling itself to be in an imaginative realm, recognizes itself as the site of such strange and incomprehensible phenomena as conscious feelings of intrusion, imagination, and misfit, which are distinguishable from other related experiences (27). When the ego senses a break in the continuity of its activities, according to Torok, it experiences the momentary shifting of intrapsychic levels as an imaginary "misfitting" that forces it to encounter a "lower" version of itself (30). The

fantasy that then irrupts into consciousness is a symptom in its own right: "The representation of a problem seeking expression" (29). That irruption in turn enables the psychic process of introjection through which the ego mediates between interior and exterior worlds, assimilating experience through imagination, play, intellection, language art, and fantasy, all of which have equal access to the unconscious.

26. Lewis, introduction, x.

27. I am thinking here, for example, of Frankenstein's monster, who has often been read by critics as a projection of Mary Shelley herself; of Lucy Snowe, in *Villette*, who tells her story initially as that of Paulina Home, but whose narrative incorporates many elements of Brontë's own biography; and of Dr. Jekyll and Mr. Hyde, who are not only doubles but also projections of Mr. Utterson, the narrator, who can be seen as a version of Robert Louis Stevenson's father.

28. Walpole viewed his letters as the centerpiece of his chronicle. Ketton-Cremer indicates that he chose his principal correspondents with great care so that they would be precisely positioned in relation to his interests, and he appointed their substitutes when they died. All were expected to return his letters to him for editing, annotation, and, often, alteration, and these he organized into an extensive social history (*Horace Walpole*, 127, 131–32).

29. Of Walpole's biographers, Lewis is the most dismissive of the rumors, observing both that "[i]f the Walpoles had any doubts about Horace's paternity they were very charitable about it" and that "[s]o far as we know," Horace did not know the gossip about his birth (*Horace Walpole*, 12). While Ketton-Cremer is also dubious, Gwynn accepts the opinion expressed by Lady Mary Wortley Montague in her journals that contemporary opinion "did not doubt" Horace's illegitimacy and, on the basis of similarities of appearance and temperament, believed Hervey to have been his father. Gwynn quotes an observation attributed to Lady Mary that "mankind was divided into men, women, and Herveys," suggesting that it was in part on the basis of his effeminacy that Horace was thought to have been Hervey's son (*The Life of Horace Walpole*, 16).

30. Ketton-Cremer, *Horace Walpole*, 29.

31. Lewis describes a dynamic between Horace and Sir Robert that seemed to change during the time immediately before and after Sir Robert lost his office. Ultimately, Robert left Horace a handsome fortune, and Horace became "a violent champion of his father, heaping abuse upon Sir Robert's enemies, extolling his virtues, and making his faults attractive" (*Horace Walpole*, 20). Still Lewis believes that "beneath this outward loyalty lay quite different emotions" (20), which he characterizes as a continuing "latent hostility " on the part of the son (24).

32. Lewis, *Horace Walpole*, 72.

33. Lewis, *Horace Walpole*, 76.

34. Ketton-Cremer, *Horace Walpole*, 248–49.

35. Ketton-Cremer, *Horace Walpole*, 211.

36. Gwynn reports that after his mother's death, Horace wrote to his

friend Charles Lyttleton: "You have often been witness to my happiness and by that may partly figure what I feel for losing so fond a mother. If my loss consisted solely in being deprived of one that loved me so much, it would feel lighter to me than it now does, for I doated on her" (*Life of Horace Walpole*, 27).

37. Lewis, *Horace Walpole*, 19.

38. The first time that Walpole offered Conway money was in 1744, when he hoped to enable his cousin to marry; the second was in 1764, when Conway lost his court position. In 1744, Walpole wrote to Conway, as Ketton-Cremer reports, "If I ever felt much for anything (which I know may be questioned), it was certainly for my mother. I look on you as my nearest relation by her, and I think I can never do enough to show my gratitude and affection to her" (*Horace Walpole*, 103).

39. Ketton-Cremer writes of Walpole: "He could be petty and malicious. He had a queer feminine element which occasionally rose to the surface in the form of violent jealousy or spite. He gossiped with old ladies for days on end; he was fond of china and goldfish and little dogs; he committed every architectural absurdity in the building and adornment of his house; he once stuck sweet-peas in his hair and sang to a roomful of dowagers at their card-tables" (*Horace Walpole*, 21). Ketton-Cremer believes that Walpole was "a natural celibate" (52). Gwynn says that he is unable to throw any light on Walpole's sexual history, but does not see him as "a man of strong passion" (*Life of Horace Walpole*, 83). Lewis explicitly brushes off the possibility that Walpole was a homosexual, discounting some remarks in the correspondence that others have read differently: "a handful of letters written in extravagant high spirits in the manner of the time are not proof of it, and none has come to light" (*Horace Walpole*, 36). More recently, Eve Kosofsky Sedgwick has written of Walpole, Beckford, and Matthew Lewis as in some significant sense having been homosexual, "Beckford notoriously, Lewis probably, Walpole iffily." She adds that despite the fact that Walpole's life was "staggeringly well-documented, we cannot tell how far he was homosexual, because of the close protective coloration given by the aristocratic milieu" (*Between Men: English Literature and Male Homosocial Desire*, 92–93). In "Literature and Homosexuality in the Late Eighteenth Century," George Haggerty picks up on Sedgwick's argument and looks specifically to Walpole's letters to Lord Lincoln and Harry Conway (the letters discounted by Lewis) for evidence of Walpole's homosexuality (344).

40. All three of Walpole's biographers describe Walpole's penchant for close friendships with much older women. During the four years (1753–77) that Walpole contributed to the periodical *The World*, he wrote a paper in which he argued—ironically but not insignificantly—that old women were the most satisfactory objects for love (Ketton-Cremer, *Horace Walpole*, 168).

41. Gwynn reports, for example, that Walpole wrote to his friend George Montaque that Madame Du Deffand was "the best and sincerest of friends, who loves me as much as my mother did" (*Life of Horace Walpole*, 223).

42. Walpole, "Preface to the 1781 Edition," in *The Mysterious Mother*,

265. All references to the play are to this edition, which is cited parenthetically in the text.

43. In his postscript to *The Mysterious Mother*, Walpole writes that the subject of his play is "more truly horrid than even that of Oedipus," and observes: "From the time that I first undertook the foregoing scenes, I never flattered myself that they would be appropriate to appear on the stage. The subject is so horrid, that I thought it would shock, rather than give satisfaction to an audience. Still I found it so truly tragic in the essential springs of terror and pity, that I could not resist the impulse of adapting it to the scene, though it could never be practicable to produce it there" (253–54).

44. Ketton-Cremer, *Horace Walpole*, 284.

45. Lewis, *Horace Walpole*, 163.

46. Walpole, postscript to *The Mysterious Mother*, 254.

47. Lewis suggests the ways in which Walpole was deeply divided within and between his relationships with his mother and father, and the extent to which he was the ambivalent product of his parents' contradictory influences: "Horace had Sir Robert's powers of persuasion, shrewdness, ambition, gift of friendship, and passion for collecting. Lady Walpole reinforced her son's love of the arts and heightened his taste for the ridiculous. Both contributed to his inner uncertainties: his mother by her possessiveness and hatred of his father; Sir Robert by his initial aloofness, by the rejection of Horace's mother, and by his power. From childhood, Horace was pulled back and forth between love and hatred, fear and confidence, desire for money and contempt for it, pride and humility, idealism and disillusionment, his flair for friendship and his dislike of people at too close quarters" (*Horace Walpole*, 188).

48. Freud, "The Uncanny," 369–70. The uncanny can be seen as Freud's conceptualization of the sublime, another version of which is Julia Kristeva's theory of abjection.

49. Near the conclusion of his essay "The Uncanny"—after having followed an extremely circuitous route that seems to suggest the process of his own struggle with the uncanny—Freud writes: "It often happens that male patients declare that they feel there is something uncanny about the female genital organs. This *unheimlich* place, however, is the entrance to the former *heim* (home) of all human beings, to the place where everyone dwelt once upon a time and in the beginning" (398–99). He adds, "the *unheimlich* is what was once *heimisch*, home-like, familiar; the prefix 'un' is the token of repression" (399). To the extent that Freud identifies the mother's body as the primal uncanny object, "The Uncanny" can be read as an essay on melancholia.

50. Torok, "The Illness of Mourning," 117.

51. Torok, "The Illness of Mourning," 118.

52. Abraham and Torok, "Mourning or Melancholia," 136.

53. Nicolas Abraham and Maria Torok, "The Lost Object—Me: Notes on Endocryptic Identification," 141. Of course, in "Mourning and Melancholia," Freud observes that in the case of melancholia, the libido is not withdrawn

from the lost love object and transferred to a new one; rather, the ego identifies with the abandoned object (159).

54. Abraham and Torok, "Mourning or Melancholia," 136.
55. Abraham and Torok, "The Lost Object—Me," 142.
56. Ketton-Cremer, *Horace Walpole*, 341.
57. Ketton-Cremer, *Horace Walpole*, 352.
58. Abraham and Torok, "Mourning or Melancholia," 130.

CONCLUSION

1. I am drawing here on the concept of "nachtraglichkeit," which J. Laplanche and J. B. Pontalis define as "A term frequently used by Freud in connection with his view of psychical temporality and causality: experiences, impressions and memory traces may be revised at a later date to fit in with fresh experiences or with the attainment of a new stage of development. They may in that event be endowed not only with a new meaning but also with psychical effectiveness" ("Deferred Action; Deferred," 111). Although Freud used this concept in relation to traumatic events, I am using it to suggest that the interpretation of texts is always to some extent an act of "nachtraglichkeit."

2. For example, there are strong fantastic elements in Dickens's novels, which are often associated with his criminal men and fallen women. These fantastic subtexts reveal the profound resentments and thwarted desires that the social system produces but cannot reconcile. Charlotte Brontë's *Villette* is a striking composite text that provides insight into the shared structure of personal, cultural, and textual melancholia, while Mary Shelley's *Frankenstein* is an exemplary Romantic fiction in which interpsychic relations are appropriated and transformed for the intrapsychic dynamic.

3. Of course, it was with the publication of Dorothy Dinnerstein's *Mermaid and the Minotaur* in 1976 and Nancy Chodorow's *Reproduction of Mothering: Psychoanalysis and the Sociology of Gender* in 1978 that the feminist psychoanalytic project was inaugurated. The list of theorists who have contributed to this project is too long—and the relations among them too complicated—to detail here. In the writing of this book, I have found the work of three people particularly important. For me Mary Jacobus established a model of feminist psychoanalytic theory and criticism with *Reading Woman: Essays in Feminist Criticism* and *First Things: The Maternal Imaginary in Literature, Art, Psychoanalysis*. Jessica Benjamin's work has been exceptionally influential and I refer to it often in these pages. With so many other feminists, I am also much indebted to Judith Butler. In relation to this chapter, *The Psychic Life of Power: Theories of Subjection* has been especially helpful.

4. In a well-known passage in his essay "Female Sexuality," which was published in 1931, Freud writes: "Everything connected with this first mother-attachment has in analysis seemed to me so elusive, lost in a past so dim and shadowy, so hard to resuscitate, that it seemed as if it had undergone some specially inexorable repression" (195).

5. As J. Laplanche and J. B. Pontalis point out in "Object-Relation(ship),"
although the term "object-relationship" does occur occasionally in Freud's
writing, the idea plays no part in Freud's conceptual scheme (278). Feminist
object-relations theorists belong to the larger psychoanalytic movement that
has become dominant in the United States and England since the 1930s.
Although there are many variations among object-relations theories, all insist
that the individual should not be considered in isolation, but should be examined in its interactions with others. In other words, the subject constitutes
its own world of objects and those objects, in turn, shape the subject's actions.

6. In *The Shadow of the Object: Psychoanalysis of the Unthought Unknown*,
Christopher Bollas argues that the infant experiences the mother not as an
object but as "a process of transformation." Because this early experience of
transformation endures into adult life, the subject is moved to seek objects
which will have a similar potential for self-transformation (14). One's life
can therefore be seen as a quest for a symbolic equivalent for the first transformative object. According to Bollas, that equivalent can be found in art, in
nature, in a love relationship, in prized possessions, and in adventures of
various sorts.

7. In *Bonds of Love: Psychoanalysis, Feminism, and the Problem of Domination*
and *Like Subjects, Love Objects: Essays on Recognition and Sexual Difference*,
Jessica Benjamin emphasizes the significant loss experienced by male and
female children as a result of the imposed denial of cross-gender identifications. In "Melancholy Gender/Refused Identification," in *The Psychic Life
of Power*, Judith Butler emphasizes the ways in which the ritualized prohibition of homosexual love—and, indeed, all rigid forms of gender and sexual
identification—creates personal and cultural melancholia: "What ensues is
a culture of gender melancholy in which masculinity and femininity emerge
as the traces of an ungrieved and ungrievable love" (140).

8. In "Sympathy for the Devil: Notes on Sexuality and Aggression, with
Special Reference to Pornography" (the final chapter of *Like Subjects, Love
Objects*, 175–211), Jessica Benjamin suggests that the fear of difference in
heterosexual relations can lead either to repudiation or to complementarity,
both of which can be seen as defenses against the struggle for recognition.
I find the former represented in fantastic narratives, the latter in realist narratives. Later in this chapter I examine the third possibility that Benjamin
discusses—an intersubjectivity that allows for mutual recognition. In explaining the historical subordination of women, Benjamin argues that the
heterosexual oedipal structure, which is central to gender organization and
development, is "the paradigmatic expression of splitting: the subject simultaneously denies the other's subjectivity and makes her, instead, into the
object that embodies the split-off parts of the self" (*Like Subjects, Love Objects*,
18). It is the oedipal disruption of the male child's identification with the
mother that establishes the complementary gender structure. Benjamin also
argues, however, that identificatory tendencies may be—and often are—
maintained alongside object love. The complementarity that then results
is of a different sort, and produces different attitudes toward oppositional

differences (73). The gender indeterminacy that I locate in fantastic texts is grounded in this "overinclusive" position.

9. Jessica Benjamin first theorized relations of erotic domination in 1980 in "The Bonds of Love: Erotic Domination and Rational Violence." She extended her analysis in *Bonds of Love* and *Like Subject, Love Objects*. In "Sympathy for the Devil," she added a provocative discussion of aggression, violence, and pornography.

10. In *Between Men: English Literature and Male Homosocial Desire* and *Epistemology of the Closet*, Eve Kosofsky Sedgwick examines such paranoid, homosocial, fantastic texts and theorizes the social and psychological dynamics that produce them.

11. In *The Psychic Life of Power*, Butler writes, "The ego comes into being on the condition of the 'trace' of the other, who is, at that moment of emergence, already at a distance. To accept the autonomy of the ego is to forget that trace, and to accept that trace is to embark upon a process of mourning that can never be complete, for no final severance could take place without dissolving the ego" (196).

12. For example, the relational possibility that Sterne conceptualizes for his male characters has a great deal in common with the one that Jessica Benjamin aligns with the "overinclusive position" available to men *and* women. In *Like Subjects, Love Objects*, she writes: "Each love object embodies multiple possibilities of sameness and difference, of masculinity and femininity, and love relationships may serve a multitude of functions. In each relationship the axis of similarity and complementarity is aligned somewhat differently with the axis of gender" (128). Comparing an erotic to a pornographic sexuality, she explains: "But what makes sexuality erotic is the survival of the other throughout the exercise of power, which in turn makes the expression of power part of symbolic play" (206). In *Straight Male Modern: A Cultural Critique of Psychoanalysis*, John Brenkman also conceptualizes such a subject, as do Julian Henriques and the other authors of *Changing the Subject: Psychology, Social Regulation, and Subjectivity*. All are concerned to define a psychoanalytic theory that is responsive to social and political influences.

Works Cited

Abraham, Nicolas, and Maria Torok. "The Lost Object—Me: Notes on Endocryptic Identification." In *The Shell and the Kernel: Renewals of Psychoanalysis*. Ed. and trans. Nicholas Rand. Vol. 1. Chicago: University of Chicago Press, 1994. 139–56.

———. "Mourning or Melancholia: Introjection versus Incorporation." In
The Shell and the Kernel: Renewals of Psychoanalysis. Ed. and trans. Nicholas
Rand. Vol. 1. Chicago: University of Chicago Press, 1994. 125–38.

———. "A Poetics of Psychoanalysis: The Lost Object—Me." *Sub-Stance* 43.2
(1984): 3–18.

———. *The Shell and the Kernel: Renewals of Psychoanalysis*. Ed. and trans.
Nicholas Rand. Vol. 1. Chicago: University of Chicago Press, 1994.

Allen, Dennis W. "Sexuality/Textuality in *Tristram Shandy*." *Studies in English Literature, 1500–1900* 25 (1987): 651–70.

Amussen, Susan D. *An Ordered Society: Gender and Class in Early Modern
England*. Oxford: Blackwell, 1988.

Anderson, Benedict. *Imagined Communities: Reflections on the Origin and
Spread of Nationalism*. 2nd ed. New York: Verso, 1991.

Armstrong, Nancy. *Desire and Domestic Fiction: A Political History of the Novel*.
New York: Oxford University Press, 1987.

Bakhtin, Mikhail. *Problems of Dostoevsky's Poetics*. Ed. and trans. Caryl Em-
erson. Minneapolis: University of Minnesota Press, 1984.

Ballaster, Ros. *Seductive Forms: Women's Amatory Fiction from 1684 to 1740*.
New York: Oxford University Press, 1992.

Barker-Benfield, G. J. *The Culture of Sensibility: Sex and Society in Eighteenth-
Century Britain*. Chicago: University of Chicago Press, 1992.

Bender, John. *Imagining the Penitentiary: Fiction and the Architecture of Mind
in Eighteenth-Century England*. Chicago: University of Chicago Press,
1987.

Benjamin, Jessica. *The Bonds of Love: Psychoanalysis, Feminism, and the Problem
of Domination*. New York: Pantheon, 1988.

———. "The Bonds of Love: Rational Violence and Erotic Domination." *Feminist Studies* 6 (1980): 14–74.

———. *Like Subjects, Love Objects: Essays on Recognition and Sexual Difference*.
New Haven: Yale University Press, 1995.

Benjamin, Walter. *Illuminations*. Ed. Hannah Arendt, trans. Harry Zohn.
New York: Schocken Books, 1968.

Bhabha, Homi. "The Other Question: Difference, Discrimination, and the

Discourse of Colonialism." In *Literature, Politics, and Theory: Papers from the Essex Conference, 1976–84,* ed. Francis Barker et al. New York: Methuen, 1986. 148–72.

Blaut, J. M. *The Colonizer's Model of the World: Geographical Diffusionism and Eurocentric History.* New York: Guilford Press, 1993.

Bollas, Christopher. *The Shadow of the Object: Psychoanalysis of the Unthought Unknown.* New York: Columbia University Press, 1987.

Bordo, Susan. "The Cartesian Masculinization of Thought." *Signs: Journal of Women in Culture and Society* 11 (1983): 439–56.

Braudy, Leo. "Daniel Defoe and the Anxieties of Autobiography." In *Modern Critical Views: Daniel Defoe,* ed. Harold Bloom. New York: Chelsea House, 1987. 107–23.

———. "Penetration and Impenetrability in *Clarissa*." In *New Aspects of the Eighteenth Century,* ed. Philip Harth. New York: Columbia University Press, 1974. 177–206.

Braverman, Richard. "Crusoe's Legacy." *Studies in the Novel* 8 (1986): 1–26.

Brenkman, John. *Culture and Domination.* Ithaca: Cornell University Press, 1985.

———. *Straight Male Modern: A Cultural Critique of Psychoanalysis.* New York: Routledge, 1993.

Butler, Judith. *Gender Trouble: Feminism and the Subversion of Identity.* New York: Routledge, 1990.

———. "The Lesbian Phallus and the Morphological Imaginary." *Differences* 4.1 (1992): 133–71.

———. *The Psychic Life of Power: Theories in Subjection.* Stanford: Stanford University Press, 1997.

Cahn, Susan. *Industry of Devotion: The Transformation of Women's Work in England, 1500–1660.* New York: Columbia University Press, 1987.

Caillois, Roger. *Man, Play, and Games.* Trans. M. Barasch. [New York]: Free Press of Glencoe, 1961.

Castle, Terry J. "Amy, Who Knew My Disease: A Psychosexual Pattern in Defoe's *Roxana*." *ELH* 46 (1979): 81–96.

———. *Clarissa's Ciphers: Meaning and Disruption in Richardson's* Clarissa. Ithaca: Cornell University Press, 1982.

Chabor, Lois. "Matriarchal Mirror: Women and Capital in *Moll Flanders*." *PMLA* 97 (1982): 212–26.

Chodorow, Nancy. *The Reproduction of Mothering: Psychoanalysis and the Sociology of Gender.* Berkeley: University of California Press, 1978.

Clark, Alice. *Working Life of Women in the Seventeenth Century.* 1919. Reprint, Boston: Routledge and Kegan Paul, 1982.

Davis, Lennard J. *Factual Fictions: The Origins of the English Novel.* New York: Columbia University Press, 1983.

———. *Resisting Novels: Ideology and Fiction.* New York: Methuen, 1987.

Day, William Patrick. *In the Circles of Fear and Desire: A Study of Gothic Fantasy.* Chicago: University of Chicago Press, 1985.

Defoe, Daniel. *The Life and Strange Surprizing Adventures of Robinson Crusoe of York, Mariner* (1719). Ed. J. Donald Crowley. New York: Oxford University Press, 1981.

——. *Moll Flanders* (1722). Ed. James Sutherland. Boston: Houghton Mifflin, 1959.

——. *Roxana: The Fortunate Mistress* (1724). Ed. David Blewett. New York: Penguin, 1982.

DeLamotte, Eugenia C. *Perils of the Night: A Feminist Study of Nineteenth-Century Gothic.* New York: Oxford University Press, 1990.

Deleuze, Gilles. *Masochism: An Interpretation of Coldness and Cruelty.* Trans. Jean McNeil. New York: George Braziller, 1971.

Dinnerstein, Dorothy. *The Mermaid and the Minotaur.* New York: Harper and Row, 1976.

Durant, David. "Roxana's Fictions." In *Modern Critical Views: Daniel Defoe,* ed. Harold Bloom. New York: Chelsea House, 1987. 225–36.

Eagleton, Terry. *The Rape of Clarissa: Writing, Sexuality, and Class Struggle in Samuel Richardson.* Minneapolis: University of Minnesota Press, 1982.

Ehlers, Leigh. "Mrs. Shandy's 'Lint and Basilicon': The Importance of Women in *Tristram Shandy.*" *South Atlantic Review* 46 (1981): 61–73.

Elias, Norbert. *The Civilizing Process.* Vol. 1, *The History of Manners.* Trans. Edmund Jephcott. New York: Pantheon, 1978.

Elliott, Anthony, and Stephen Frosch, eds. *Psychoanalysis in Contexts: Paths between Theory and Modern Culture.* New York: Routledge, 1995.

Faller, Lincoln. *Crime and Defoe: A New Kind of Writing.* New York: Cambridge University Press, 1993.

Fanon, Franz. *Black Skin, White Masks.* Trans. Charles Lam Markmann. New York: Grove, 1967.

Faurot, Ruth. "Mrs. Shandy Observed." *Studies in English Literature, 1500–1900* 10 (1970): 579–89.

Felman, Shoshana, ed. *Literature and Psychoanalysis: The Question of Reading, Otherwise.* Baltimore: Johns Hopkins University Press, 1982.

Fiedler, Leslie A. *Love and Death in the American Novel.* 1960. Reprint, New York: Stein and Day, 1966.

Filmer, Sir Robert. *Patriarcha and Other Political Works* (1653). Ed. Peter Laslett. Oxford: Blackwell, 1949.

Flint, Christopher. "Orphaning the Family: The Role of Kinship in *Robinson Crusoe.*" *ELH* 55 (1988): 381–419.

Foster, James O. "*Robinson Crusoe* and the Uses of the Imagination." *Journal of English and German Philology* 91 (1992): 179–202.

Freud, Sigmund. "A Child Is Being Beaten" (1919). In *Sexuality and the Psychology of Love.* Ed. Philip Rieff, trans. Alix and James Strachey. New York: Collier, 1963. 107–32.

——. *The Ego and the Id* (1923). Trans. and ed. James Strachey. New York: W. W. Norton, 1960.

——. "Female Sexuality" (1931). In *Sexuality and the Psychology of Love.* Ed. Philip Rieff, trans. Joan Riviere. New York: Collier, 1963. 194–211.

————. "Humour" (1928). In *The Standard Edition of the Complete Psychological Works of Sigmund Freud*. Ed. James Strachey and Anna Freud, trans. Joan Riviere. Vol. 21. London: Hogarth Press, 1961. 160–66.

————. "Mourning and Melancholia" (1917). In *Collected Papers*. Ed. Ernest Jones, trans. Joan Riviere. Vol. 4. New York: Basic Books, 1959. 152–70.

————. "A Special Kind of Object Choice Made by Men" (1910). In *Sexuality and the Psychology of Love*. Ed. Philip Rieff, trans. Joan Riviere. New York: Collier, 1963. 49–57.

————. "The Uncanny" (1919). In *Collected Papers*. Ed. Ernest Jones, trans. Joan Riviere. Vol. 4. New York: Basic Books, 1959. 369–70.

————. "The Unconscious" (1915). In *Collected Papers*. Ed. Ernest Jones, trans. Joan Riviere. Vol. 4. New York: Basic Books, 1959. 98–136.

Gallagher, Catherine. *Nobody's Story: The Vanishing Acts of Women Writers in the Marketplace, 1670–1820*. Berkeley: University of California Press, 1994.

Gallop, Jane. "Beyond the Phallus." In *Thinking through the Body*. New York: Columbia University Press, 1988. 119–34.

Ganner, Michael. "Genres for the Prosecution: Pornography and the Gothic." *PMLA* 14 (1999): 1043–66.

Gilman, Sander. *Difference and Pathology: Stereotypes of Sexuality, Race, and Madness*. Ithaca: Cornell University Press, 1985.

Gwynn, Stephen. *The Life of Horace Walpole*. London: Thornton Butterworth, 1932.

Haggerty, George. "Literature and Homosexuality in the Late Eighteenth Century." *Studies in the Novel* 18 (1986): 341–52.

————. *Unnatural Affections: Women and Fiction in the Later Eighteenth Century*. Bloomington: Indiana University Press, 1998.

Haywood, Eliza Fowler. *Memoirs of a Certain Island Adjacent to the Kingdom of Utopia*. 1725–26. Reprint, New York: Garland, 1972.

Hegel, Georg Wilhelm Friedrich. *Phenomenology of Spirit* (1807). Trans. A. V. Miller. Oxford: Clarendon Press, 1977.

Henriques, Julian, et al. *Changing the Subject: Psychology, Social Regulation, and Subjectivity*. London: Methuen, 1984.

Hentzi, Gary. "Holes in the Heart: *Moll Flanders*, *Roxana*, and 'Agreeable Crime.' " *Boundary 2*. 18 (1991): 174–200.

Hill, Bridget. *Women, Work, and Sexual Politics in Eighteenth-Century England*. Oxford: Blackwell, 1989.

Hill, Christopher. "Clarissa Harlowe and Her Times." In *Puritanism and Revolution: Studies in Interpretation of the English Revolution of the Seventeenth Century*. 1958. Reprint, London: Secker and Warburg, 1997. 332–56.

Hoffmann, E. T. A. "The Sandman" (1817). In *Tales of Hoffmann*. Trans. R. J. Hollingdale. New York: Penguin, 1982. 85–125.

Hogg, James. *The Private Memoirs and Confessions of a Justified Sinner*. 1824. Reprint, New York: Grove Press, 1959.

Horney, Karen. "The Dread of Woman: Observations on a Specific Difference

in the Dread Felt by Men and Women Respectively for the Opposite Sex."
IJPA 13 (1932): 348–60.

Hughes, Peter. "War within Doors: Erotic Heroism and the Implosion of
Texts." *English Studies* 60 (1979): 402–21.

Hulme, Peter. *Colonial Encounters: Europe and the Native Caribbean, 1492–1797.*
New York: Methuen, 1986.

Hunter, John Paul. "Clocks, Calendars, and Names: The Troubles of Tristram
and the Aesthetics of Uncertainty." In *Rhetorics of Order/Ordering Rhetorics
in English Neoclassical Literature,* ed. J. Douglas Canfield and J. Paul Hunter. Newark: University of Delaware Press, 1989. 173–98.

Ian, Marcia. *Remembering the Phallic Mother: Psychoanalysis, Modernism, and
the Fetish.* Ithaca: Cornell University Press, 1993.

Irigaray, Luce. "The Blind Spot of an Old Dream of Symmetry" (1974). In
Speculum of the Other Woman. Trans. Gillian C. Gill. Ithaca: Cornell University Press, 1985. 11–129.

———. "The Bodily Encounter with the Mother." In *The Irigaray Reader,* ed.
Margaret Whitford. Cambridge, Mass.: Blackwell, 1991. 34–46.

Iser, Wolfgang. *Tristram Shandy.* Trans. David Henry Wilson. New York:
Cambridge University Press, 1988.

Jackson, Rosemary. *Fantasy: The Literature of Subversion.* New York: Methuen,
1981.

Jacobus, Mary. *First Things: The Maternal Imaginary in Literature, Art, Psychoanalysis.* New York: Routledge, 1995.

———. *Reading Woman: Essays in Feminist Criticism.* New York: Columbia
University Press, 1986.

Johnson, Claudia L. "The Sex of Suffering: *The Mysteries of Udolpho.*" In *Equiv-
ocal Beings: Politics, Gender, and Sentimentality in the 1790s: Wollstonecraft,
Radcliffe, Burney, Austen.* Chicago: University of Chicago Press, 1995. 95–
116.

Keller, Evelyn. *Reflections on Gender and Science.* New Haven: Yale University
Press, 1985.

Ketton-Cremer, Robert Wyndham. *Horace Walpole: A Biography.* New York:
Longmans, Green, 1940.

Kibbie, Ann Louise. "Monstrous Generation: The Birth of Capital in Defoe's
Moll Flanders and *Roxana.*" *PMLA* 10 (1995): 1023–34.

Kilgour, Maggie. *The Rise of the Gothic Novel.* London: Routledge, 1995.

Klein, Jurgen. "Laurence Sterne's Novel of Consciousness: Identities of
Selves and World Constructions in *Tristram Shandy.*" *Studies on Voltaire
and the Eighteenth Century* 265 (1989): 1544–47.

Kohut, Heinz. *The Analysis of the Self.* New York: International Universities
Press, 1971.

———. *The Restoration of the Self.* New York: International Universities Press,
1977.

Kristeva, Julia. *Black Sun: Depression and Melancholia.* Trans. Leon Roudiez.
New York: Columbia University Press, 1989.

————. "An Interview with Julia Kristeva." *Critical Texts* 3.3 (1986): 5–13.

————. *Powers of Horror: An Essay on Abjection.* Trans. Leon Roudiez. New York: Columbia University Press, 1982.

————. "Revolution in Poetic Language." In *The Kristeva Reader,* ed. Toril Moi. New York: Columbia University Press, 1986. 89–136.

————. "Woman's Time." Trans. Alice Jardine and Harry Blake. *Signs: Journal of Women in Culture and Society* 7 (1988): 13–35.

Lacan, Jacques. *The Four Fundamental Concepts of Psychoanalysis.* Ed. Jacques-Alain Miller, trans. Alan Sheridan. London: Hogarth Press, 1977.

————. "God and the Jouissance of the Woman." In *Feminine Sexuality: Jacques Lacan and the ecole freudienne.* Ed. Juliet Mitchell and Jacqueline Rose, trans. Jacqueline Rose. New York: W. W. Norton, 1982. 137–48

————. "Guiding Remarks for a Congress on Feminine Sexuality." In *Feminine Sexuality: Jacques Lacan and the ecole freudienne.* Ed. Juliet Mitchell and Jacqueline Rose, trans. Jacqueline Rose. New York: W. W. Norton, 1982. 86–98.

————. "A Love Letter." In *Feminine Sexuality: Jacques Lacan and the ecole freudienne.* Ed. Juliet Mitchell and Jacqueline Rose, trans. Jacqueline Rose. New York: W. W. Norton, 1982. 149–61.

————. "The Mirror Stage as Formative of the I." In *Ecrits: A Selection.* Trans. Alan Sheridan. New York: W. W. Norton, 1977. 1–7.

Lanham, Richard. Tristram Shandy: *The Games of Pleasure.* Berkeley: University of California Press, 1973.

Laplanche, J., and J. B. Pontalis. "Deferred Action; Deferred." In *The Language of Psychoanalysis.* Trans. Donald Nicholson-Smith. New York: W. W. Norton, 1973. 111–14.

————. "Narcissism." In *The Language of Psychoanalysis.* Trans. Donald Nicholson Smith. New York: W. W. Norton, 1973. 255–57.

————. "Object-Relation(ship)." In *The Language of Psychoanalysis.* Trans. Donald Nicholson Smith. New York: W. W. Norton, 1973. 278–81.

————. "Primal Phantasies." In *The Language of Psychoanalysis.* Trans. Donald Nicholson-Smith. New York: W. W. Norton, 1973. 331–33.

————. "Sublimation." In *The Language of Psychoanalysis.* Trans. Donald Nicholson-Smith. New York: W. W. Norton, 1973. 431–34.

Laqueur, Thomas. *Making Sex: Body and Gender from the Greeks to Freud.* Cambridge, Mass.: Harvard University Press, 1990.

Leites, Edmund. *The Puritan Conscience and Modern Sexuality.* New Haven: Yale University Press, 1986.

Lewis, W. S. *Horace Walpole.* Bollingen Series, 35. A. W. Mellon Lectures in the Fine Arts, 9. New York: Pantheon, 1960.

————. Introduction to *The Castle of Otranto, a Gothic Story,* by Horace Walpole. London: Oxford University Press, 1964. vii–xvi.

Locke, John. *Two Treatises of Government: A Critical Edition.* Ed. Peter Laslett. London: Cambridge University Press, 1960.

Loewald, Hans. "The Waning of the Oedipus Complex." *Journal of the American Psychoanalytic Association* 27 (1979): 751–75.

Lukács, Georg. "Reification and the Consciousness of the Proletariat." In *History and Class Consciousness: Studies in Marxist Dialectics*. Trans. Rodney Livingstone. Cambridge, Mass.: MIT Press, 1971. 83–222.

Macksey, Richard. " 'Alas, Poor Yorick': Sterne Thoughts." *Modern Language Notes* 98 (1983): 1006–20.

Manley, Delarivier. *The New Atalantis* (1709). Ed. Ros Ballaster. New York: Penguin, 1992.

Marcuse, Herbert. *Eros and Civilization: A Philosophical Inquiry into Freud*. New York: Vintage, 1955.

Masse, Michelle A. *In the Name of Love: Women, Masochism, and the Gothic*. Ithaca: Cornell University Press, 1992.

McKeon, Michael. "Historicizing Patriarchy: The Emergence of Gender Difference in England, 1660–1760." *Eighteenth Century Studies* 28 (1995): 295–322.

———. *The Origins of the English Novel, 1600–1740*. Baltimore: Johns Hopkins University Press, 1987.

Memmi, Albert. *Dominated Man: Notes towards a Portrait*. Boston: Beacon Press, 1968.

Mitchell, Juliet. *Psychoanalysis and Feminism: Freud, Reich, Laing, and Women*. New York: Vintage, 1975.

Moglen, Helene. *The Philosophical Irony of Laurence Sterne*. Gainesville: Florida University Press, 1975.

———. "Redeeming History: Toni Morrison's *Beloved*." *Cultural Critique*, no. 24 (spring 1993): 17–40.

———. "(Un)Gendering the Subject: Towards a Feminist Theory of the Novel." *Genre* 25 (1992): 65–89.

Moretti, Franco. *Signs Taken for Wonders: Essays in the Sociology of Literary Forms*. Trans. Susan Fischer, David Forgacs, and David Miller. New York: Verso, 1988.

Nussbaum, Felicity. *Torrid Zones: Maternity, Sexuality, and Empire in Eighteenth-Century English Narratives*. Baltimore: Johns Hopkins University Press, 1995.

Perry, Ruth. "Words for Sex: The Verbal-Sexual Continuum in *Tristram Shandy*." *Studies in the Novel* 20 (1988): 27–42.

Poovey, Mary. *The Proper Lady and the Woman Writer: Ideology as Style in the Works of Mary Wollstonecraft, Mary Shelley, and Jane Austen*. Chicago: University of Chicago Press, 1984.

Praz, Mario. *The Romantic Agony*. Trans. Angus Davidson. 1933. Reprint, New York: Oxford University Press, 1970.

Preston, John. *The Created Self: The Reader's Role in Eighteenth-Century Fiction*. London: Heinemann, 1970.

Punter, David. *The Literature of Terror: A History of Gothic Fictions from 1765 to the Present Day*. New York: Longmans, 1980.

Rand, Nicholas. "Introduction: Renewals of Psychoanalysis." In Nicolas Abraham and Maria Torok, *The Shell and the Kernel: Renewals of Psychoanalysis*. Chicago: University of Chicago Press, 1994. 1–22.

Randall, Richard S. *Freedom and Taboo: Pornography and the Politics of a Self Divided*. Berkeley: University of California Press, 1989.

Reed, Joel. "Nationalism and Geoculture in Defoe's History of Writing." *Modern Language Quarterly* 56 (1995): 31–52.

Reich, Theodor. *Masochism in Sex and Society*. New York: Grove Press, 1962.

Richardson, Samuel. *Clarissa or The History of a Young Lady* (1747). Ed. Angus Ross. New York: Penguin, 1988.

Richter, David H. "The Unguarded Prison: Reception Theory, Structural Marxism, and the History of the Gothic Novel." *Eighteenth Century* 30.3 (1989): 3–17.

Rose, Jacqueline. *States of Fantasy*. Oxford: Clarendon Press, 1996.

Rowbotham, Sheila. *Hidden from History*. New York: Pantheon, 1974.

Schwartz, Daniel R. "The Importance of Ian Watt's *The Rise of the Novel*." *Journal of Narrative Technique* 13 (1983): 59–73.

Sedgwick, Eve Kosofsky. *Between Men: English Literature and Male Homosocial Desire*. New York: Columbia University Press, 1985.

———. *Epistemology of the Closet*. Berkeley: University of California Press, 1990.

Seidel, Michael. *Robinson Crusoe, Island Myths, and the Novel*. Boston: Twayne, 1991.

Showalter, Elaine. "Critical Cross-Dressing: Male Feminists and the Woman of the Year." *Raritan* 3.2 (1983): 130–49.

Silverman, Kaja. "The Lacanian Phallus." *Differences* 4.1 (1992): 84–115.

———. *Male Subjectivity at the Margins*. New York: Routledge, 1992.

Spencer, Jane. *The Rise of the Woman Novelist: From Aphra Behn to Jane Austen*. New York: Oxford University Press, 1986.

Stallybrass, Peter, and Allon White. *The Politics and Poetics of Transgression*. London: Methuen, 1986.

Sterne, Laurence. *A Sentimental Journey with The Journal to Eliza and A Political Romance*. Ed. Ian Jack. Oxford: Oxford University Press, 1984.

———. *Tristram Shandy* (1759–67). Ed. Ian Watt. Boston: Houghton Mifflin, 1965.

Thomas, Calvin. "*Tristram Shandy*'s Consent to Incompleteness: Discourse, Disavowal, Disruption." *Literature and Psychology* 36.3 (1990): 44–62.

Todd, Janet. *The Sign of Angellica: Women, Writing, and Fiction, 1660–1800*. London: Virago Press, 1989.

Todorov, Tzvetan. *The Fantastic: A Structural Approach to a Literary Genre*. Trans. Richard Howard. Ithaca: Cornell University Press, 1975.

Torok, Maria. "Fantasy: An Attempt to Define Its Structure and Operations." In *The Shell and the Kernel: Renewals of Psychoanalysis*. Ed. and trans. Nicholas Rand. Vol. 1. Chicago: University of Chicago Press, 1994. 27–36.

———. "The Illness of Mourning and the Fantasy of the Exquisite Corpse." In *The Shell and the Kernel: Renewals of Psychoanalysis*. Ed. and trans. Nicholas Rand. Vol. 1. Chicago: University of Chicago Press, 1994. 107–24

Trumbach, Randolph. *The Rise of the Egalitarian Family*. New York: Academic, 1976.

———. "Sex, Gender, and Social Identity in Modern Culture: Male Sodomy and Female Prostitution in Enlightenment London." *Journal of the History of Sexuality* 2 (1991): 186–203.

Turner, James Grantham. "The Libertine Sublime: Love and Death in Restoration England." *Studies in Eighteenth-Century Culture* 19 (1989): 99–115.

———. "Lovelace and the Paradoxes of Libertinism." In *Samuel Richardson: Tercentenary Essays*, ed. Margaret Anne Doody and Peter Sabor. New York: Cambridge University Press, 1989. 70–88.

Vickery, Amanda. *The Gentleman's Daughter: Women's Lives in Georgian England*. New Haven: Yale University Press, 1998.

Walpole, Horace. *The Castle of Otranto, a Gothic Story* (1764). Ed. W. S. Lewis. London: Oxford University Press, 1964.

———. *The Mysterious Mother* (1781). Ed. Montaque Summers. Boston: Houghton Mifflin; London: Constable, 1925.

Warner, William Beatty. *Reading Clarissa: The Struggles of Interpretation*. New Haven: Yale University Press, 1979.

Watt, Ian. *The Rise of the Novel*. Berkeley: University of California Press, 1959.

Weiskel, Thomas. *The Romantic Sublime: Studies in the Structure and Psychology of Transcendence*. Baltimore: Johns Hopkins University Press, 1976.

Whyte, Lancelot Law. *The Unconscious before Freud*. New York: Basic Books, 1960.

Wiegman, Robyn. "Economies of the Body: Gendered Sites in *Robinson Crusoe* and *Roxana*." *Criticism* 31.1 (1989): 33–51.

Williams, Anne. *Art of Darkness: A Poetics of Gothic*. Chicago: University of Chicago Press, 1995.

Williams, Linda. *Hard Core: Power, Pleasure, and the Frenzy of the Visible*. Berkeley: University of California Press, 1989.

Williams, Raymond. "Forms of Fiction in 1848." In *Literature, Politics, and Theory: Papers from the Essex Conference, 1976–84*, ed. Francis Barker et al. New York: Methuen, 1986. 1–16.

———. *Marxism and Literature*. New York: Oxford University Press, 1977.

Wilt, Judith. "He Could Go No Farther: A Modest Proposal about Lovelace and Clarissa." *PMLA* 92 (1977): 19–32.

Winnicott, D. W. *Playing and Reality*. New York: Basic Books, 1971.

Index

Abjection, 10, 142, 181n48
Abraham, Nicolas, 13, 110, 124–26, 133, 135, 136, 137, 144, 172n13, 178nn16, 18
Absurd, comic, 88
Affectivity: and *Clarissa*, 83; and connectedness, 37; and domestic sphere, 30; and erotics, 107; and family, 20, 33; and fantastic narrative, 10; and femininity, 34; and gothic literature, 8; and individualism, 5, 7, 8, 83; and individuality, 37; and language, 10, 124; and maternal relations, 74, 141, 142; and *Moll Flanders*, 20, 35, 37, 40; and rationality, 160n26; and *Robinson Crusoe*, 22, 30, 33, 37; and *Roxana*, 20, 35, 37, 48; and structure of feeling, 52, 59, 161n32, 164n6; and the sublime, 10; and *Tristram Shandy*, 103, 106; and women, 20, 51, 74
Alienation: and capitalism, 30, 42, 53; and *The Castle of Otranto*, 110, 122, 123, 134; and *Clarissa*, 11, 84; and colonialism, 158n13; and commodification, 39; and fantastic narrative, 10, 53; and *Moll Flanders*, 36, 39, 42, 44, 47; and object-relations theory, 55; and paternal relations, 122, 123, 134; and psychoanalysis, 140; and reproductive relations, 42, 90, 91; and *Robinson Crusoe*, 24, 26–27, 30, 34; and *Roxana*, 36, 44, 47; and self, 10, 26, 47, 53, 112, 140, 165n14; and self-awareness, 139; and sublime, 111, 112; and tragedy, 53; and *Tristram Shandy*, 89, 91
Allegory: and *Clarissa*, 82, 84; and fantastic narrative, 22; and paternal relations, 32; and picaresque, 25; and Puritanism, 22; and realist narrative, 22, 25, 26, 32, 82; and regression, 82; and religion, 19, 32, 82, 83, 84; and *Robinson Crusoe*, 19, 22, 24–26, 32; and self, 25, 84; and sentimentality, 84; and

temporality, 156n8; and *Tristram Shandy*, 101
Allen, Dennis W., 175n31
Ambisexuality, 94, 106, 175n31
Anderson, Benedict, 156n8, 158n16
Androgyny, 79, 84, 106, 169n29
Anti-hero, 8–9, 110, 118, 154n21, 154n22
Anxiety: and *The Castle of Otranto*, 121, 123, 124; and castration, 97, 101; and *Clarissa*, 11, 63, 121, 168n27; and difference, 96; and family, 36, 133; and incest, 38, 159n22; and masculinity, 121, 168n27; and maternal relations, 124, 141; and *Moll Flanders*, 36, 38; and paternal relations, 121; and *Robinson Crusoe*, 26–27, 30, 32, 34, 36; and *Roxana*, 36; and sexuality, 11, 63; and sublime, 112, 169n30; and *Tristram Shandy*, 90, 91, 96, 97, 100, 101, 107, 121, 171nn10, 11
Appropriation: and *The Castle of Otranto*, 123, 143; and *Clarissa*, 71, 76–77, 84, 143; and *Moll Flanders*, 42; and otherness, 109; and pornographic imagination, 60; and reproductive relations, 91; and *Robinson Crusoe*, 31, 33, 34; and *Tristram Shandy*, 91, 94, 105, 106, 144; of women's roles by men, 33, 91, 93–94, 105, 123
Aristocracy: and *The Castle of Otranto*, 124, 134; and *Clarissa*, 61, 62
Armstrong, Nancy, 57, 149–50n2, 155n27
Authorship, and gender, 153n17, 156n30
Autobiography, spiritual, 22, 24–25
Autonomy: and bourgeoisie, 54; and *The Castle of Otranto*, 110, 118, 127; and *Clarissa*, 13, 62, 67, 71, 72, 81, 82, 83, 118; and ego, 184n11; and fantastic narrative, 7, 19; and femininity, 48, 72, 82; and identity, 59; and ideology, 36–37; and individualism, 4, 17, 25, 36–37; and individuality, 31;

195

Autonomy (*continued*)
and interiority, 26; and masculinity,
21, 28, 34, 59; and *Moll Flanders*, 36–
37, 38, 51; and psychoanalysis,
165n14; and realist narrative, 6, 19,
25, 54; and repression, 21; and *Robinson Crusoe*, 19, 21, 22–23, 25–29, 31,
32, 34, 35, 37; and *Roxana*, 36–37, 44,
47, 48, 49; and self, 26, 71, 83, 144,
161n35, 165n14; and subjectivity, 139;
and *Tristram Shandy*, 144, 145; and
women, 20, 35–36

Bakhtin, Mikhail, 155n25, 170n2
Ballaster, Ros, 149n2
Barker-Benfield, G. J., 151n7
Beckett, Samuel, 88
Beckford, William, 180n39
Benjamin, Jessica, 13, 165–68nn, 182n3,
183–84nn
Benjamin, Walter, 156n8, 161n33
Bhaba, Homi, 158n13
Bimodality, 1, 21, 55, 58, 60, 109, 139,
140, 145, 146
Blaut, J. M., 157n2
Body: and *Clarissa*, 67, 81, 82, 83; and
commodification, 39, 44, 82, 160n28;
and fantastic narrative, 60; and gender, 60; and Lacanian theory, 104–5,
174n30; and masculinity, 97, 107; and
maternal relations, 34, 92, 103, 106,
107, 126, 133, 142, 174nn, 181n49;
and pornographic imagination, 60;
and reproductive relations, 20, 36, 42;
and *Robinson Crusoe*, 34; and *Roxana*,
47, 160n28; and *Tristram Shandy*, 94,
97, 106, 107, 144; ungendered, 60;
and women, 3, 35, 36, 42, 47, 60,
107
Bollas, Christopher, 183n6
Boundary: and *Clarissa*, 71, 73; and fantastic narrative, 10, 110–11; and realist narrative, 10; and self, 71, 73, 94,
165n14; and *Tristram Shandy*, 94, 144,
145
Bourgeoisie: and autonomy, 54; and
Clarissa, 62; and family, 62, 123, 133,
140, 159n20; and *Moll Flanders*, 43;
and *Pamela*, 58
Braudy, Leo, 165n12
Braverman, Richard, 158n15
Brenkman, John, 160n26, 184n12
Brontë, Charlotte, 153–54nn, 155n26,
161n30, 179n27, 182n2
Brontë, Emily, 88, 153n17, 155n26
Burke, Edmund, 111, 177n13

Butler, Judith, 173n20, 178n18, 182n3,
183n7, 184n11
Byron, George Gordon, 130

Caillois, Roger, 172n16
Capitalism: and alienation, 30, 42, 53;
and *The Castle of Otranto*, 110, 123;
and *Clarissa*, 60; and Defoe's life, 17;
and difference, 60; and family, 36, 38,
159n23; and fantastic narrative, 7,
150n3; and femininity, 43; and gender, 1, 2; and ideology, 28, 32, 59;
and incest, 159n23; and individualism, 4, 17, 19, 28, 31, 35, 39, 54, 59;
and materialism, 8; and *Moll Flanders*, 35, 38, 42–43, 159n19; and novelistic form, 1; and object-relations
theory, 53; and patriarchy, 7, 38, 60,
123; and pornographic imagination,
59; and realist narrative, 53, 150n3;
and reproductive relations, 42,
159n19; and *Robinson Crusoe*, 20, 28,
30–32, 34; and *Roxana*, 20, 35, 159n19;
and self, 31, 53; and sex-gender system, 1–2, 110; and sexuality, 60; and
subjectivity, 52; and women, 35, 42,
159n19
Carnivalesque, 106, 155n25, 170n2
Carroll, Lewis, 88
The Castle of Otranto (Walpole): and alienation, 110, 122, 123, 134; and anxiety, 121, 123, 124; and appropriation,
123, 143; and aristocracy, 124, 134;
and autonomy, 110, 118, 127; and bimodality, 145; and capitalism, 110,
123; and comedy, 113, 115, 117, 121,
122; and death, 134, 135; and desire,
110, 113, 122, 124, 133, 134; and difference, 11, 117, 121, 124; and dividedness, 127; and domination, 123;
and dream, 112, 113, 114, 127, 136;
and egotism, 110, 118; and erotics,
123; and family, 11, 119, 120, 121,
122, 123–24; and fantastic narrative,
11, 109–10, 116, 117, 118, 124, 127,
135; and gender, 11, 117, 145; and
gothic literature, 13, 87, 109–10, 118,
119, 155n26; and heterosexuality, 123;
and hierarchy, 121; and homoeroticism, 136; and hysteria, 118; and
identity, 119; and imagination, 117;
and incest, 110, 122, 123, 134, 135;
and incorporation, 133; and individualism, 117, 118, 123, 124; and instrumentalization, 117, 118; and interaction of narrative modes, 11, 110, 115–

16, 117, 124; and interiority, 110; and introjection, 133; and irony, 123; and language, 117, 124; and libertinism, 123; and loss, 11, 13, 110, 124, 134; and marriage, 121, 123, 135; and masculinity, 110, 117; and masochism, 120; and maternal relations, 120, 123, 124, 135–36, 142, 143, 144; and melancholia, 11, 110, 124, 127, 133, 134, 135, 144; and melodrama, 117, 145; and misogyny, 120, 123, 124; and mourning, 110, 113, 118; and narcissism, 118; and nihilism, 123; and objectification, 117; and oedipal struggle, 119; and paranoia, 118, 124; and parody, 110, 113; and paternal relations, 110, 117, 119, 121, 122, 123–24, 127, 134; and patriarchy, 117, 119, 120, 123–24; and perversity, 110, 117; and political relations, 119, 124, 177n14; and pornography, 122–23, 143; and possessiveness, 117, 118, 123, 124; and power, 117, 119, 121, 123–24; and preservative repression, 133; and private sphere, 121; and property, 119; and psychological relations, 117–19, 122–24, 127, 132, 133–36; and public sphere, 121; publication of, 170n3, 175n2; and rape, 143; and reader response, 118; and realist narrative, 11, 110, 116, 124; and recognition, 144; and regression, 136; and reproductive relations, 121, 124; and sadism, 120; and self, 110, 117, 118, 119, 123, 133; and self-awareness, 110; and sex-gender system, 110, 123, 124; and sexuality, 11, 120, 122–23, 134, 135, 145; and social class, 134; and solipsism, 110, 117; and subjectivity, 117, 120, 127, 145; and the sublime, 123, 136; and the supernatural, 112, 114–15, 117, 133; and tragedy, 113, 115, 121; and the uncanny, 133; and Walpole's life, 110, 116–17, 127, 129, 136, 177n13, 177n14; and women, 119–21
Castle, Terry, 69, 163–64n5
Castration: and anxiety, 97; and *Clarissa*, 78, 79; and Lacanian theory, 13, 104, 106, 173n19, 174n22; and language, 97, 98, 174n22; and maternal relations, 78, 92, 93; and *Tristram Shandy*, 13, 92, 93, 97, 98, 106, 107
Chabor, Lois, 159n19
Children: and gender identity, 166–67n18; and *Moll Flanders*, 20, 37, 43–

44; and psychoanalytic theory, 140, 141; and *Roxana*, 20, 44, 47, 49–50
Chodorow, Nancy, 182n3
Clarissa (Richardson): and affectivity, 83; and alienation, 11, 84; and allegory, 82, 84; and androgyny, 79, 83, 169n29; and anxiety, 11, 63, 121, 168n27; and appropriation, 71, 76–77, 84, 143; and aristocracy, 61, 62; and autonomy, 13, 62, 67, 71, 72, 81, 82, 83, 118; and bimodality, 58, 60, 145; and bisexuality, 79; and body, 67, 81, 82, 83; and boundary, 71, 73; and bourgeoisie, 62; and capitalism, 60; and castration, 78, 79; and colonialism, 82; and comedy, 65; and commodification, 62, 82; and connectedness, 71, 72, 79, 80, 142; and contradiction, 62, 68, 71, 76, 83, 164–65n9; and deconstruction, 163n5; and dependency, 67; and desire, 62, 66, 70, 71, 74, 122, 142, 143; and difference, 60, 66, 70, 73, 74, 75, 76, 78, 84–85, 142; and disintegration, 81, 83; and dividedness, 70, 80, 85, 109; and domination, 13, 65, 66, 68, 75, 168n27; and doubleness, 161n30, 168n24; and dream, 78, 79; and economic relations, 61–63; and erasure, 71, 84; and erotics, 13, 65–66, 68, 72, 75, 79, 85, 143, 168n27; and family, 61–64, 67, 68, 69, 70, 72, 83, 142; and fantastic narrative, 11, 57, 60, 61, 70, 71, 75, 77, 78, 82, 84, 85, 118, 163n1, 165n13; and femininity, 62, 70, 72, 74, 79, 81, 82, 85; and feminism, 13, 163–64n5; and fetishism, 76, 78; and gender, 11, 13, 60, 61, 65, 66, 70, 72, 74, 79, 80, 83, 84, 109, 142, 145, 166n16; and gothic literature, 81, 165n13; and heterosexuality, 60, 65, 73, 142; and homosociality, 143; and identification, 72, 78, 79, 85, 142, 169n29; and identity, 67, 71; and ideology, 62, 69, 83, 109; and impotence, 75, 79, 85; and individualism, 69, 83, 109, 118, 163n1; and integration, 84; and interaction of narrative modes, 11, 59, 60, 61, 70, 82, 84, 85; and libertinism, 59, 61, 69, 75, 162n38; and love, 73, 79; and marriage, 61, 62, 66, 67, 68, 69, 73; and martyrdom, 81, 82, 83, 169n29; and masculinity, 60, 62, 66, 70, 72, 73, 77, 78, 79, 85; and masochism, 66, 72, 80, 83, 163n1, 165n13; and mastery, 73; and materialism, 62, 67; and maternal relations, 63, 66, 67,

Clarissa (Richardson) (*continued*)
72, 75, 77–79, 80, 81, 142, 143, 144,
168n27; and matriarchy, 64; and melancholia, 144; and middle class, 61;
and misogyny, 63, 68; and morality,
62, 67, 80, 81, 82, 163n1; and murder,
61; and mutuality, 70–71, 142, 168n27;
and narcissism, 66, 68, 69, 70, 72, 81,
93; and objectification, 62, 65, 85; and
oceanic experience, 84; and omnipotence, 79; and otherness, 74, 78, 85,
143; and parody, 77, 81; and paternal
relations, 62–63, 68, 72, 80, 82, 83;
and patriarchy, 60, 63, 64, 80, 82, 83,
120; and penetration, 68, 76, 81,
165n12; and perversity, 163n1; and
pornography, 59–60, 66, 75, 76, 80,
84, 85, 143, 145; and possession, 69,
79; and possessiveness, 79; and
poststructuralism, 57; and power, 62,
63, 65, 66, 68, 73, 79, 80; and property, 62, 63, 67, 82; and prostitution,
61, 76, 77; and psychological relations, 60, 61, 71–85; and Puritanism,
164–65n9; and rape, 61, 65, 70, 76–78,
80, 81, 83, 85; and rationality, 71; and
reader response, 60, 85, 118, 168n26;
and realist narrative, 11, 57, 60, 61,
68, 69, 70, 71, 74, 75, 77, 80, 82, 83,
84, 85, 163n1, 165n13, 166n16; and
reciprocity, 83, 143; and recognition,
13, 71, 142, 144; and regression, 75,
80; and religion, 64, 72, 81, 82, 83, 84,
169n29; and sadism, 60, 63, 66, 72,
73, 75, 79, 80, 163n1, 168n27; and sadomasochism, 163n1; and self, 68, 70,
71, 73, 80, 82, 83, 84–85; and self-
preservation, 70; and sentimentality,
83, 84, 85; and sex-gender system, 60;
and sexuality, 60, 63, 64, 66, 69, 74,
75, 77, 83, 84, 145, 163n1; and social
class, 62, 63, 66; and socialization, 77;
and solipsism, 75, 78, 83, 85; and
subjectivity, 68–69, 71, 75, 80, 84, 109,
145; and sublime, 61, 82, 83, 84, 112;
and tragedy, 60, 85; and ungendered
condition, 60, 61
Clark, Alice, 151n6
Class. *See* Social class
Collins, Wilkie, 155n26, 161n30
Colonialism: and alienation, 158n13;
and *Clarissa*, 82; and contradiction, 29;
and diffusionism, 157n12; and otherness, 158n13; and race, 157–58n13;
and religion, 29; and *Robinson Crusoe*,
29, 31, 51, 157n11; and self, 158n13

Comedy: and the absurd, 88; and *The
Castle of Otranto*, 113, 115, 117, 121,
122; and *Clarissa*, 65; and fantastic
narrative, 102, 103–4, 105; and *Pamela*, 58; and realist narrative, 53, 107;
and sentimentality, 87; and sublime,
87, 102, 105, 106, 107; and *Tristram
Shandy*, 13, 87, 91, 95, 102, 103–4, 105,
106, 107, 117, 144
Commodification: and alienation, 39;
and body, 39, 44, 82, 160n28; and
Clarissa, 62, 82; and desire, 39; and
family, 36; and *Moll Flanders*, 36, 39,
42–43, 44; and reification, 39, 160n25,
160n26; and *Robinson Crusoe*, 34; and
Roxana, 36, 44, 47, 160n28; and self,
54; and sexuality, 43; and women, 36,
39
Complementarity, 142, 183n8, 184n12
Connectedness: and affectivity, 37; and
Clarissa, 71, 72, 79, 80, 142; and erotics, 107, 108; and fictionality, 146;
and heterosexuality, 60; and homosociality, 143; and individuality, 37, 60;
and power, 165n14; and reciprocity,
37, 143; and reproductive relations,
42; and *Tristram Shandy*, 107, 108,
144, 145
Consciousness: and contradiction, 47;
divided, 51; and fantastic narrative,
30, 47; and gothic literature, 111; and
ideology, 52, 55; and individualism,
5, 19, 51, 159n22; and interaction of
narrative modes, 22; and irrationalism, 47; and middle class, 57; and
modernity, 52, 109; and *Moll Flanders*,
47, 159n22; and object-relations theory, 52, 55; and *Pamela*, 57; and Puritanism, 22; and realist narrative, 140;
and *Robinson Crusoe*, 22, 30; and Romanticism, 140; and *Roxana*, 47, 140
Contradiction: and bimodality, 55; and
Clarissa, 62, 68, 71, 76, 83, 164–65n9;
and colonialism, 29; and consciousness, 47; and fantastic narrative, 35;
and gender, 36; and ideology, 20, 21,
139; and individualism, 55; and *Moll
Flanders*, 39–40, 47, 55; and Puritanism, 165–21n9; and realist narrative,
19, 21, 35; and *Robinson Crusoe*, 28,
29, 32, 35, 55; and *Roxana*, 20, 46–47,
48, 51, 55, 142, 145; and sex-gender
system, 1; and subjectivity, 46
Criminality, 37, 38, 40–43, 50–51, 182n2
Cross-gender identification, 51, 60,
183n7

Death: and *The Castle of Otranto*, 134, 135; and *Clarissa*, 61, 81, 83; and fantastic narrative, 9, 135; and *The Mysterious Mother*, 134; and sexuality, 134, 135; and *Tristram Shandy*, 102, 103

Deconstruction: and *Clarissa*, 163n5; and fantastic narrative, 110–11; and gothic literature, 111; and *Tristram Shandy*, 88

Defoe, Daniel: life of, 17–19, 52; works of, 13, 19–22, 52–55, 144, 149n1. See also *Moll Flanders; Robinson Crusoe; Roxana*

Deleuze, Gilles, 168n26

Dependency: and *Clarissa*, 67; and masculinity, 28, 35, 59; and *Robinson Crusoe*, 23, 28, 35

Desire: and *The Castle of Otranto*, 110, 113, 122, 124, 133, 134; and *Clarissa*, 62, 66, 70, 71, 74, 122, 142, 143; and commodification, 39; and fantastic narrative, 7, 9, 12, 60, 74, 85, 88, 103, 112, 153n17, 154n24, 176n3; and femininity, 58, 74, 153n17, 153n18, 166n16; and gothic literature, 8, 153n18; and homosociality, 94; and incest, 110, 122, 134; and lack, 101; and loss, 13, 134; and masculinity, 60, 94, 153n17, 153n18; and masochism, 66; and materialism, 7; and maternal relations, 124, 132, 141; and melancholia, 125; and *Moll Flanders*, 35, 38, 39, 44; and mourning, 134; and *The Mysterious Mother*, 134; and *Pamela*, 58; and paternal relations, 134, 166n16; and perversity, 5; and phallic economy, 104; and pornographic imagination, 60; and *Robinson Crusoe*, 26, 30, 32; and *Roxana*, 35, 44, 46, 49, 50; and sex-gender system, 142, 143; and subjectivity, 88; and *Tristram Shandy*, 93, 94, 101, 103, 104; and the uncanny, 132

Dialectics, Hegelian, 165n14

Dickens, Charles, 155n26, 156n30, 161n30, 170n2, 182n2

Difference: and anxiety, 96; and capitalism, 60; and *The Castle of Otranto*, 117, 121, 124; and *Clarissa*, 60, 66, 70, 73, 74, 75, 76, 78, 84–85, 142; and fantastic narrative, 7, 9, 103–4; and gender, 1, 4, 14, 28, 32, 59, 60, 70, 84, 102, 103, 117, 151n5, 162n44, 173n17; and heterosexuality, 183n8; and hierarchy, 10, 94, 103, 107, 121, 144; and

Lacanian theory, 12–13; and maternal relations, 124; and melancholia, 7, 11; and men, 74; and naturalization, 73; and patriarchy, 60; and pornography, 59, 85, 167n20; and power, 59, 66; and psychoanalysis, 12–13; and race, 28; and realist narrative, 5, 7, 10, 73, 108; and reproductive relations, 3, 90; and *Robinson Crusoe*, 28, 29, 32; and scientific ideology, 3; and self, 84–85; and sex-gender system, 3–4; sexual, 2, 3, 9, 13, 60, 74, 75, 83–84, 89, 103, 143, 167n20; and *Tristram Shandy*, 89, 90, 93, 94, 96, 102, 117, 143, 144, 173n17; and women, 74

Dinnerstein, Dorothy, 182n3

Disintegration: and *Clarissa*, 81, 83; and *Robinson Crusoe*, 25; and self, 25, 103

Displacement: and family, 20; and gender, 33; and *Robinson Crusoe*, 20, 32, 33; and *Tristram Shandy*, 93, 107; and women, 33

Dissenters, 17, 18

Dividedness: and *The Castle of Otranto*, 127; and *Clarissa*, 70, 80, 85, 109; and consciousness, 51; and fantastic narrative, 7, 20, 88, 127; and hysteria, 51; and individualism, 5, 51, 109; and labor, 2, 3, 12, 33, 34, 51, 58, 77, 88, 121, 163n3; and Lacanian theory, 104; and *Pamela*, 58; and Richardson's life, 85; and *Robinson Crusoe*, 26, 28, 30, 33, 34, 109; and *Roxana*, 47–48, 50, 51, 109; and self, 5, 7, 26, 28, 30, 50, 55, 80, 87, 97, 133, 152n13, 183n8; and subjectivity, 19, 88, 89, 109, 127, 139, 183n8; and tragedy, 47; and *Tristram Shandy*, 87, 89, 95, 97, 109

Domestication: and nature, 34; and *Robinson Crusoe*, 34

Domestic sphere: and affectivity, 30; and inequality, 30; and *Moll Flanders*, 37, 44; and novelistic form, 149n2; and realist narrative, 6; and *Robinson Crusoe*, 30, 33; and *Roxana*, 44, 45; and women, 2, 37

Domination: and *The Castle of Otranto*, 123; and *Clarissa*, 13, 65, 66, 68, 75, 168n27; and erotics, 9, 13, 68, 72, 75, 123, 143, 166nn, 168n27, 183n9; and fantastic narrative, 9; and gender, 13, 141; and Hegelian theory, 165n14; and pornography, 143; and *Robinson Crusoe*, 27, 30; and self, 165n14; and women, 123

Dostoevsky, Fyodor, 170n2
Doubleness: and bimodal fiction, 139, 140, 147; and *Clarissa*, 161n30, 168n24; and literary tradition, 161n30; and *Roxana*, 48, 50; and *Tristram Shandy*, 95, 102
Dracula (Stoker), 88, 155n26
Dream: and *The Castle of Otranto*, 112, 113, 114, 127, 136; and *Clarissa*, 78, 79; and *Robinson Crusoe*, 27–28

Eagleton, Terry, 69, 163–64n5
Economic relations: and *Clarissa*, 61–63; and criminality, 43; and Defoe's life, 17–18; and family, 2, 36, 159n20; and gender, 1, 2; and men, 2; and *Moll Flanders*, 36, 39; in *Robinson Crusoe*, 22–23, 26, 30–31; and *Roxana*, 20, 36, 44–45, 49; and sex-gender system, 1–3; and sexuality, 43, 62; and women, 2, 36, 123, 151n6
Ego, 111, 117, 125, 126, 134–35, 152n15, 178–79nn17, 18, 25, 184n11
Egotism, 6, 8, 20, 23–24, 110, 118
Ehlers, Leigh A., 171n11
Elias, Norbert, 5, 152n13, 155n25
Eliot, George, 162n38
Emotion. *See* Affectivity
Empiricism, 88, 149n1
Enlightenment, 10, 12, 116, 117, 158n16
Epistemology, 10, 11, 88, 170n4, 170n5
Erasure: and *Clarissa*, 71, 84; and maternal relations, 91, 101, 172n14; and *Robinson Crusoe*, 20, 31, 33; and *Tristram Shandy*, 91, 101, 142; and women, 20, 31, 33
Erotics: and affectivity, 107; and *The Castle of Otranto*, 123; and *Clarissa*, 13, 65–66, 68, 72, 75, 79, 85, 143, 168n27; and community, 107; and connectedness, 107, 108; and domination, 9, 13, 68, 72, 75, 123, 143, 166nn, 168n27, 184n9; and family, 123; and fantastic narrative, 9; and heroism, 177n15; and indeterminacy, 103; and Lacanian theory, 105; and maternal relations, 129; and *Moll Flanders*, 39; and *Robinson Crusoe*, 33, 143; and *Roxana*, 44, 48, 143; and self-transcendence, 105; and *Tristram Shandy*, 94, 107, 108, 143
Exchange value, 30, 43
Exploitation: and *Moll Flanders*, 36, 39, 41; and pornography, 167n20; and *Robinson Crusoe*, 28, 31, 34, 35, 37; and *Roxana*, 36, 44, 45; and subjectivity, 41

Family: and affectivity, 20, 33; and anxiety, 36, 133; and bourgeoisie, 62, 123, 133, 140, 159n20; and capitalism, 36, 38, 159n23; and *The Castle of Otranto*, 11, 119, 120, 121, 122, 123–24; and *Clarissa*, 61–64, 67, 68, 69, 70, 72, 83, 142; and commodification, 36; and displacement, 20; and economic relations, 2, 36, 159n20; and erotics, 123; extended, 36, 93; and fantastic narrative, 9, 112; and gothic literature, 8, 119, 122; and heterosexuality, 93, 166n18; and ideology, 159n20; and incest, 38–39; and individualism, 37; and instrumentalization, 47; and middle class, 2, 61, 159n20; and *Moll Flanders*, 35, 36, 37–39; nuclear, 2, 36, 38, 93; and patriarchy, 1–2, 9, 38, 64, 83; and perversity, 38; and private sphere, 2, 5; and realist narrative, 9, 93; and *Robinson Crusoe*, 20, 22–23, 25, 28, 32–33, 36, 37, 158–59n18; and *Roxana*, 20, 35, 36, 37, 47, 49–50; and self, 119; and sex-gender system, 37; and social class, 7, 159n20; and socialization, 36; and *Tristram Shandy*, 93; and working class, 159n20
Fanon, Franz, 157n13, 164n6
Fantastic narrative: and affectivity, 10; and alienation, 53; and allegory, 22; and autonomy, 7, 19; and boundary, 7, 110–11; and capitalism, 7, 150n3; and *The Castle of Otranto*, 11, 109–10, 116, 117, 118, 124, 127, 135; and *Clarissa*, 11, 57, 60, 61, 70, 71, 75, 77, 78, 82, 84, 85, 118, 163n1, 165n13; and comedy, 102, 103–4, 105; and consciousness, 30, 47; and contradiction, 35; and cross-gender representation, 60; and death, 9, 135; and deconstruction, 110–11; and desire, 7, 9, 12, 60, 74, 85, 88, 103, 112, 153n17, 154n24, 176n3; and Dickens's works, 182n2; and difference, 7, 103–4; and dividedness, 7, 20, 88, 127; and domination, 9; and erotics, 9; and family, 9, 112; and femininity, 77; and gender, 34, 60, 61, 72, 85, 88, 140, 153n17, 154n24, 184n8; and gothic literature, 7–8, 87–88, 109–10, 111, 150n3, 176n3; and Hegelian theory, 165n14; and heterosexuality, 9, 74; and homosexuality, 9; and homosociality, 143; and horror genre, 87–88; and identification, 60, 132; and ideology, 139; and impotence, 60; and in-

cest, 9, 75, 112; and indeterminacy, 7, 10, 14; and individualism, 7, 21–22; and integration, 7, 21; and interiority, 7, 48, 88, 110; and loss, 137; and love, 73–74; and marriage, 8, 9; and masculinity, 8–9, 34, 60; and materialism, 7; and maternal relations, 9, 75, 77; and melancholia, 7, 14, 125, 126–27, 143; and misogyny, 9; and modernism, 7, 10, 109; and *Moll Flanders*, 41, 42; and mourning, 143; and mutuality, 143; and *The Mysterious Mother*, 110, 132; and narcissism, 112; and necrophilia, 135; and object-relations theory, 53, 54–55; and objectification, 9; and otherness, 14, 29; and paranoia, 7, 9, 143; and paternal relations, 9; and patriarchy, 7; and picaresque, 21, 46, 49; and pornography, 60, 75, 84, 164n7; and postmodernism, 8, 109; and power, 60, 77; and psychoanalysis, 12, 13, 55, 124–27, 140, 154n24; and psychological relations, 10, 60, 61, 88, 111, 150n3, 155n26; and realist narrative, 1, 10–11, 14–15, 19–20, 22, 28, 30, 34, 49, 51, 60, 61, 70, 82, 84, 85, 87, 88, 102, 109, 110, 116, 124, 145, 154n24, 155n26; and regression, 10, 60, 75; and repression, 126, 127; and *Robinson Crusoe*, 11, 19–20, 21, 22, 26–30, 31, 34, 35, 118; and romance genre, 8, 10, 88, 150n3; and Romanticism, 8, 109; and *Roxana*, 21, 44, 46, 47, 48, 49, 50, 51; and sadism, 72; and satire, 170n2; and self, 7, 10, 14, 30, 53, 55, 61, 74, 95, 103, 112; and self-awareness, 7, 9, 31, 34; and self-reflection, 7, 46; and sex-gender system, 7; and sexuality, 8, 9, 72, 75, 77, 88; and social context, 88; and solipsism, 8–9, 60, 75, 88; and subjectivity, 9, 10, 11, 54, 88, 89, 127, 154n24; and the sublime, 10, 61, 84, 102, 104, 105, 107, 112, 177n15; and the supernatural, 112, 154n24; and tragedy, 8, 53, 103, 110; and *Tristram Shandy*, 11, 87, 88, 89, 93, 95, 102, 103–4, 107, 145; and the uncanny, 133, 154n24; and ungendered condition, 60, 61
Fantasy, psychoanalytic theory of, 126–27, 178–79n25
Faurot, Ruth, 171n11
Feeling. *See* Affectivity
Felman, Shoshana, 155–56nn28–29
Female traits. *See* Femininity

Femininity: and affectivity, 34; and autonomy, 48, 72, 82; and capitalism, 43; and *Clarissa*, 62, 70, 72, 74, 79, 81, 82, 85; and desire, 58, 74, 153n17, 153n18, 166n16; and fantastic narrative, 77; and gothic literature, 8; and identification, 60; and identity, 2, 43; and ideology, 22, 35, 43; and impotence, 85; and individualism, 19, 20–22, 35, 37, 41, 42, 44, 51, 52; and interiority, 3, 155n27; and Lacanian theory, 173n19; and masochism, 8, 66, 72, 153n19, 166n15, 166n16; and maternal relations, 74; and *Moll Flanders*, 35, 39, 40, 41, 42, 45, 51; and narcissism, 66; and nature, 33–34; and objectification, 85; and otherness, 85; and paternal relations, 166n16; and perversity, 37; and possessiveness, 42, 51; and power, 77; and realist narrative, 42, 45, 75; and *Robinson Crusoe*, 32–34; and *Roxana*, 21, 35, 44, 45, 46, 48, 160n28; and self-awareness, 8, 51; and sensibility, 151n7; and subjectivity, 47, 75, 145, 150n2, 153n17; and *Tristram Shandy*, 93, 107, 145
Feminism: and *Clarissa*, 13, 163–64n5; and gender, 142, 146; and Hegelian theory, 165n14; and indeterminacy, 103; and individualism, 51–52; and Lacanian theory, 173n20; and maternal relations, 141–42; and melancholia, 146; and object-relations theory, 13, 141, 165–66n14, 183n5; and pornographic imagination, 142; and psychoanalysis, 141–42, 145, 146, 182n3, 183n5; and reproductive relations, 91; and romance genre, 149n2; and *Roxana*, 45, 51, 160n28; and sex-gender system, 142, 146; and *Tristram Shandy*, 145, 170–171n8, 171n11
Ferguson, Frances, 163n5
Fetishism: and *Clarissa*, 76, 78; and *Tristram Shandy*, 93, 97
Feudalism, 1, 177n13
Fiedler, Leslie, 165n13
Fielding, Henry, 57, 149n1, 169–70nn1–2, 175n1
Filmer, Robert, 150n4, 171n10
Flint, Christopher, 158n18
Foster, James, 156nn2, 7
Foucault, Michel, 150n2
Fragmentation, psychic, 7, 11, 80, 81, 97, 102, 117, 133

Frankenstein (Shelley), 88, 153n17, 154n23, 155n26, 179n27, 182n2
Freud, Sigmund, 12–13, 55, 88, 89, 92, 94, 117, 140–41, 152nn14–15, 161n34, 162nn, 165n11, 166n15, 167n19, 170n6, 172nn13–15, 178n25, 182n4, 183n5; and humor, 173–74n21; and hysteria, 47; and melancholia, 125–26, 168–69n28, 172n13, 178nn17–18, 181–82n53; and mourning, 125–26, 172n13; and nachtraglichkeit, 182n1; and oedipal struggle, 133, 141, 158n17; and sublimation, 111, 176n4; and the uncanny, 10, 132, 181n48, 181n49

Gallagher, Catherine, 149n2
Gallop, Jane, 173n20, 174n22
Ganner, Michael, 164n8
Gaze, 98, 144
Gender: and authorship, 153n17, 156n30; and body, 60; and capitalism, 1, 2; and *The Castle of Otranto*, 11, 117, 145; and *Clarissa*, 11, 13, 60, 61, 65, 66, 70, 72, 74, 79, 80, 83, 84, 109, 142, 145, 166n16; and complementarity, 183n8, 184n12; and contradiction, 36; and cross-gender identification, 51, 60, 183n7; and difference, 1, 4, 11, 14, 28, 32, 59, 60, 66, 70, 84, 102, 103, 117, 151n5, 162n44, 173n17; and displacement, 33; and domination, 13, 141; and economic relations, 1, 2; and fantastic narrative, 34, 60, 72, 85, 88, 140, 153n17, 154n24, 184n8; and feminism, 142, 146; and identification, 60, 85, 183n7, 183n8; and identity, 12, 55, 166–67n18; and ideology, 21; and indeterminacy, 102–3, 144; and inequality, 6, 141; and interaction of narrative modes, 14, 85, 154n24; and labor, 2, 51, 77, 88, 121, 153n17; and Lacanian theory, 13, 162n44; and medievalism, 116; and melancholia, 11, 142, 143, 144, 183n7; and middle class, 1, 2; and *Moll Flanders*, 20, 21; and naturalization, 58; and nature, 33; and oedipal struggle, 183n8; and patriarchy, 151n5; and pornographic imagination, 59, 60–61; and power, 59, 66; and psychoanalysis, 12, 162n44, 165n14; and reader response, 60, 85; and realist narrative, 6, 7, 74, 153n17, 154n24, 166n16; and *Robinson Crusoe*, 11, 28, 32, 34, 109, 145; and *Roxana*, 21, 109, 145; and self, 21, 61; and social class, 1–2, 3, 151n5; and subjec-

tivity, 2, 4, 12, 14, 80, 102, 109, 149n2, 154n24; and tragedy, 142; and *Tristram Shandy*, 102, 109, 117, 142, 144, 145, 171nn, 173n17, 175n31; and ungendered condition, 12, 69, 61
Gilman, Sander, 164n6
Godwin, William, 154n23, 155n26
Gogol, N. V., 170n2
Gothic literature: and affectivity, 8; and *The Castle of Otranto*, 13, 87, 109–10, 118, 119, 155n26; and *Clarissa*, 81, 165n13; and consciousness, 111; and deconstruction, 111; and desire, 8, 153n18; and egotism, 8; and family, 8, 119, 122; and fantastic narrative, 7–8, 87–88, 109–10, 111, 150n3, 176n3; and femininity, 8; and feudalism, 177n13; and homosexuality, 154n23; and horror genre, 87; and imprisonment, 177n9; and individualism, 8; and irony, 123; and irrationalism, 111; and libertinism, 123, 162n38; and marriage, 8; and masculinity, 8; and masochism, 8, 153n19, 165n13, 166n15; and melancholia, 124–25; and melodrama, 87; and *The Mysterious Mother*, 13, 127; and paranoia, 9, 154n23; and patriarchy, 8; and political relations, 177n13; and pornography, 164n8; and possessiveness, 8; and psychoanalysis, 110, 117, 124–25, 134, 166n15; and romance genre, 111, 150n3, 154n21; and sadism, 8, 166n15; and self, 119; and self-awareness, 8, 9; and self-control, 8; and sexuality, 8; and solipsism, 8–9; and sublime, 123; and the supernatural, 10, 111, 150n3, 175n3, 177n9; and tragedy, 87; and *Tristram Shandy*, 87
Gray, Thomas, 175n1
Gwynn, Stephen, 175n1, 179–80n36, 180nn39, 41

Haggerty, George, 180n39
Hardy, Thomas, 155n26
Harley, Robert, 18
Hawthorne, Nathaniel, 161n30
Hegel, G. W. F., 72, 165
Henriques, Julian, 184n12
Heterosexuality, 3, 9, 60, 65, 66, 73–74, 93, 123, 142, 143, 145, 166n18, 183n8
Hierarchy: and *The Castle of Otranto*, 121; and difference, 10, 94, 103, 107, 121; and pornographic imagination, 59; and realist narrative, 10, 30, 34; and *Robinson Crusoe*, 28, 29,

30, 34; and *Tristram Shandy*, 94, 103, 144
Hill, Christopher, 164–65n9
Hoffmann, E. T. A., 132
Hogg, James, 154n23
Homoeroticism, 9, 133, 136
Homophobia, 9, 154n23
Homosexuality, 9, 129, 166n18, 180n39, 183n7
Homosociality, 33, 93–94, 105, 143, 145
Horney, Karen, 168n25
Horror genre, 87–88
Hughes, Peter, 177n15
Hulme, Peter, 157n11
Hunter, John Paul, 170n8
Hysteria: and *The Castle of Otranto*, 118; and dividedness, 51; and psychoanalysis, 47, 51; and *Roxana*, 47, 51; and women, 47, 51

Idealization: and paternal relations, 94, 101; and Phallus, 101, 105; and *Tristram Shandy*, 93, 94, 98, 100, 101; and women, 93
Identification: and *Clarissa*, 72, 78, 79, 85, 142, 169n29; cross-gender, 51, 60, 183n7; and fantastic narrative, 60, 132; and femininity, 60; and fictionality, 146; and gender, 12, 60, 85, 183nn7–8; and masculinity, 60; and maternal relations, 60, 168n27, 193n8; and melancholia, 172n13; and *The Mysterious Mother*, 132; and oedipal struggle, 183n8; and pornographic imagination, 60; and realist narrative, 72; and sex-gender system, 139, 142, 143; and sexuality, 168n26, 183n7; and *Tristram Shandy*, 94
Identity: and autonomy, 59; and *The Castle of Otranto*, 119; and *Clarissa*, 67, 71; and femininity, 2, 43; and gender, 55, 166–67n18; and ideology, 43; and masculinity, 2, 28, 59, 166–67n18; and *Moll Flanders*, 41–42; and paternal relations, 90; and race, 157–58n13; and realist narrative, 139; and reproductive relations, 90; and *Robinson Crusoe*, 28, 29, 31–32, 34; and *Roxana*, 50; and sexuality, 41, 168n26; and *Tristram Shandy*, 90, 170n5
Ideology: and autonomy, 36–37; and capitalism, 28, 32, 59; and *Clarissa*, 62, 69, 83, 109; and consciousness, 52, 55; and contradiction, 20, 21, 139; and family, 159n20; and fantastic narrative, 139; and femininity, 22, 35,

43; and gender, 21; and identity, 43; and individualism, 19, 22, 28, 35, 57, 59, 109, 165n9; and instrumentalization, 36–37; and interaction of narrative modes, 11; and libertinism, 69; and marriage, 3; and masculinity, 32, 69, 165n9; and *Moll Flanders*, 20, 35, 36–37; and nationalism, 28; and object-relations theory, 13, 52, 55; and *Pamela*, 57; and pornographic imagination, 59; and prostitution, 3; and psychological relations, 21, 52, 55; and realist narrative, 6, 21; and religion, 83; and reproductive relations, 20; and *Robinson Crusoe*, 28, 36–37, 109; and *Roxana*, 20, 21, 35, 36–37, 109; and science, 3; and self, 21; and sexuality, 3, 35; and structure of feeling, 161n32; and *Tristram Shandy*, 109
Imagination, 111, 117
Imperialism, and *Robinson Crusoe*, 20, 23, 33, 34
Impotence: and *Clarissa*, 75, 79, 85; and fantastic narrative, 60; and femininity, 85; and libertinism, 75; and *Tristram Shandy*, 92, 93, 97, 100, 101
Incest: and anxiety, 38, 159n22; and capitalism, 159n23; and *The Castle of Otranto*, 110, 122, 123, 134, 135; and desire, 9, 110, 122, 134; and fantastic narrative, 9, 75, 112; and loss, 134; and *Moll Flanders*, 38–39, 159n22; and *The Mysterious Mother*, 130, 131, 134, 136
Inchbald, Elizabeth, 150n3
Incorporation, 125–26, 133, 135
Indeterminacy, 1, 7, 10, 11, 14, 83, 107, 144, 192–93, 104
Individualism: and affectivity, 5, 7, 8, 83; and autonomy, 4, 17, 25, 36–37; and capitalism, 4, 17, 19, 28, 31, 35, 39, 54, 59; and *The Castle of Otranto*, 117, 118, 123, 124; and *Clarissa*, 69, 83, 109, 118, 163n1; and consciousness, 5, 19, 51, 159n22; and contradiction, 55; and Defoe's life, 17, 52; and dividedness, 5, 51, 109; and family, 37; and fantastic narrative, 7, 21–22; and femininity, 19, 20–22, 35, 37, 41, 42, 44, 51, 52; and feminism, 51–52; and gothic literature, 8; and ideology, 19, 22, 28, 35, 57, 59, 109, 165n9; and instrumentalization, 4–5, 36–37; and masculinity, 19, 35, 41, 52, 69, 165n9; and maternal relations, 43, 142; and middle class, 149n1; and

Individualism (*continued*)
  Moll Flanders, 19, 20, 21, 35, 36–37, 39, 41, 42–44, 55, 159n22; and nationalism, 31; and object-relations theory, 54, 55; and *Pamela*, 57; and picaresque, 22; and pornographic imagination, 59; possessive, 7, 8, 19, 20, 30, 35, 42, 51, 117, 118, 123, 124, 165n9; and realist narrative, 5, 22, 26, 30; and *Robinson Crusoe*, 19–20, 21, 22, 25, 26, 30, 31, 35, 36–37, 44, 52, 55, 109; and *Roxana*, 19, 20, 21, 35, 36–37, 44, 49, 51–52, 55, 109, 142; and self, 31, 54; and self-awareness, 4, 10, 22; and self-consciousness, 152n15; and sex-gender system, 19, 35, 37, 44; and solipsism, 83, 117; and subjectivity, 30; and tragedy, 95; and *Tristram Shandy*, 95, 109
Individuality: and affectivity, 37; and autonomy, 31; and connectedness, 37, 60; and masculinity, 19, 33, 34–35, 166n16; and *Moll Flanders*, 37; and narcissism, 53–54; and political relations, 34; possessive, 35; and realist narrative, 33; and reciprocity, 37; and *Robinson Crusoe*, 19, 31, 33, 34, 37; and *Roxana*, 37; and sexuality, 37; and *Tristram Shandy*, 145
Inequality: and domestic sphere, 30; and gender, 6, 141; and realist narrative, 5, 6; and *Robinson Crusoe*, 29, 30; and sex-gender system, 123
Instrumentalization: and *The Castle of Otranto*, 117, 118; and family, 47; and ideology, 36–37; and individualism, 4–5, 36–37; and *Moll Flanders*, 35, 37, 38, 44, 45; and otherness, 10; and *Robinson Crusoe*, 31, 37; and *Roxana*, 35, 37, 44, 45, 47, 51; and sexuality, 51
Integration: and *Clarissa*, 84; and fantastic narrative, 7, 21; and maternal relations, 141; and *Moll Flanders*, 41; and object-relations theory, 53, 54; and realist narrative, 6, 10; and *Robinson Crusoe*, 24, 26, 27, 31, 54; and *Roxana*, 21; and self, 31, 41, 53, 54, 84, 93, 165n14; and subjectivity, 89; and *Tristram Shandy*, 89, 93, 102
Interiority: and autonomy, 26; and *The Castle of Otranto*, 110; and Defoe's life, 19; and fantastic narrative, 7, 48, 88, 110; and femininity, 3, 155n27; and masculinity, 3; and *Moll Flanders*, 40; and *Robinson Crusoe*, 26; and *Rox-*

ana, 46, 47, 48, 52; and socioeconomic relations, 155n27; and solipsism, 88
Intersubjectivity, 141, 144, 165n14, 183n8
Introjection, 125–26, 133, 134, 178nn17–18, 179n25
Irigaray, Luce, 167n20, 171n12, 174n23
Irony: and *The Castle of Otranto*, 123; and gothic literature, 123; and *Moll Flanders*, 35–36; and *Pamela*, 58; and *Tristram Shandy*, 88, 91, 102, 107, 117
Irrationalism: and consciousness, 47; and gothic literature, 111; and psychoanalysis, 55, 132; and *Robinson Crusoe*, 22, 25; and *Roxana*, 46, 47; and subjectivity, 55; and the uncanny, 132
Isaacs, Susan, 178n25
Iser, Wolfgang, 172n16

Jackson, Rosemary, 154n24, 176n3
Jacobinism, 18
Jacobus, Mary, 182n3
James, Henry, 154n24
Johnson, Claudia L., 153n20
Jouissance, 104–5, 106, 107, 142, 173n19, 174n25
Journal to Eliza (Sterne), 93, 105
Joyce, James, 88

Ketton-Cremer, Robert Wyndham, 176n8, 179n28, 180n38, 180n38, 39
Kilgour, Maggie, 177n13
Klein, Jurgen, 170n5
Klein, Melanie, 106, 174n30, 178n25
Knowledge, 75, 89, 99, 101, 103, 104, 106, 111, 146
Kohut, Heinz, 13, 52–55, 118, 161nn34, 37, 162nn39–44
Kristeva, Julia, 10, 103, 107, 167n22, 172n13, 174n23, 175n33, 181n48

Labor: division of, 2, 3, 12, 33, 51, 58, 77, 88, 121, 153n17, 163n3; exploitation of, 34, 36; and gender, 2, 51, 77, 88, 121, 153n17; and *Moll Flanders*, 36; and *Pamela*, 58; and *Robinson Crusoe*, 26, 30, 33, 34; and *Roxana*, 36; and women, 36, 151n6
Lacan, Jacques, 88, 157–58n13, 161n35, 162n44
Lacanian theory: and body, 104–5, 174n30; and castration, 13, 104, 106, 173n19, 174n22; and difference, 12–13; and dividedness, 104; and erotics, 105; and femininity, 173n19; and

feminism, 173n20; and gender, 13, 162n44; and homosociality, 105; and *hors-sexe*, 105; and *jouissance*, 104–5, 106, 107, 173n19, 174n25; and language, 97, 101; and materiality, 105; and maternal relations, 174n30; and mirror stage, 153n16, 161n35, 165n14; and misogyny, 13; and narcissism, 161n35; and object-relations theory, 161n35; and patriarchy, 97; and phallic economy, 104; and phallic signifier, 101, 173n19, 174nn; and the Real, 10, 103; and religion, 104–5; and self, 89, 106, 153n16, 161n35; and self-transcendence, 104–5; and sexuality, 89; and subjectivity, 13, 89, 104; and Symbolic order, 103; and *Tristram Shandy*, 13, 87, 97, 101, 103–6, 171n8, 172n15, 173nn18–20; and women, 104–5, 174n25

Lack: and desire, 101; and *Tristram Shandy*, 13, 93, 94, 97, 100, 101

Language: and affectivity, 10, 124; and *The Castle of Otranto*, 117, 124; and castration, 97, 98, 174n22; and introjection, 126; and Lacanian theory, 97, 101; and Lockean theory, 88, 99; and melancholia, 126, 146; and mourning, 126, 146; and patriarchy, 97; and primal bond, 145; and self, 89; and *Tristram Shandy*, 13, 88, 89, 95, 97, 98, 99, 101, 103, 117, 144, 145

Lanham, Richard, 172n16

Laplanche, J., 170n6, 182n1, 183n5

Laqueur, Thomas, 151–52n8

Lawrence, D. H., 155n26

Lefanu, Sheridan, 155n26

Leites, Edmund, 152n8, 163n3

Lewis, Matthew, 88, 153n18, 155n26, 164n8, 180n39

Lewis, W. S., 127, 128, 175n1, 179–81nn

Libertinism: and *The Castle of Otranto*, 123; and *Clarissa*, 59, 61, 69, 75, 162n38; and ideology, 69; and impotence, 75; and literary tradition, 162n38; and *Pamela*, 57; and pornographic imagination, 59; and the sublime, 123, 177n15

Locke, John, 88, 99, 150–51n4, 158n15, 170n4, 176n5

Loewald, Hans, 175n32

Loss: and *The Castle of Otranto*, 11, 13, 110, 124, 134; and fantastic narrative, 137; and incest, 134; and melancholia, 11, 14, 125, 126, 133; and pornographic imagination, 143; and *Tristram*

Shandy, 88, 89, 93, 97, 106, 107, 143

Love: and *Clarissa*, 73, 79; and fantastic narrative, 73–74; and heterosexuality, 74; and melancholia, 125; and realist narrative, 73; and *Robinson Crusoe*, 28, 32; and struggle for change, 147

Lukács, Georg, 160nn25, 26

McKeon, Michael, 57, 150n2, 151n5, 170n1

Macksey, Richard, 170n8, 173n18

Magical realism, 88

Male traits. *See* Masculinity

Marcuse, Herbert, 159–60n24

Marginality: and Defoe's life, 17; and Defoe's works, 28–29; and Sterne's works, 87, 169n1

Marriage: and *The Castle of Otranto*, 121, 123, 135; and *Clarissa*, 61, 62, 66, 67, 68, 69; and fantastic narrative, 8, 9; and gothic literature, 8; and heterosexuality, 65, 73; and ideology, 3; and incest, 38; and *Moll Flanders*, 36, 37, 38, 43; and *Pamela*, 57–58; and property, 62; and realist narrative, 6–7, 73; and *Robinson Crusoe*, 29, 33; and *Roxana*, 36, 44, 45–46, 49

Masculinity: and anxiety, 121, 168n27; and autonomy, 21, 28, 34, 59; and body, 97, 107; and *The Castle of Otranto*, 110, 117; and *Clarissa*, 60, 62, 66, 70, 72, 73, 77, 78, 79, 80, 85; and community, 107; and dependency, 28, 35, 59; and desire, 60, 94, 153nn17–18; and fantastic narrative, 8–9, 34, 60; and gothic literature, 8–9; and heterosexuality, 60; and homosociality, 93–94; and identification, 60; and identity, 2, 28, 59, 166–67n18; and ideology, 32, 69, 165n9; and individualism, 19, 35, 41, 52, 69, 165n9; and individuality, 19, 33, 34–35, 166n16; and interiority, 3; and masochism, 168n26; and mastery, 60; and materiality, 150n2; and maternal relations, 77–78, 166n16, 168n27; and misogyny, 60; and *Moll Flanders*, 41; and nature, 34; and otherness, 94; and *Pamela*, 58; and perversity, 110; and pornographic imagination, 59–60, 80; and possessiveness, 35; and power, 62, 79–80, 119; and psychoanalysis, 141; and rationality, 3, 34; and reader response, 60; and realist narrative, 33, 60; and repression, 21; and reproductive relations, 90–91;

Masculinity (*continued*)
and *Robinson Crusoe*, 19, 20, 21, 28, 32–35, 37; and sadism, 60, 72, 73, 166nn15–16, 168n26; and sameness, 93; and self, 85; and self-interest, 58; and sensibility, 151n7; and sexuality, 3, 167n18; and subjectivity, 33, 41, 89, 117, 145; and sublimation, 37; and *Tristram Shandy*, 89, 93–94, 101, 102–3, 145; and wholeness, 59, 60
Masochism: and *The Castle of Otranto*, 120; and *Clarissa*, 66, 72, 80, 83, 163n1, 165n13; and desire, 66; and femininity, 8, 66, 72, 153n19, 166nn15–16; and gothic literature, 8, 153n19, 165n13; and martyrdom, 169n29; and masculinity, 168n26; and narcissism, 83; and religion, 169n29; and sex-gender system, 66; and women, 66
Masse, Michelle A., 153n19, 165n13, 166n15
Master-slave relation, 165–66n14
Mastery: and *Clarissa*, 73; and masculinity, 60; and object-relations theory, 54; and *Robinson Crusoe*, 26, 28–29, 33; and self, 29, 54, 139
Materialism: and capitalism, 8; and *Clarissa*, 62, 67; and desire, 7; and fantastic narrative, 7; and middle class, 62; and sexuality, 8
Materiality: and Lacanian theory, 105; and masculinity, 150n2
Maternal relations: and affectivity, 74, 141, 142; and anxiety, 124, 141; and body, 34, 92, 103, 106, 107, 126, 133, 142, 174nn, 181n49; and *The Castle of Otranto*, 120, 123, 124, 135–36, 142, 143, 144; and castration, 78, 92, 83; and *Clarissa*, 63, 66, 67, 72, 75, 77–79, 80, 81, 142, 143, 144, 168n27; and desire, 124, 132, 141; and difference, 124; and erasure, 91, 101, 172n14; and erotics, 129; and fantastic narrative, 9, 75, 77; and femininity, 74; and feminism, 141–42; and identification, 60, 168n27, 183n8; and individualism, 43, 142; and integration, 141; and Lacanian theory, 174n30; and masculinity, 77–78, 166n16, 168n27; and melancholia, 126, 142, 144, 181n49; and middle class, 2; and *Moll Flanders*, 20, 35, 37–38, 42–43, 47; and *The Mysterious Mother*, 129, 130, 132, 133; and narcissism, 162n40; and parody, 77; and patriarchy, 77; and psychoanalysis, 91–92, 141–42, 165n14,

172n14, 182n4; and realist narrative, 7; and *Robinson Crusoe*, 22–23, 28, 32, 33–34; and *Roxana*, 20–21, 35, 44, 47, 49, 50, 51, 142; and sex-gender system, 142; and sexuality, 43, 50, 51, 74, 75, 167n23, 168n26; and socialization, 38, 77, 120; and *Tristram Shandy*, 91–93, 101, 106, 107, 142, 144–45; and Walpole's life, 128, 129, 130, 179–81nn; and wholeness, 141
Matriarchy, and *Clarissa*, 64
Maturin, Charles, 154n23, 175n3
Melancholia: and *The Castle of Otranto*, 11, 110, 124, 127, 133, 134, 135, 142, 144; and *Clarissa*, 144; and difference, 7, 11; and fantastic narrative, 7, 14, 125, 126–27, 133, 143; and feminism, 146; and gender, 11, 142, 143, 144, 183n7; and gothic literature, 124–25; and language, 126, 146; and loss, 11, 14, 125, 126, 133; and maternal relations, 126, 142, 144, 181n49; and misogyny, 14, 142, 145; and *The Mysterious Mother*, 131, 133; and pornography, 142–43; and psychoanalysis, 124–27, 133, 135, 172n13, 178nn17–18; and realist narrative, 14; and self, 125, 143; and struggle for change, 147; and the sublime, 176n6; and *Tristram Shandy*, 93, 142, 144, 145; and the uncanny, 133, 181n49; and *Villette*, 182n2; and Walpole's life, 127, 137
Melmouth the Wanderer (Maturin), 154n23, 175n3
Melodrama, 87, 117, 145
Men: and appropriation of women's roles, 91, 93–94, 105, 123; and cross-gender identification, 51; and dependence upon women, 35, 121; and difference, 74; and economic relations, 2; and identification with women, 60; and individualism, 35; and reader response, 85; and sexuality, 3, 163n3
Menippean satire, 170n2
Middle class: and *Clarissa*, 61; and consciousness, 57; and empiricism, 149n1; and family, 2, 61, 159n20; and gender, 1, 2; and individualism, 149n1; and materialism, 62; and novelistic form, 1; and *Pamela*, 57; and rationalism, 149n1; and realist narrative, 5, 11; and *Robinson Crusoe*, 23
Mirror stage, 153n16, 161n35, 165n14
Misogyny: and *The Castle of Otranto*,

120, 123, 124; and *Clarissa*, 63, 68; and fantastic narrative, 9; and Lacanian theory, 13; and masculinity, 60; and melancholia, 14, 142, 145; and *Roxana*, 21, 51; and sadism, 63; and subjectivity, 104; and *Tristram Shandy*, 13, 93, 102, 104, 106, 107, 142, 145, 171nn10, 11

Mitchell, Juliet, 159nn20, 23

Modernism: and fantastic narrative, 7, 10, 109; and self, 140; and subjectivist fiction, 155n26

Modernity: and consciousness, 52, 109; and self, 40; and self-awareness, 9, 10, 11, 13, 19, 109, 111; and sexgender system, 66, 124, 142, 146; and subjectivity, 12, 40, 54, 55, 104

Moll Flanders (Defoe): and affectivity, 20, 35, 37, 40; and alienation, 36, 39, 42, 44, 47; and anxiety, 36, 38, 159n22; and appropriation, 42; and autonomy, 36–37, 38, 51; and bourgeoisie, 43; and capitalism, 35, 38, 39, 42–43, 159n19; and children, 20, 37; and commodification, 36, 39, 42–43, 44; and consciousness, 47, 159n22; and contradiction, 39–40, 47, 55; and criminality, 37, 38, 40–43; and desire, 35, 38, 39, 44; and domestic sphere, 37, 44; and economic relations, 36, 39; and erotics, 39; and exchange value, 43; and exploitation, 36, 39, 41; and extra–marital relations, 36, 37, 40; and family, 35, 36, 37–39; and fantastic narrative, 41, 42; and femininity, 35, 37, 39, 40, 41, 42, 45, 51; and gender, 20, 21; and identity, 41–42; and ideology, 20, 35, 36–37; and incest, 38–39, 159n22; and individualism, 19, 20, 21, 35, 36–37, 39, 41, 42–44, 55, 159n22; and individuality, 37; and instrumentalization, 35, 37, 38, 44, 45; and integration, 41; and interiority, 40; and irony, 35–36; and labor, 36; and marriage, 36, 37, 38, 40, 43; and masculinity, 41; and maternal relations, 20, 35, 37–38, 42–43, 47; and morality, 40–42; and nature, 42; and objectification, 41; and patriarchy, 36, 38; and perversity, 37, 38, 39, 45; and picaresque, 20, 44; and possessiveness, 42; and private sphere, 37, 43; and prostitution, 35, 36, 37, 39, 41; and psychological relations, 20, 21; and realist narrative, 20, 42, 45, 51; and reciprocity, 37; and reification,

39, 42; and religion, 42, 156n4; and repressive de-sublimation, 159–60n24; and reproductive relations, 20, 36, 37, 42–43, 159n19; and self, 39–41; and self-awareness, 42; and self-interest, 40; and self-reflection, 44; and sex-gender system, 20, 21, 35, 37, 44; and sexuality, 35, 36, 37, 39, 41; and social embeddedness, 21, 35; and socialization, 38; and solipsism, 47; and spiritual autobiography, 156n4; and subjectivity, 41, 47; and women, 20, 35–36, 39, 42, 43, 159n19

The Monk (Lewis), 153n18, 155n26, 164n8

Morality: and *Clarissa*, 62, 67, 80, 81, 82, 163n1; and *Moll Flanders*, 40–42; and *Pamela*, 57–58; and *Robinson Crusoe*, 24; and *Roxana*, 46, 47; and self-control, 5; and subject-in-process, 175n33

Morrison, Toni, 156n30

Mourning: and *The Castle of Otranto*, 110, 113, 118; and desire, 134; and fantastic narrative, 143; and language, 126, 146; as productive work, 15; and psychoanalysis, 125, 134–35, 172n13, 184n11; and struggle for change, 147; and *Tristram Shandy*, 93; and Walpole's life, 129

Murder: and *Clarissa*, 61; and *Roxana*, 50–51

Mutuality: and *Clarissa*, 70–71, 142, 168n27; and fantastic narrative, 143; and Hegelian theory, 165n14; and sex-gender system, 143

The Mysterious Mother (Walpole): and death, 134; and desire, 133–34; and fantastic narrative, 110, 132; and gothic literature, 13, 127; and identification, 132; and incest, 130, 131, 134, 136; and incorporation, 133; and introjection, 133; and maternal relations, 129, 130, 132, 133; and melancholia, 131, 133; and paternal relations, 132–33; and preservative repression, 133; and psychological relations, 131–32, 133–36; publication of, 130; and self, 133; and the supernatural, 133; and tragedy, 110, 127, 130; and the uncanny, 133; and Walpole's life, 127, 129–32

Nachtraglichkeit, 182n1

Narcissism: and *The Castle of Otranto*, 118; and *Clarissa*, 66, 68, 69, 70, 72, 81, 83; and fantastic narrative, 112; and femininity, 66; and humor,

Narcissism (*continued*)
173n21; and incorporation, 125; and masochism, 83; and maternal relations, 162n40; and melancholia, 125; and object-relations theory, 13, 53–54, 161–62nn; and pornography, 143; and psychoanalysis, 125, 173n21; and sex-gender system, 66; and subject-in-process, 175n33; and subjectivity, 107, 144; and sublime, 162n38; and *Tristram Shandy*, 95, 107, 144; and women, 66
Nationalism, 28, 31
Naturalization: and difference, 73; and gender, 58; and *Pamela*, 58; and realist narrative, 5, 6, 73; and *Robinson Crusoe*, 29, 30
Nature: and domestication, 34; and femininity, 33–34; and gender, 33; and masculinity, 34; and *Moll Flanders*, 42; and *Robinson Crusoe*, 31
Necrophilia, 135
Nihilism, 123

Object-relations theory, 13, 52–55, 141, 161–62nn, 165n14, 183n5
Objectification: and *The Castle of Otranto*, 117; and *Clarissa*, 62, 65, 85; and fantastic narrative, 9; and femininity, 85; and *Moll Flanders*, 41; and pornography, 167n20; and realist narrative, 30; and *Robinson Crusoe*, 24, 30; and *Roxana*, 50; and women, 41, 62, 167n20
Objectivity, and psychoanalysis, 162n42
O'Brien, Mary, 91
Oceanic experience, 84
Oedipal struggle, 32–33, 75, 119, 133, 141, 158n17, 171n12, 183n8
Omnipotence, 79, 143, 165n14
Otherness: and appropriation, 109; and *Clarissa*, 74, 78, 85, 143; and colonialism, 158n13; and ego, 184n11; and fantastic narrative, 10, 29; and femininity, 85; and instrumentalization, 10; and masculinity, 94; and race, 158n13; and realist narrative, 10; and *Robinson Crusoe*, 11, 27, 29–30, 157n10; and *Roxana*, 47–48; and self, 10, 89, 94, 109, 158n13, 164n6, 165n14; and sexuality, 132; and *Tristram Shandy*, 93, 94, 97, 106, 142
Ownership, 26, 29, 62

Pamela (Richardson), 57–59, 149n2, 163n1, 170n1

Paranoia: and *The Castle of Otranto*, 118, 124; and fantastic narrative, 7, 9, 143; and gothic literature, 9, 154n23; and homosociality, 143; and *Robinson Crusoe*, 27, 29, 51
Parody: and *The Castle of Otranto*, 110, 113; and *Clarissa*, 77, 81; and maternal relations, 77
Paternal relations: and alienation, 122, 123, 134; and allegory, 32; and anxiety, 121; and *The Castle of Otranto*, 110, 117, 119, 121, 122, 123–24, 127, 134; and *Clarissa*, 62–63, 68, 72, 80, 82, 83; and desire, 134, 166n16; and fantastic narrative, 9; and femininity, 166n16; and homoeroticism, 9; and idealization, 94, 101; and identity, 90; and *The Mysterious Mother*, 132–33; and psychoanalysis, 94, 141, 172n14; and realist narrative, 6, 7, 32; and religion, 25, 32, 33; and reproductive relations, 90, 121; and *Robinson Crusoe*, 22–23, 25, 28, 30, 32–33, 158n15; and sadism, 9; and sexuality, 9, 122, 168n26; and subjectivity, 166n16; and temporality, 103; and *Tristram Shandy*, 90–91, 93–94, 101–2, 144; and Walpole's life, 128, 129, 179nn, 181n47
Patriarchy: and capitalism, 7, 38, 60, 123; and *The Castle of Otranto*, 117, 119, 120, 123–24; and *Clarissa*, 60, 63, 64, 80, 82, 83, 120; and difference, 60; and family, 1–2, 9, 38, 64, 83; and fantastic narrative, 7; and gender, 151n5; and gothic literature, 8; and Lacanian theory, 97; and language, 97; and maternal relations, 77; and medievalism, 116; and *Moll Flanders*, 36, 38; and political relations, 150n4; and *Robinson Crusoe*, 30, 32; and *Roxana*, 36, 45, 160n28; and sexuality, 60, 64; and social class, 151n5; and *Tristram Shandy*, 97, 117, 144, 171n10
Penis, 92, 94, 100–101, 106, 173n20, 174n22; and penis/breast, 92, 106, 174n30
Perry, Ruth, 171nn
Perversity: and *The Castle of Otranto*, 110, 117; and *Clarissa*, 163n1; and desire, 5; and family, 38; and femininity, 37; and masculinity, 110; and *Moll Flanders*, 37, 38, 39, 45; and *Roxana*, 37, 45, 47; and *Tristram Shandy*, 102, 107, 144
Phallic economy, 94, 104

Phallic signifier, 101, 173n19, 174nn
Phallus, 101, 102, 105–6, 173n20
Picaresque: and allegory, 25; and Defoe's life, 19; and fantastic narrative,
21, 46, 49; and individualism, 22; and
Moll Flanders, 20, 44; and realist narrative, 6, 19, 20, 22, 46; and *Robinson
Crusoe*, 22, 25, 46; and *Roxana*, 21, 45,
49
Poe, Edgar Allan, 135, 161n30
Political relations: and *The Castle of
Otranto*, 119, 124, 177n14; and Defoe's life, 17–18; and gothic literature,
177n13; and individuality, 34; and
patriarchy, 150n4; and *Robinson Crusoe*, 19, 30, 31, 34; and Walpole's life,
116–17, 128–29, 177n13
Pontalis, J. B., 170n6, 182n1, 183n5
Pope, Alexander, 175n1
Pornography: and *The Castle of Otranto*,
122–23, 143; and *Clarissa*, 59–60, 66,
75, 76, 80, 84, 85, 143, 145; and difference, 59, 85, 167n20; and domination,
143; and exploitation, 167n20; and
fantastic narrative, 60, 75, 84, 164n7;
and feminism, 142; and film, 167n20;
and gothic literature, 164n8; and heterosexuality, 66; and ideology, 59;
and imagination, 59–60, 66, 75, 80,
142; and knowledge, 75; and masculinity, 59–60, 80; and melancholia,
142–43; and narcissism, 143; and
objectification, 167n20; and reader response, 60; and realist narrative, 59,
60, 164n7; and romance, 76; and sadism, 143, 164n7; and sadomasochism, 163n3; and subjectivity, 75;
and sublime, 84
Possessiveness: and *The Castle of
Otranto*, 117, 118, 123, 124; and *Clarissa*, 79, 118; and femininity, 42, 51;
and gothic literature, 8; and individualism, 7, 19, 20, 30, 35, 42, 51, 117,
118, 123, 124, 165n9; and individuality, 35; and masculinity, 35; and *Moll
Flanders*, 42; and *Robinson Crusoe*, 19,
30, 35; and *Roxana*, 20, 44, 51; and
subjectivity, 30
Postmodernism, 52, 53, 87, 109, 161n31
Poststructuralism, 57
Power: and *The Castle of Otranto*, 117,
119, 121, 123–24; and *Clarissa*, 62, 63,
65, 66, 68, 73, 79, 80; and connectedness, 165n14; and difference, 59, 66;
and fantastic narrative, 60, 77; and
femininity, 77; and gender, 59, 66;

and masculinity, 62, 79–80, 119; and
pornographic imagination, 59–60;
and reproductive relations, 124; and
Robinson Crusoe, 26, 27, 28, 31; and
sexuality, 63, 79, 163n3; and *Tristram
Shandy*, 98, 101, 117
Praz, Mario, 165n13
Primal scene, 89–90, 170n6
Private sphere: and *The Castle of Otranto*,
121; and family, 2, 5; and *Moll Flanders*, 37, 43; and pornographic imagination, 59; and socioeconomic relations, 2, 3; and women, 2, 43
Property: and *The Castle of Otranto*, 119;
and *Clarissa*, 62, 63, 66, 82; and marriage, 62; and *Robinson Crusoe*, 30, 32;
and *Tristram Shandy*, 90
Prostitution: and *Clarissa*, 61, 76, 77;
and ideology, 3; and *Moll Flanders*,
35, 36, 37, 39, 41; and *Roxana*, 21, 35,
36, 46, 48
Psychoanalysis: and alienation, 140;
and autonomy, 165n14; and bimodality, 55, 140; and childhood, 140, 141;
and difference, 12–13; and ego, 111,
117, 125, 126, 134–35, 178–79nn,
184n11; and fantastic narrative, 12,
13, 55, 124–27, 140, 154n24; and fantasy, 125–26, 178–79n25; and feminism, 141, 145, 146, 182n3, 183n5;
and gender, 12, 162n44, 165n14; and
gothic literature, 110, 117, 124–25,
134, 166n15; and Hegelian theory,
165n14; and humor, 173–74n21; and
hysteria, 47, 51; and introjection, 125–
26, 134, 178nn17–18, 179n25; and irrationalism, 55, 132; and literary criticism, 155n28; and masculinity, 141;
and maternal relations, 91–92, 141–
42, 165n14, 172n14, 182n4; and melancholia, 124–27, 133, 135, 172n13,
178nn17–18, 181–82n53; and mourning, 125, 134–35, 172n13, 184n11; and
narcissism, 125, 173n21; and object-
relations theory, 13, 52–55, 141, 161–
62nn, 165n14, 183n5; and objectivity,
162n42; and oedipal struggle, 32–33,
75, 133, 141, 158n17, 171n12, 183n8;
and paternal relations, 94, 141,
172n14; and primal scene, 89–90,
170n6; and race, 157–58n13; and repression, 126, 159–60n24; and self, 12,
52–55, 89, 140, 165n14; and self-
consciousness, 165n14; and sex-
gender system, 141, 146; and socialization, 13, 167n19; and solipsism,

Psychoanalysis (*continued*)
165n14; and subjectivity, 13, 52, 55,
89; and sublimation, 111, 176n4; and
superego, 111, 140, 168–69n28,
174n21; and the uncanny, 132–33,
181nn48–49; and the unconscious, 12,
125, 126, 132, 136, 137, 140–41,
152nn14–15, 172n13, 178–79n25; and
women, 47, 51, 165n11
Psychological relations: and *The Castle
of Otranto*, 117–19, 122–24, 127,
132, 133–36; and *Clarissa*, 60, 61,
71–85; and fantastic narrative, 10,
60, 61, 88, 111, 150n3, 155n26; and
ideology, 21, 52, 55; and *Moll Flanders*, 20, 21; and *The Mysterious
Mother*, 131–32, 133–36; and object-
relations theory, 52–55; and *Pamela*,
58; and race, 157–58n13, 164n6; and
Robinson Crusoe, 19, 25–26, 28, 30, 32;
and *Roxana*, 47–48, 50; and *Tristram
Shandy*, 88–107; and wholeness, 25,
59, 60
Public sphere, 2, 3, 6, 59, 121, 152n13
Puritanism, 1, 22, 164–65n9

Race: and colonialism, 157–58n13; and
difference, 28; and identity, 157–
58n13; and otherness, 158n13; and
psychological relations, 157–58n13,
164n6; and *Robinson Crusoe*, 28, 157–
58n13
Radcliffe, Ann, 88, 153–54nn, 155n26,
177n9
Rape: and *The Castle of Otranto*, 143;
and *Clarissa*, 61, 65, 70, 76–78, 80, 81,
83, 85, 143
Rationalism, 12, 88, 149n1, 152n15
Rationality: and affectivity, 160n26; and
Clarissa, 71; and masculinity, 3, 34;
and object-relations theory, 54, 55;
and *Robinson Crusoe*, 26, 27; and *Tristram Shandy*, 102
Reader response, 60, 85, 118, 168n26
Real, the, Lacanian concept of, 10, 103
Realist narrative: and allegory, 22, 25,
26, 32, 82; and autonomy, 6, 19, 25,
54; and boundary, 10; and capitalism,
53, 150n3; and *The Castle of Otranto*,
11, 110, 116, 124; and *Clarissa*, 11, 57,
60, 61, 68, 69, 70, 71, 74, 75, 77, 80,
82, 83, 84, 85, 163n1, 165n13, 166n16;
and comedy, 53, 107; and consciousness, 140; and contradiction, 19, 21,
35; and difference, 5, 7, 10, 73, 108;
and domestic sphere, 6; and family,

9, 93; and fantastic narrative, 1, 10–
11, 14–15, 19–20, 22, 28, 30, 34, 49,
51, 60, 61, 70, 82, 84, 85, 87, 88, 95,
102, 109, 110, 116, 124, 145, 154n24,
155n26; and femininity, 42, 45, 75;
and gender, 6, 7, 74, 153n17, 154n24,
166n16; and hierarchy, 10, 30, 34;
and homosociality, 143; and identification, 72; and identity, 139; and ideology, 6, 21; and individualism, 5, 22,
26, 30; and individuality, 33; and inequality, 5, 6; and integration, 6, 10;
and introjection, 126; and love, 73;
and marriage, 6–7, 73; and masculinity, 33, 60; and maternal relations, 7;
and melancholia, 14; and middle
class, 5, 11; and *Moll Flanders*, 20, 42,
45, 51; and naturalization, 5, 6, 73;
and object-relations theory, 54; and
objectification, 30; and otherness, 10;
and *Pamela*, 57–58; and paternal relations, 6, 7, 32; and picaresque, 6, 19,
20, 22, 46; and pornography, 59, 60,
164n7; and public sphere, 6; and *Robinson Crusoe*, 11, 19, 21, 22, 23, 25, 26,
28, 30, 31, 33, 34–35, 46, 51; and romance genre, 150n3; and Romanticism, 140; and *Roxana*, 20–21, 44, 45,
49, 51; and self, 10, 25, 30, 31, 40, 54,
68; and self-awareness, 6; and self-
interest, 6; and sexuality, 75; and social context, 140; and subjectivity, 89,
139, 154n24; and sublime, 61, 83, 84;
and superego, 140; and tragedy, 102;
and *Tristram Shandy*, 11, 87, 88, 89,
93, 95, 102, 107, 145; and Victorian
period, 155n26; and wholeness, 6,
117, 139; and women, 35
Reciprocity: and *Clarissa*, 83; and
connectedness, 37, 143; and individuality, 37; and *Moll Flanders*, 37; and
Robinson Crusoe, 23, 37, 143; and *Roxana*, 37, 143; and *Tristram Shandy*,
143, 144
Recognition, 13, 71, 89, 142, 143, 144,
146, 165n14, 183n8
Regression: and allegory, 82; and *The
Castle of Otranto*, 136; and *Clarissa*,
75, 80, 82; and fantastic narrative, 10,
60, 75; and pornographic imagination, 60
Reich, Theodor, 169n29
Reification: and commodification, 39,
160nn25–26; and *Moll Flanders*, 39, 42;
and self, 39; and self-preservation,
160n26; and sexuality, 160n26; and

subjectivity, 160n25, 160n26; and women, 160n26

Religion: and allegory, 19, 32, 82, 83, 84; and *Clarissa*, 64, 72, 81, 82, 83, 84, 169n29; and colonialism, 29; and Defoe's life, 17–18; and ideology, 83; and Lacanian theory, 104–5; and masochism, 169n29; and medievalism, 116; and *Moll Flanders*, 42, 156n4; and paternal relations, 25, 32, 33; and *Robinson Crusoe*, 19, 24–26, 28, 29, 31, 33; and *Roxana*, 46, 47; and self, 26, 84; and sentimentality, 84; and sublime, 82, 83, 84, 169n30

Repression: and autonomy, 21; and de-sublimation, 159–60n24; and masculinity, 21; and melancholia, 126, 127, 135; preservative, 126, 127, 133

Reproductive relations: and alienation, 42, 90, 91; and appropriation, 91; and body, 20, 36, 42; and capitalism, 42, 159n19; and *The Castle of Otranto*, 121, 124; and connectedness, 42; and difference, 3, 90; and feminism, 91; and homunculus theory, 91, 171n10; and identity, 90; and ideology, 20; and legal relations, 91; and masculinity, 90–91; and men's dependence on women, 121; and *Moll Flanders*, 20, 36, 37, 42–43, 159n19; and paternal relations, 90, 121; and power, 124; and *Roxana*, 36, 159n19; and temporality, 42; and *Tristram Shandy*, 90–91, 105; and women, 3, 36, 42, 90, 91, 105, 121

Richardson, Samuel, 85, 149n1, 175n1. See also *Clarissa; Pamela*

Richter, David H., 177n9

Robinson Crusoe (Defoe): and affectivity, 22, 30, 33, 37; and alienation, 24, 26–27, 30, 34; and allegory, 19, 22, 24–26, 32; and anxiety, 26–27, 30, 32, 34, 36; and appropriation, 31, 33, 34; and autonomy, 19, 21, 22–23, 25–29, 31, 32, 34, 35, 37; and bimodality, 145; and body, 34; and capitalism, 20, 28, 30–32, 34; and colonialism, 29, 31, 51, 157n11; and commodification, 34; and consciousness, 22, 30; and contradiction, 28, 29, 32, 35, 55; and Defoe's life, 22; and dependency, 23, 28, 35; and desire, 26, 30, 32; and difference, 28, 29, 32; and disintegration, 25; and displacement, 20, 32, 33; and dividedness, 26, 28, 30, 33, 34, 109; and domestication, 34; and domestic

sphere, 30, 33; and domination, 27, 30; and dream, 27–28; and economic relations, 22–23, 26, 30–31; and egotism, 20, 23–24; and erasure, 31, 33; and erotics, 33, 143; and exchange value, 30; and exploitation, 28, 31, 34, 35, 37; and family, 20, 22–23, 25, 28, 32–33, 36, 37, 158–59n18; and fantastic narrative, 11, 19–20, 21, 22, 26–30, 31, 34, 35, 118; and femininity, 32–34; and gender, 11, 28, 32, 34, 109, 145; and hierarchy, 28, 29, 30, 34; and homosociality, 33, 143; and identity, 28, 29, 31–32, 34; and ideology, 28, 32, 36–37, 109; and imperialism, 20, 23, 33, 34; and individualism, 19–20, 21, 22, 25, 26, 30, 31, 35, 36–37, 44, 52, 55, 109; and individuality, 19, 31, 33, 34, 37; and inequality, 29, 30; and instrumentalization, 31, 37; and integration, 24, 26, 27, 31, 54; and interaction of narrative modes, 11, 19–20, 21, 22, 25, 26, 28, 30, 32, 34, 46; and interiority, 26; and irrationalism, 22, 25; and labor, 26, 30, 33, 34; and love, 28, 32; and marginality, 28–29; and marriage, 29, 33; and masculinity, 19, 20, 21, 28, 32–35, 37; and mastery, 26, 28–29, 33; and maternal relations, 22–23, 28, 32, 33–34; and middle class, 23; and morality, 24; and nationalism, 28, 31; and naturalization, 29, 30; and nature, 31; and objectification, 24, 30; and oedipal struggle, 32–33; and otherness, 11, 27, 29–30, 157n10; and ownership, 26, 29; and paranoia, 27, 29, 51; and paternal relations, 22–23, 25, 28, 30, 32–33, 158n15; and patriarchy, 30, 32; and picaresque, 22, 25, 46; and political relations, 19, 30, 31, 34; and possession, 22–23, 30, 34, 69; and possessiveness, 19, 30, 35; and power, 26, 27, 28, 31; and property, 30, 32; and psychological relations, 19, 25–26, 28, 30, 32; and Puritanism, 22, 25; and race, 28, 157–58n13; and rationality, 26, 27; and realist narrative, 11, 19, 21, 22, 23, 25, 26, 28, 30, 31, 33, 34–35, 46, 51; and reciprocity, 23, 37, 143; and religion, 19, 24–26, 28, 29, 31, 33; and self, 22–26, 29, 31; and self-awareness, 19, 21, 31, 34; and self-preservation, 23; and sex-gender system, 21, 44; and sexuality, 32, 33, 37, 145; and slavery, 23–24; and social

Robinson Crusoe (Defoe) (*continued*)
class, 23, 31, 32, 143; and social embeddedness, 23; and solipsism, 27;
and spiritual autobiography, 22, 24–
25; and subjectivity, 11, 33, 109, 145;
and sublimation, 33; and sublime,
112; and surplus value, 26, 30; and
temporality, 24, 26, 157n8; and uncanny, 27; and wholeness, 25; and
women, 20, 31–32, 33, 37; and xenophobia, 29
Romance genre, 8, 10, 76, 88, 111,
149n2, 150n3, 154n21
Romanticism: and consciousness, 140;
and doubleness, 161n30; and fantastic narrative, 7, 109; and *Frankenstein*,
182n2; and libertinism, 162n38; and
object-relations theory, 52, 54, 55;
and realist narrative, 140; and sadomasochism, 163n1; and self, 140
Roxana (Defoe): and affectivity, 20, 35,
37, 48; and alienation, 36, 44, 47; and
anxiety, 36; and autonomy, 36–37, 44,
47, 48, 49; and bimodality, 21, 145;
and body, 47, 160n28; and capitalism,
20, 35, 159n19; and children, 20, 44,
47, 49–50; and commodification, 36,
44, 47, 160n28; and consciousness, 47,
140; and contradiction, 20, 46–47, 48,
51, 55, 142, 145; and criminality, 50–
51; and cross-gender identification,
51; and desire, 35, 44, 46, 49, 50; and
dividedness, 47–48, 50, 51, 109; and
domestic sphere, 44, 45; and doubleness, 48, 50; and economic relations,
20, 36, 44–45, 49; and erotics, 44, 49,
143; and exploitation, 36; and extra-
marital relations, 20, 36, 44, 45, 48, 49;
and family, 20, 35, 36, 37, 47, 49–50;
and fantastic narrative, 21, 44, 46, 47,
48, 49, 50, 51; and femininity, 21, 35,
37, 44, 45, 46, 48, 160n28; and feminism, 45, 51, 160n28; and gender, 21,
109, 145; and homosociality, 143; and
hysteria, 47, 51; and identity, 50; and
ideology, 20, 21, 35, 36–37, 109; and
individualism, 19, 20, 21, 35, 36–37,
44, 49, 51–52, 55, 109, 142; and individuality, 37; and instrumentalization, 35, 37, 44, 45, 46, 51; and
integration, 21; and interaction of
narrative modes, 21, 46, 49, 51; and
interiority, 46, 47, 48, 52; and irrationalism, 46, 47; and labor, 36; and
marriage, 36, 44, 45–46, 49; and maternal relations, 20–21, 35, 44, 47, 49,
50, 51, 142; and misogyny, 21, 51;
and morality, 46, 47; and murder, 50–
51; and objectification, 50; and otherness, 47–48; and patriarchy, 36, 45,
160n28; and perversity, 37, 45, 47;
and picaresque, 21, 45, 49; and possessiveness, 20, 44, 51; and prostitution, 21, 35, 36, 46, 48; and psychological relations, 47–48, 50; and
realist narrative, 20–21, 44, 45, 49, 51;
and reciprocity, 37, 143; and religion,
46, 47; and repressive de-sublimation, 159n24; and reproductive relations, 36, 159n19; and self, 46–48,
50; and self-awareness, 46, 51; and
self-consciousness, 45; and self-
preservation, 47; and self-reflection,
46; and sex-gender system, 20, 35, 37;
and sexuality, 35, 36, 37, 44, 48, 49,
50, 51, 145; and slavery, 160n28; and
social class, 143; and social embeddedness, 35; and subjectivity, 21, 46–
47, 109, 145; and sublime, 112; and
tragedy, 21, 47; and women, 35–36, 51

Sade, Marquis de, 75, 163n1
Sadism: and *The Castle of Otranto*, 120;
and *Clarissa*, 60, 63, 66, 72, 73, 75, 79,
80, 163n1, 168n27; and fantastic narrative, 72; and gothic literature, 8;
and masculinity, 60, 72, 73, 166nn15–
16, 168n26; and melancholia, 178n17;
and misogyny, 63; and paternal relations, 9; and pornographic imagination, 143, 164n7; and sexuality, 63
Sadomasochism: and *Clarissa*, 163n1;
and pornography, 163n3; and Romanticism, 163n1
Sartre, Jean-Paul, 72
Satire, 170n2
Scientific ideology, 3
Scientific skepticism, 152n15
Sedgwick, Eve Kosofsky, 154n23,
180n39, 184n9
Self: and alienation, 10, 26, 47, 53, 112,
140, 165n14; and allegory, 25, 84; and
androgyny, 84; and autonomy, 26,
71, 83, 144, 161n35, 165n14; and
boundary, 71, 73, 94, 165n14; and
capitalism, 31, 53; and *The Castle of
Otranto*, 110, 117, 118, 119, 123, 133;
centered, 22; and *Clarissa*, 68, 70, 71,
73, 80, 82, 83, 84–85; and colonialism,
158n13; and commodification, 54; decentered, 22; and difference, 84–85;
and disintegration, 25, 103; divided,

5, 7, 26, 28, 30, 50, 55, 80, 87, 97, 133, 152n13, 183n8; and domination, 165n14; and family, 119; and fantastic narrative, 7, 10, 14, 30, 53, 55, 61, 74, 95, 103, 112; and gender, 21, 61; and gothic literature, 119; and Hegelian theory, 165n14; and ideology, 21; and indeterminacy, 107; and individualism, 31, 54; and integration, 31, 41, 53, 54, 84, 93, 165n14; and Lacanian theory, 89, 106, 153n16, 161n35; and language, 89; and masculinity, 85; and mastery, 29, 54, 139; and melancholia, 125, 143; and modernism, 140; and modernity, 40; and *Moll Flanders*, 39–41; and mourning, 126; and otherness, 10, 14, 89, 94, 109, 158n13, 164n6, 165n14; and pornographic imagination, 61; and postmodernism, 53; and psychoanalysis, 12, 52–55, 89, 140, 165n14; and Puritanism, 22, 25; and realist narrative, 10, 25, 30, 31, 40, 54, 68; and recognition, 89, 143, 165n14; and reification, 39; and religion, 26, 84; and representation, 53–54; and *Robinson Crusoe*, 22–26, 29, 31; and Romanticism, 140; and *Roxana*, 46–48, 50; and sex-gender system, 3–4; and sublimation, 111; and sublime, 111; and *Tristram Shandy*, 87, 89, 93, 94–95, 97, 144; and the uncanny, 109, 132; ungendered, 61

Self-awareness: and alienation, 139; and *The Castle of Otranto*, 110; and egotism, 6; and fantastic narrative, 7, 9, 31, 34; and femininity, 8, 51; and gothic literature, 8, 9; and individualism, 4, 10, 22; and interaction of narrative modes, 11; and modernity, 9, 10, 11, 13, 19, 109, 111; and *Moll Flanders*, 42; and realist narrative, 6; and *Robinson Crusoe*, 19, 21, 31, 34; and *Roxana*, 46, 51; and solipsism, 5, 110; and subjectivity, 139; and sublime, 111–12; and *Tristram Shandy*, 109

Self-consciousness: and Hegelian theory, 165n14; and individualism, 152n15; and psychoanalysis, 165n14; and *Roxana*, 45; and *Tristram Shandy*, 97, 145; and the unconscious, 152n15; and women, 97

Self-control, 5, 8, 152n13

Self-interest, 5, 6, 40, 58

Self-preservation, 23, 47, 70, 160n26

Self-reflection: and fantastic narrative,

7, 46; and *Moll Flanders*, 44; and *Roxana*, 46; and *Tristram Shandy*, 96, 102

Self-transcendence: and Lacanian theory, 104–5; and the sublime, 102, 105, 111; and *Tristram Shandy*, 102, 107

Sentimentality: and *Clarissa*, 83, 84, 85; and comedy, 87; and *Tristram Shandy*, 87, 106

A Sentimental Journey (Sterne), 93, 105

Sex-gender system: and capitalism, 1–2, 110; and *The Castle of Otranto*, 110, 123, 124; and *Clarissa*, 60; and contradiction, 1; and desire, 142, 143; and difference, 3–4, 58; and economic relations, 1–3; and family, 37; and fantastic narrative, 7; and feminism, 142, 146; and heterosexuality, 143; and identification, 139, 142, 143; and individualism, 19, 35, 37, 44; and inequality, 123; and interaction of narrative modes, 1; and masochism, 66; and maternal relations, 142; and modernity, 66, 124, 142, 146; and *Moll Flanders*, 20, 21, 35, 37, 44; and mutuality, 143; and narcissism, 66; and novelistic form, 1, 4, 149n2; and *Pamela*, 57–58; and psychoanalysis, 141, 146; and *Robinson Crusoe*, 21, 44; and *Roxana*, 20, 35, 37; and self, 3–4; and social class, 4, 57; and subjectivity, 1, 12

Sexuality: and anxiety, 11, 63; and capitalism, 60; and *The Castle of Otranto*, 11, 120, 122–23, 134, 135, 145; and *Clarissa*, 60, 63, 64, 66, 69, 74, 75, 77, 83, 84, 145, 163n1; and commodification, 43; and criminality, 43; and death, 134, 135; and difference, 2, 3, 9, 13, 60, 74, 75, 84, 89, 93, 103, 143, 167n20; and economic relations, 43, 62; and fantastic narrative, 8, 9, 72, 75, 77, 88; and gothic literature, 8; and heroism, 177n15; and identification, 168n26, 183n7; and identity, 41, 168n26; and ideology, 3, 35; and indeterminacy, 83, 102–3; and individuality, 37; and instrumentalization, 51; and Lacanian theory, 89; and masculinity, 3, 167n18; and materialism, 8; and maternal relations, 43, 50, 51, 74, 77, 167n23, 168n26; and *Moll Flanders*, 35, 36, 37, 39, 41; and otherness, 132; and *Pamela*, 57–58; and paternal relations, 9, 122, 168n26; and patriarchy, 60, 64; and pornographic imagination, 60; and power, 63, 79, 163n3; and realist nar-

Sexuality (*continued*)
rative, 75; and reification, 160n26;
and *Robinson Crusoe*, 32, 33, 37, 145;
and *Roxana*, 35, 36, 37, 44, 48, 49, 50,
51, 145; and sadism, 63; and social
class, 69, 150n2; and sublimation, 57,
176n4; and the sublime, 177n15; and
Tristram Shandy, 11, 93, 95, 103; and
the uncanny, 132; and Walpole's life,
180n39; and women, 3, 35, 36, 74,
120, 152n8, 167n20
Shakespeare, William, 175n1
Shelley, Mary, 88, 153n17, 154n23,
155n26, 161n30, 179n27, 182n2
Showalter, Elaine, 164n5
Silverman, Kaja, 173n20
Slavery: and *Clarissa*, 67; and *Robinson
Crusoe*, 23–24; and *Roxana*, 160n28
Smollett, Tobias, 175n1
Social class: and *The Castle of Otranto*,
134; and *Clarissa*, 62, 63, 66; and family, 7, 159n20; and gender, 1–2, 3,
151n5; and medievalism, 116; and
Pamela, 57–58; and patriarchy, 151n5;
and *Robinson Crusoe*, 23, 31, 32, 143;
and *Roxana*, 143; and sex-gender system, 4, 57; and sexuality, 69, 150n2;
and *Tristram Shandy*, 173n17
Social context: and fantastic narrative,
88; and realist narrative, 140
Social embeddedness: and knowledge,
89; and *Moll Flanders*, 21, 35; and
Robinson Crusoe, 23; and *Roxana*, 35;
and *Tristram Shandy*, 89, 95
Socialization: and *Clarissa*, 77; and family, 36; and maternal relations, 38, 77,
120; and *Moll Flanders*, 38; and psychoanalysis, 13, 167n19
Solipsism: and *The Castle of Otranto*,
110, 117; and *Clarissa*, 75, 78, 83, 85;
and fantastic narrative, 8–9; and
78, 88; and gothic literature, 8–9; and
Hegelian theory, 165n14; and individualism, 83, 117; and interiority, 88;
and *Moll Flanders*, 47; and pornographic imagination, 60; and psychoanalysis, 165n14; and *Robinson Crusoe*, 27; and self-awareness, 5, 110;
and *Tristram Shandy*, 94, 95, 106
Spencer, Jane, 149n2
Spiritual autobiography, 22, 24–25,
156n4
Stallybrass, Peter, 154–55n25
Sterne, Laurence. See *Tristram Shandy*
Stevenson, Robert Louis, 155n26,
161n30, 179n27

Stoker, Bram, 88, 155n26, 161n30
Subjectivity: and autonomy, 139; and
capitalism, 52; and *The Castle of
Otranto*, 117, 120, 127, 145; and *Clarissa*, 68–69, 71, 75, 80, 84, 109, 145;
and contradiction, 46; and desire, 88;
divided, 19, 88, 89, 109, 127, 139,
183n8; and domination, 139; and empiricism, 88; and exploitation, 41; and
fantastic narrative, 9, 10, 11, 54, 88,
89, 127, 154n24; and femininity, 47,
75, 145, 150n2, 153n17; and gender,
2, 4, 12, 14, 80, 102, 109, 149n2,
154n24; and indeterminacy, 1; and
individualism, 30; and integration, 89;
and irrationalism, 55; and knowledge, 88; and Lacanian theory, 13,
89, 104; and masculinity, 33, 41, 89,
117, 145; and misogyny, 104; and
modernity, 12, 40, 54, 55, 104; and
Moll Flanders, 41, 47; and narcissism,
107, 144; and object-relations theory,
13, 52, 54; and paternal relations,
166n16; and performance, 102; and
pornography, 75; and possessiveness,
30; and psychoanalysis, 13, 52, 55, 89;
and rationalism, 88; and realist narrative, 89, 139, 154n24; and reification, 160nn25–26; and *Robinson Crusoe*, 11, 30, 33, 109, 145; and *Roxana*,
21, 46–47, 109, 145; and self-
awareness, 139; and sex-gender system, 1, 12; and *Tristram Shandy*, 88–
89, 93, 94, 97, 102, 104, 109, 144–
45; and ungendered condition, 12;
and women, 120
Sublimation: and masculinity, 37; and
Pamela, 57; and repressive de-
sublimation, 159–60n24; and *Robinson
Crusoe*, 33, 37; and self, 111; and sexuality, 57, 176n4; and *Tristram
Shandy*, 95
Sublime: and affectivity, 10; and alienation, 111, 112; and anxiety, 112,
169n30; and *The Castle of Otranto*,
123, 136; and *Clarissa*, 61, 82, 83, 84,
112; and comedy, 87, 102, 105, 106,
107; and fantastic narrative, 10, 61,
84, 102, 104, 105, 107, 112, 177n15;
and gothic literature, 123; and imagination, 111; and libertinism, 123,
177n15; and melancholia, 176n6; and
narcissism, 162n38; negative, 84, 112,
136, 176n6, 177n15; and pornography, 84; and realist narrative, 61, 83,
84; and religion, 82, 83, 84, 169n30;

and *Robinson Crusoe*, 112; and *Roxana*, 112; and self-awareness, 111–12; and self-transcendence, 102, 105, 111; and sexuality, 177n15; and the supernatural, 111; and tragedy, 107; and *Tristram Shandy*, 87, 102, 104, 105, 106, 107, 112; and the uncanny, 181n48
Superego, 111, 140, 152n15, 168–69n28, 174n21
Supernatural, the, 10, 111, 112, 114–15, 117, 133, 150n3, 154n24, 175n3, 177n9
Supplementarity, 103, 104
Surplus value, 26, 30
Surrealism, 112, 117
Swift, Jonathan, 170n2
Symbolic order, 103

Temporality, 24, 26, 42, 52, 87, 103, 139, 156n8, 161n33
Thomas, Calvin, 171n8
Time. *See* Temporality
Todd, Janet, 149n2
Todorov, Tzvetan, 154n24
Torok, Maria, 13, 110, 124–26, 133, 134–35, 136, 137, 144, 172n13, 178nn
Tragedy: and alienation, 53; and *The Castle of Otranto*, 113, 115, 121; and *Clarissa*, 60, 85; and dividedness, 47; and fantastic narrative, 8, 53, 103, 110; and gender, 142; and gothic literature, 87; and individualism, 95; and melodrama, 87; and *The Mysterious Mother*, 110, 127, 130; and realist narrative, 102; and *Roxana*, 21, 47; and sublime, 107; and *Tristram Shandy*, 95, 102
Tristram Shandy (Sterne): and affectivity, 103, 106; and alienation, 89, 91; and allegory, 101; and ambisexuality, 106, 175n31; and ambivalence, 106; and androgyny, 106; and anxiety, 90, 91, 96, 97, 100, 101, 107, 121, 171nn; and appropriation, 91, 94, 105, 106, 144; and autonomy, 144, 145; and body, 94, 97, 106, 107, 144; and boundary, 94, 144, 145; and breast/penis, 92, 106; and carnivalesque, 106; and castration, 13, 92, 93, 97, 98, 106, 107; and comedy, 13, 87, 91, 95, 102, 103–4, 105, 106, 107, 117, 144; and community, 107; and connectedness, 107, 108, 144, 145; and desire, 93, 94, 101, 103, 104; and difference, 89, 90, 93, 94, 96, 102, 103, 117, 143, 144, 173n17; and displacement, 93, 107;

and dividedness, 87, 89, 95, 97, 109; and doubleness, 95, 102; and empiricism, 88; and epistemology, 11, 88, 170nn4–5; and erasure, 91, 101, 142; and erotics, 94, 107, 108, 143; and family, 93; and fantastic narrative, 11, 87, 88, 89, 93, 95, 102, 103–4, 107, 145; and femininity, 93, 107, 145; and feminism, 145, 171nn; and fetishism, 93, 97; and gaze, 98, 144; and gender, 102, 109, 117, 142, 144, 145, 171nn, 173n17, 175n31; and gothic literature, 87; and heterosexuality, 145; and hierarchy, 94, 103, 144; and hobbyhorse, 95–97, 102, 144, 172–73nn15–16, 173n19; and homosociality, 93–94, 143, 145; and idealization, 93, 94, 98, 100, 101; and identification, 94; and identity, 90, 170n5; and ideology, 109; and imagination, 117; and impotence, 92, 93, 97, 100, 101; and indeterminacy, 11, 102–3, 104, 107, 144; and individualism, 95, 109; and individuality, 145; and integration, 89, 102; and interaction of narrative modes, 11, 87, 88, 89, 95, 102, 145; and intersubjectivity, 144; and irony, 88, 91, 102, 107, 117; and *jouissance*, 104–5, 106, 107; and knowledge, 89, 99, 101, 103, 104, 106; and Lacanian theory, 13, 87, 97, 101, 103–6, 171n8, 172n15, 173nn18–20; and lack, 13, 93, 94, 97, 100, 101; and language, 13, 88, 89, 95, 97, 98, 99, 101, 103, 117, 144, 145; and legal relations, 91; and Lockean theory, 88, 99, 170n4; and loss, 88, 89, 93, 97, 106, 107, 143; and marginality, 87; and masculinity, 89, 93–94, 101, 102–3, 145; and maternal relations, 91–93, 101, 106, 107, 142, 144–45; and melancholia, 93, 142, 144, 145; and misogyny, 13, 93, 102, 104, 106, 107, 142, 145, 171nn; and naming, 98, 106; and narcissism, 95, 107, 144; and nose, 92, 97, 99–101; and otherness, 93, 94, 97, 106, 142; and paternal relations, 90–91, 93–94, 101–2; and patriarchy, 97, 117, 171n10; and penis, 92, 94, 100–101, 106; and performance, 102; and phallic economy, 94, 104; and Phallus, 101, 102, 105–6; and polymorphous perversity, 107, 144; and postmodernism, 87; and power, 98, 101, 117; and primal scene, 89–90; and property, 90; publication of, 170n3; and rationalism, 88; and ra-

Tristram Shandy (Sterne) (*continued*)
tionality, 102; and realist narrative,
11, 87, 88, 89, 93, 95, 102, 107, 145;
and reciprocity, 143, 144; and recognition, 89, 142, 144; and reproductive
relations, 90–91, 105; and sameness,
93; and self, 87, 89, 93, 94–95, 97,
144; and self-awareness, 109; and
self-consciousness, 97, 145; and
self-reflection, 96, 102; and self-
transcendence, 102, 107; and sentimentality, 87, 106; and sexuality,
11, 93, 95, 103; and social class,
173n17; and social embeddedness, 89,
95; and solipsism, 94, 95, 106; and
subjectivity, 88–89, 93, 94, 97, 102,
104, 107, 109, 144–45; and sublimation, 95; and sublime, 87, 102, 104,
105, 106, 107, 112; and temporality,
87, 103; and tragedy, 95, 102; and
wholeness, 93, 94; and women, 93,
94, 97, 105, 107, 173n17
Trumbach, Randolph, 166–67n18
Turner, James Grantham, 177n15

Uncanny, 10, 27, 109, 132–33, 142,
154n24, 181nn48–49
Unconscious, 5, 10, 12, 125, 126, 132,
136, 137, 140–41, 152n14, 152n15,
172n13, 178–79n25
Ungendered condition, 12, 60, 61

Victorian period, 155n26, 161n30
Villette (Brontë), 153–54n21, 155n26,
179n27, 182n2

Walpole, Horace, 87–88, 109–10, 112,
116–17, 127–30, 136, 137, 175nn1–2,
176n8, 177nn13–14, 179–81nn. See
also *The Mysterious Mother; The Castle
of Otranto*
Warner, William, 69, 163nn4–5
Watt, Ian, 5, 57, 59, 69, 149n1, 150n2,
162–63n1, 169n1
Weiskel, Thomas, 169n30, 176nn5–6
White, Allon, 154–55n25
Wholeness: and *The Castle of Otranto*,
117; and masculinity, 59, 60; and maternal relations, 141; and pornographic imagination, 59–60; and
realist narrative, 6, 117, 139; and reli-

gion, 25; and *Robinson Crusoe*, 25;
and *Tristram Shandy*, 93, 94
Whyte, Lancelot Law, 152n15
Wiegman, Robyn, 160n28
Wilde, Oscar, 155n26
Williams, Linda, 163n3, 167nn20–21,
168n26
Williams, Raymond, 161n32, 164n6
Wilt, Judith, 168n24
Winnicott, D. W., 96, 172n16
Women: and affectivity, 20, 51, 74; and
autonomy, 20, 35–36; and biological
determinism, 35; and body, 3, 35, 36,
42, 47, 60, 107; and capitalism, 35, 42,
159n19; and *The Castle of Otranto*, 119–
21; and commodification, 36, 39; and
difference, 3, 74; and displacement,
33; and domestic sphere, 2, 37; and
domination, 123; and economic relations, 2, 36, 123, 151n6; and erasure,
20, 31, 33; and exclusion, 93, 107; and
exploitation, 39; and hysteria, 47, 51;
and idealization, 93; and individualism, 20, 35; and labor, 36, 151n6,
163n3; and Lacanian theory, 104–5,
174n25; and lack, 97; and legal
relations, 123; and masochism, 66;
men's dependence upon, 35, 121;
men's identification with, 60; men's
usurpation of, 33, 91, 93–94, 105, 123;
and *Moll Flanders*, 20, 35–36, 39, 42,
43, 159n19; and narcissism, 66; and
objectification, 41, 62, 167n20; and
private sphere, 2, 43; and psychoanalysis, 47, 51, 165n11; and reader
response, 85; and realist narrative, 35;
and reification, 160n26; and reproductive relations, 3, 36, 42, 90, 91,
105, 121; and *Robinson Crusoe*, 20, 31–
32, 33, 37; and *Roxana*, 35–36, 51; and
scientific ideology, 3; and self-
consciousness, 97; and sensibility,
151n7; and sexuality, 3, 35, 36, 74,
120, 152n8, 163n3, 167n20; and subjectivity, 120; and temporality, 103;
and *Tristram Shandy*, 93, 94, 97, 105,
107, 173n17
Woolf, Virginia, 155n26
Working class, and family, 159n20

Xenophobia, and *Robinson Crusoe*, 29

Text: 10/13 Palatino
Display: Palatino
Composition: Binghamton Valley Composition, LLCA

Index: Andrew Joron